The Illustrated
Armada
Handbook

David A. Thomas

HARRAP
London

First published in Great Britain 1988
by HARRAP Ltd
19-23 Ludgate Hill London EC4M 7PD

ISBN 0 245 54591–3

Designed by Jim Weaver

Phototypeset by Falcon Graphic Art Ltd
Wallington, Surrey

Printed by Butler & Tanner Limited, Frome

Contents

Acknowledgements

I wish to acknowledge the help and wise counsel of a number of people who kindly put their services at my disposal in a manner quite above what one could reasonably expect. In particular I am indebted to the staff of the Reading Room at the National Maritime Museum for their unfailing help and courtesy. The Photographic Section also gave enormous help, and I single out Anne Carvell for her kind assistance on several occasions. I am also appreciative of the help given by the staff of the British Library, the Rijksmuseum of Amsterdam and the staffs of the reference libraries of the County of Essex at Chelmsford and Harlow, and especially of the London Borough of Redbridge Central Reference Library. The National Portrait Gallery were most kind, and I enjoyed the good-natured help of Laurence N.W. Flanagan, Keeper of Antiquities at the Ulster Museum. Margaret Prendiville of the Irish Tourist Board in London kindly made available a wide selection of photographs. I appreciated the help of Dr Richard Luckett, Pepys Librarian and Keeper of the Old Library, and Assistant Librarian Mrs E.M. Coleman. The staff of the Science Museum were helpful in a number of ways, and I am grateful too to Major Idris Morgan-Williams for his courteous attention to my enquiries. The staff of the Plymouth City Art and Museum Collection, especially Miss M.B. Attrill, Keeper of Arts and Mrs C. Gaskell-Brown of the Drake Project, were most helpful and gave guidance. Alan Green provided photographic help; and help with translations from Italian and Spanish by Juan Ruiz Palma was much appreciated. The typing of the final manuscript was by Mrs Pat Palmer, to whom I give my thanks.

Picture credits

National Portrait Gallery
British Library
National Maritime Museum
Woburn Abbey
Diputado General de Vizcaya, Bilbao
Ulster Museum
Rijksmuseum-Stichting, Amsterdam
Irish Tourist Board
Major Idris Morgan-Williams
City of Bristol Museum & Art Gallery
Plymouth City Museum & Art Gallery
Buckland Abbey
National Galleries of Scotland
Magdalene College, Cambridge
Musées Royaux des Beaux Arts de Belgique

Museo Naval, Madrid
Tate Gallery
St Faith's Church, Gaywood, King's Lynn
Stedelijk Museum de Lakenhal, Leiden
Patrimonio Nacional, Madrid
Ministero peri Beni Culturali e Ambientali, Firenze

The front cover illustration is an oil painting on a panel 44" x 56½" by an unknown artist, painted c.1590. The heraldic treatment of the painting is thought to have been a design for a tapestry. (National Maritime Museum).

1. The Queen's Head

*T*O THE ENGLISH it was known as the Spanish fleet. To the Spanish and Portuguese who watched it assembling for months in Lisbon harbour it was known as the *Felicissima* (or Most Fortunate) Armada. And when it was ready to embark on the *Empresa* or 'Enterprise of England' this prodigious fleet was nicknamed — with a touch of arrogance — the Invincible Armada. But comprehensive defeat gave a patina of mockery to the word which opponents of Spain have not been slow to dwell upon, although the Spaniards themselves have been quite content to ignore the ridicule and to accept the title *Invincible* for four centuries.

To the rest of the world this fleet became known as the Spanish Armada, though perhaps it should more correctly have been called the 'First Armada'. It was, in fact, the first of four which were marshalled and launched by the ageing King Philip II — a megalomaniac if ever there was one — three of them against the heretic English.

The first, and the greatest by far, bore down upon England in the unusually cold, thunderously overcast, storm-bound summer of 1588. The decisive defeats in the battles of that summer which together constituted the Armada Campaign impelled Philip to postpone any immediate repetition, and it was eight years later, in 1596, when he ordered the second Armada to assault England. No explanation has been given why he chose November as the time for invasion; any naval man worth his salt could have told him it is one of the worst storm-filled months in the Atlantic. The fleet was wrecked almost before it was out of sight of its own Spanish coastline.

In the following year the third Armada came nearest to success, when the chance to invade Cornwall was within its grasp — only to be thwarted at the last moment by a northerly gale as the fleet approached Falmouth.

The fourth Armada — the last in Philip's series of invasion attempts, which only his death in 1598 brought to an end — was not directed against England but had the objective of reinforcing the Spanish army in Flanders. The fleet sailed up-Channel quite undetected by English ships till it reached the sanctuary of Calais: an Armada version of the 1942 Channel Dash.

What manner of man, then, was Philip II, who wielded such power that he could direct 'the greatest navy that ever swam upon the sea' against his political and religious rival in England? And what of the Duke of Medina Sidonia, that self-effacing, much maligned, enigmatic Supremo of the Armada, and the fine commanders, the noble and soldierly Don Juan Martinez de Recalde, the magnificent Marquis of Santa Cruz, Don Pedro de Valdes who surrendered without a fight and Don Diego Flores de Valdes who commanded the Castilian squadron?

What strength or guile did Philip's arch-rival Queen Elizabeth I of England possess, and how could she have the audacity to taunt and harass him, to thumb her nose at the King of the greatest and most powerful nation in the world? The irascible, shrewd and

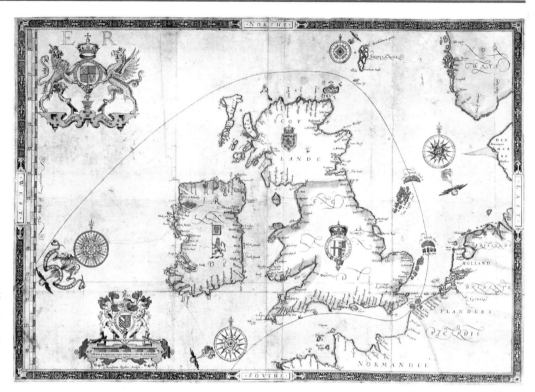

Robert Adams's chart of the British Isles and North-west Europe in 1588 showing the track of the Armada through the North Sea on its voyage north-about to Spain.

tactless Pope Sixtus V had been driven to mutter that the emperor of half the world was defied by a woman who was queen of half an island.

And what of Elizabeth's statesmen and advisers, the men of her Navy Royal, the commanders, noblemen, officers and even the simple mariners — the word sailor had yet to be adopted commonly? These men had to repel a vast threatened invasion of these islands, a peril only experienced in later centuries to anything like the same degree in Napoleon's days and in the hot, tense summer of 1940.

The campaign, too, with its sequence of battles off Plymouth, Portland, the Isle of Wight, Calais and Gravelines — frequently treated dismissively as of less consequence than the effect of the Atlantic storms — needs describing as a decorated backdrop to the colourful personalities on centre stage. It was carried through at a pedestrian pace no faster than a comfortable amble, averaging a speed of a little more than two knots — and it deserves careful scrutiny and review. This review will accord it its proper place in maritime history, perhaps as one of the greatest, most significant and decisive defeats in the annals of war at sea.

*   *   *

The Anglo-Spanish war of the sixteenth century never had a formal beginning and historians have ever since speculated as to the most acceptable date: this need not concern us here. The fact is that Philip and Elizabeth were locked in personal antagonism for practically the whole of Elizabeth's long reign, save for brief periods of uneasy peace such as when he offered her marriage, and the five years following his death.

The 27-year-old Prince Philip married Queen Mary of England, eleven years his senior, in a ceremony of political convenience at Winchester Cathedral in July 1554. Mary (Elizabeth's stepsister, and daughter to Catherine of Aragon), was a devout

King Philip II of Spain was a profoundly religious man who spent hours a day kneeling in prayer. He was a brooding fatalist, yet nursed a fanatical belief that God was on his side. Even after the defeat of the Armada his belief was unshaken.

The Calendar in 1588

*I*N 1582 Pope Gregory XIII proclaimed a new calendar which was adopted by many countries of western Europe over the next few years. The calendar has survived the test of time: it is used to this day. This new-style Gregorian Calendar (sometimes referred to as NS) replaced what was known as the Old Style (or OS) Julian Calendar.

England, with her conservative reluctance to change, clung to the past for more than a century and a half, confusing the general reader, and even students, with differing dates of historical events.

Thus at the time of the Armada campaign England's dates differed from those of many other Continental countries by a margin of ten days, with the result that the first day's battle with the Armada is recorded by Englishmen as having taken place on 21 July, while many other countries — including Spain — date it as 31 July.

Fortunately, the days of the week remain the same whatever numerical date is employed: 31 July was a Sunday in Rome and Madrid: 21 July was also a Sunday in London and Plymouth.

Some historians have adopted a clumsy device, expressing the anomaly as a fraction, thus $\frac{21}{31}$ July, but this seems unnecessarily pedantic: if there is any question or doubt about a date, the bracketed insertion of OS or NS is used. Otherwise it has seemed sensible to follow the Continental system throughout this book.

Catholic, ruthlessly determined to impose her faith upon the English. She later had the bishops Latimer and Ridley burnt at the stake, together with Archbishop Cranmer. She plunged the country into a bitter blood-bath, and because of her remorseless persecution of the Protestants she earned the nickname 'Bloody' Mary.

At the end of August 1555 Philip left Mary to return to the Continent to ascend his own Spanish throne. He was probably glad to escape the unsympathetic English court, where he had never felt at ease, to return to Madrid. In November 1558 Mary died at Lambeth Palace after a life that had been one long tragedy.

In another display of Anglo-Spanish solidarity Philip offered marriage to his sister-in-law Elizabeth, the new Queen of England. It was to be one of numerous such offers that Elizabeth received from several suitors over the years and which she toyed with for a time before they were finally cast aside. In some ways this typified the woman — she was a mistress in the art of delay and prevarication.

But the years of uneasy peace, of undeclared and open war between England and Spain, were more than a long period of personal tussle between the two monarchs. The rivalry was dynastic and political, it was predominantly religious, it was economic in that it stemmed from greed and it made war as inevitable as the sunrise. Two events which helped precipitate the conflict were of climactic importance. The first was the execution by beheading of Mary, Queen of Scots and the second, a few months later, was Drake's raid on Cadiz — his so-called singeing of the King of Spain's beard. The year was 1587, and it is to these formidable and fateful events that we must now direct our attention.

*   *   *

Elizabeth's cousin Mary, Queen of Scots, was nearly nine years younger than herself, and ever since she was born she had been a thorn in Elizabeth's side. Right to the very end, as she prepared for her execution, Mary still proclaimed her right to the throne of England. She never achieved that, of course, but there is some irony in the fact that it was her son who ultimately won the English crown, and not a son of Elizabeth.

Mary had led a life of incredible intrigue, of many ordeals and terrible disasters which she bore with amazing fortitude. She succeeded to the Scottish throne as an infant — just one week old — on the death of her father, James V of Scotland. In 1548, not yet six, the little princess was betrothed to the young Dauphin of France, a convenient political arrangement which culminated in her marriage at the age of fifteen. She spent the intervening years in Paris under the influence and hawk eyes of her mother-in-law, Catherine de Medici.

The tall, attractive teenager enjoyed the Parisian court life, though Francis, her husband, was handicapped and retarded. As soon as news reached Paris of Mary I's death the King of France immediately proclaimed his daughter-in-law to be the rightful claimant to the throne of England — a throne which Elizabeth, in the absence of a male inheritor of the Tudor line, claimed for herself.

Protestant England accepted Elizabeth's claim, although to the Catholics she was merely the bastard daughter of Henry VIII and Anne Boleyn. She was accepted without hesitation and with much rejoicing, but then almost anyone would have been welcomed after 'Bloody' Mary. The claim of Mary, Queen of Scots, the only alternative and legitimate claim, was looked at askance by the English. For a start, she was married to the Dauphin and this put her out of court, while the thought of knuckling down again to the edicts of Rome after the other Mary's reign of terror was simply too much to bear. The popular Princess Elizabeth was altogether more acceptable, more comfortable and safe as Queen of England. Within a few years the Dauphin was crowned king, died of an abscess in his ear and left Mary, at eighteen, a widow.

In August 1561 she received an invitation from the Scottish parliament to take up her own crown in Scotland. She arrived on 19 August at Leith and almost immediately met opposition to her religious faith. Many expected her to denounce her catholicism. Far from it. She alienated herself by her powerful Catholic views and tastes. Mary further annoyed Elizabeth when she wrote to her asking that she be named as the rightful successor to the English crown.

Mary hoped to marry Don Carlos, heir to the Spanish throne, but so opposed to this was Elizabeth that Lord Darnley was sent from London to dissuade the young Mary. Darnley, the dashing young courtier (himself a claimant to the English throne), met Mary at Wemyss Castle on the rocky coast of Fife, and both fell in love at first sight. Their marriage, however, was a disaster, even though the union did produce a son who would later unify the crowns of the two nations and become James VI of Scotland and James I of England. Soon after their marriage Mary was faced with the murder of Rizzio and then that of Darnley himself, whose strangled body was found in the garden of Kirk o' Field House: her innocence or guilt of any implication have never been established. There followed her affair and marriage with Bothwell, who had been tried and acquitted of Darnley's murder. In rapid succession she abdicated, escaped from Lochleven Castle and was defeated at the battle of Langside. In 1568 she escaped across the Solway Firth and landed at Workington in Cumbria, rashly committing herself to the hospitality of Queen Elizabeth. It was a fatal step, one consequence of which — twenty years later — was the launching of the Armada against England.

Elizabeth's hospitality was cruel; she imprisoned her cousin for nearly twenty years. Mary was *persona non grata*, and it is small wonder that she was imprisoned, when even in confinement she posed a threat to Elizabeth. As the years passed and Elizabeth could no longer bear children to perpetuate the line, Mary continued to pose another

This cartoon appeared as the frontispiece to Dr John Dee's *General and Rare Memorials Portraying to the Perfect Arte of Navigation*, 1577. It depicts the ship of Europe steered by Elizabeth and manned by Burghley, Leicester and Walsingham.

threat through her son. True, the baby had been taken away from his mother at the age of ten months and had been brought up a strict Protestant in Scotland, but he was a legitimate successor to Elizabeth, and that must have rankled with her. James was a sickly lad, backward, shambling, awkward and unattractive.

Even in prison Mary was a centre for intrigue. In 1577 she made a will leaving all her rights to the English throne to Philip, King of Spain. It was a gesture which some saw as an invitation for Philip to come and rescue the distressed maiden.

Elizabeth's advisers, the Council — especially Walsingham, Burghley and Leicester — saw Mary's possible succession to the throne as a great danger not only to England but to themselves in particular: their heads would be the first to roll. They had every reason to urge on Elizabeth the execution of Mary.

To many foreign and English Catholics Mary remained a romantic princess, brutally imprisoned. In fact her incarceration could hardly be described as brutal: she was allowed an entourage of forty, was permitted to hunt and to visit a spa to take the waters.

Elizabeth resisted all arguments for Mary's trial and her head. Royal persons, she insisted, were not executed. Deviously she sought a way out of her dilemma. Her idea may have been to persuade the Scots to accept the return of their queen on the understanding that they would then execute her, thereby keeping Elizabeth's hands as free of blood as Pontius Pilate's. But each of the regents reigning in Mary's stead died in office before negotiations and terms could be completed.

Mary's rivalry and relentless determination reached new heights in another ambitious plot in the autumn of 1586. It was led by Sir Anthony Babington, a staunch but misguided Catholic from Derbyshire. He proposed that six Catholics should kill Elizabeth. The Duke of Guise would wait with an army in Normandy to march on London. Babington himself would free Mary with a hundred chosen men and raise the new queen's standard. The plot was discovered, and smashed. It precipitated Mary's trial, and she was brought to Fotheringhay Castle in Northamptonshire in September 1586 to face thirty-six noblemen, privy councillors and judges, both Protestant and Catholic.

Mary refused to attend the trial, questioning the court's validity until she received a brief note from Elizabeth holding out a veiled hint of clemency. She defended herself for two days, displaying much vigour and ability. The trial was adjourned for fourteen days before reconvening at Westminster, in the Star Chamber, the ancient tribunal of state charged with the duty of trying offences against the government, unfettered by the ordinary rules of law — a sort of Privy Council entrusted with judicial duties. The verdict, of course, was a foregone conclusion. The warrant simply needed the Queen's signature . . . and this Elizabeth was conspicuously disinclined to give. While she continued for two months to procrastinate and agonize over her conscience she allowed Mary to write letters. Mary took advantage of this and promptly wrote to the Pope — Sixtus V — to the influential Duke of Guise, to Mendoza, the Spanish ambassador in Paris, to archbishops and other Catholic dignitaries and to Philip of Spain.

Pressure of all sorts was being applied to Elizabeth, both for clemency and for death. Mary's letter to Elizabeth herself made the Queen cry. But her Councillors' persuasion won the day. In a torment of mental agony she signed the death warrant . . . and later tried to blame anyone and everyone for delivering and processing the document bearing her permission. The date was Wednesday 11 February 1587.

One week later, on the 18th, Mary — the heir apparent to the throne of England — was executed by beheading at Fotheringhay Castle. She had been for two decades the cynosure for English and even European Catholics: now, beheaded, she became a beacon of religious faith, a martyr whose spilled blood called out for Catholic

The Execution of Mary, Queen of Scots

OF ALL the reasons which brought about the war between Protestant England and Catholic Spain in 1588 only one other was as catalytic as the beheading of Mary, Queen of Scots. This was Drake's raid on Cadiz, which came a few months after Mary's execution.

The scene at Fotheringhay Castle was one of sombre blackness. Black velvet drapes adorned the walls, the stairs and the knee-high platform itself, on which was placed an ordinary wooden chopping block. Two hundred or more invited spectators, all of them knights, gentlemen, dignitaries, sat and stood in awed silence, trying hard to keep out the chill of the day — let alone of the occasion, for they had assembled at seven o'clock this winter morning.

Mary, prima donna to the end, appeared for her last performance three hours later, on the arm of an official, accompanied by six attendants. She too was draped in black, relieved only by a white frill at her throat and by her auburn hair (in reality a wig) piled high on her head. As she sat to await proceedings she looked a pathetic, lonely, plump figure, barely recognizable as Mary Stuart, Queen of Scotland, Dowager Queen of France, claimant to the English throne.

She cut short the Dean of Peterborough, dithering over his words: 'I shall die as I have lived,' she declared, 'in the true and holy Catholic faith . . .' Silencing the Dean further, she held aloft her crucifix for all to see and prayed for the people of England, for the soul of Elizabeth, for the forgiveness of her enemies.

Her ladies-in-waiting disrobed her to her red chemise and she knelt by the block, bent her head: '*In manus tuas, domine . . .*' The axe fell once, twice, blood flowed, the head rolled. Right to the end Mary held her audience spellbound . . .

The execution of Mary, Queen of Scots, is depicted in this German print with Mary clutching her crucifix, proclaiming to the very end her faith as a Catholic. Noblemen, councillors, lords and gentlemen watch stonily while outside some servants burn all her clothes to prevent them being secreted away as a martyr's memorabilia. Her execution ended the hopes of Catholic Europe that England would return to the Church of Rome. As a consequence, war with Spain became inevitable.

Mary, Queen of Scots, was born in December 1542, nine years later than her cousin Elizabeth. Her father, James V of Scotland, died at the age of thirty when she was only a week old. When she was not yet six she was betrothed to the Dauphin of France. All her life she opposed Elizabeth and claimed the English crown for herself. Eventually Elizabeth signed the warrant for her execution, which took place on 18 February 1587 at Fotheringhay Castle in Northamptonshire, helping to precipitate the Armada campaign the following year.

vengeance. Shock waves of horror and outrage swept Europe — especially Spain. In France, when the news was received some weeks after the event, the Court went into mourning and a requiem Mass was held in Notre Dame attended by Mary's brother-in-law, Henry III, her mother-in-law, Catherine de Medici, and her cousins, the Guises. In Rome Pope Sixtus is said to have received the news sadly. To the Spanish ambassador in the Vatican Sixtus repeated his rash but conditional pledge of a million ducats payable to Philip II as soon as the invading Spaniards set foot in England.

In Spain the reactions of anger and shock were equally as violent as in Paris. The Duke of Parma, on assignment in Flanders, wrote to Philip:

> This cruel act must be the last of many which she of England has performed and that of our Lord will be served if she receives the punishment she deserved for so many years . . .

He went on to urge forward preparations for the invasion of England, cloaking them with continuing negotiations for peace:

> For the reasons I have so often put before your Majesty we must be able to achieve our aims if we are called on to undertake any of the many parts which fall to us . . . Above all, I beg your Majesty that neither on this nor on other occasions will you relax in any way in regard to your preparations for the prosecution of the war and the *Empresa* which was conceived in your Majesty's heart.

2. Background to an enterprise

*D*ON ALVARO DE BAZAN, first Marquis of Santa Cruz and Captain General of the Ocean Seas, may not have been the originator of the *Empresa*, but it was he who planned it and was chosen to mount it.

Santa Cruz bestrode the Spanish naval scene like a colossus. Historians have described him as the Nelson of Spain, and compared him with De Ruyter of the Netherlands. In Spanish eyes he occupied a position rather akin to Drake, Howard and Hawkins all rolled into one. He was unquestionably the architect of the first Armada. In the 1580s he had built the then modern Spanish navy, administered it with efficiency, without corruption and — perhaps most importantly — had commanded it in battle with distinction and triumph. One eminent naval historian classified him unequivocally: 'He *was* the Spanish navy.' In a word, the Marquis of Santa Cruz was an institution.

The splendid sixteenth-century painting of him by an unknown artist seems to do justice to the word pictures handed down through the past four centuries and to have captured the spirit of the man. He exhibits the demeanour, the arrogance, leadership-quality, the unbending pride of that highly exclusive class of Spanish nobility called a Don: in a land that teemed with nobility of high-sounding names, of high birth, landed wealth and inherited titles, Santa Cruz stood higher than most.

He had to his credit two naval victories, the more creditable of which was Lepanto in 1571. That victory was analogous in some respects to Nelson's when as a captain in the British line he was instrumental in winning the battle of Cape St Vincent more than two centuries later. At Lepanto, Santa Cruz was the commander of the reserve Spanish fleet, of more than 100 ships, eighty of them galleys, and 21,000 fighting men, but it was his timely commitment of this reserve force to battle and his assured handling of the fleet which 'converted a colleague's error into a Turkish rout'. It was masterly.

Lepanto was a watershed. It was the last battle fought by galleys, and, although many fleets would still retain them for years to come, this encounter marked the beginning of the end of oared vessels and the transition to sail. It was as significant a transition as the nineteenth-century change from sail to steam propulsion.

The Christian ships were commanded by the 24-year-old Don John of Austria, younger illegitimate brother of Philip II. His huge, impressive fleet defeated the might of Turkish naval forces commanded by Ali Pasha in a battle characterized by gruesome hand-to-hand fighting. No one should fire, Don Juan had instructed bloodthirstily, 'until near enough to be splashed with the blood of an enemy'. The bloodshed was awesome, the numbers killed and wounded horrendous. Among the wounded was a man named Cervantes: his left hand was lopped off in the fighting, but his life was spared to give the world the masterpiece *Don Quixote*.

Following Spain's annexation of Portugal in 1580, Santa Cruz fought the naval battle of Terceira off the Azores in 1582. Although he was greatly outnumbered, he captured

Don Alvaro de Bazan, first Marquis of Santa Cruz. His death on the eve of the projected invasion of England delayed it for several months, and command of the enterprise devolved upon the Duke of Medina Sidonia.

Philip of Spain offered a reward of £40,000 (perhaps £4 million in today's values) for 'the pirate' Sir Francis Drake — dead or alive. This portrait of Drake by M. Gheerhaerts the Younger is in the Plymouth City Museum and Art Gallery.

the enemy flagship and the Admiral, Strozzi, while the victory paved the way for the capture of the Azores the following year. Spanish naval officers' morale was high: they were heard to brag, 'Now that we have all of Portugal, England is ours!' The date was 1583, the bragging premature.

In Madrid Philip settled back to give his attention not so much to England, but to another thorn in his side — the Netherlands. He could reflect comfortably on the situation. His empire was the greatest since that of ancient Rome.

He could remind himself further that Spain enjoyed peace — uneasy, it is true, but peace of a sort nevertheless — and prosperity beyond his dreams: her colonies in South America, the West Indies, the Philippines and elsewhere were providing treasure and wealth of enormous value. But north-western Europe lay in shadow, oppressive as if under a thundercloud, and soon a challenge to Spain's supremacy arose over the horizon in the form of a Dutch-French-English axis.

Worse still, in August 1585 Queen Elizabeth undertook to supply military aid to the Netherlands: an army of no less than 6,000 soldiers and 1,000 cavalry, under the Earl of Leicester, who later took over as governor-general of the allied armies. Even more worrying, Philip was receiving intelligence that Elizabeth was preparing to dispatch a piratical fleet commanded by Sir Francis Drake to attack Spanish shipping and property in the West Indies.

An Elizabethan Diary 1558–1603

1558 Elizabeth succeeded to the throne at the age of twenty-five. Cecil became Secretary of State (→1572). Mary, Queen of Scots, married Francis, Dauphin of France.

1559 Protestantism re-established. Matthew Parker became Archbishop of Canterbury (→1575). John Knox returned to Scotland. Civil war in Scotland. Peace with France. Francis II became king of France (→1560).

1560 Mysterious death of Amy Robsart, Lady Dudley (wife of the future Earl of Leicester). War in Scotland ended.

1561 Mary, Queen of Scots, returned to Scotland from France.

1562 John Hawkins sold West African slaves in the West Indies.

1565 Mary, Queen of Scots, married Darnley. Moray's rebellion in Scotland repressed.

1566 Rizzio murdered. Probable date of introduction of tobacco into England.

1567 Darnley murdered. Mary, Queen of Scots, married Bothwell. She was defeated at Carberry Hill and imprisoned at Loch Leven. She abdicated. Moray became regent for the infant James VI, who was to reign over Scotland for nearly sixty years.

1568 Mary escaped from Scotland and fled to England. Elizabeth imprisoned her. Attempts made to colonize Ireland with Protestants. Spanish treasure ships seized.

1569 Northern rebellion broke out.

1570 Pope excommunicated Elizabeth I. Moray assassinated. Lennox became regent of Scotland.

1572 Cecil became Lord Treasurer (→1598). Morton became regent of Scotland. Duke of Norfolk executed. Elizabeth began negotiations to marry the Duke of Alençon, brother to Charles IX.

1576 Archbishop of Canterbury Grindal installed. Frobisher expedition failed to discover NW Passage.

1577 Grindal suspended from office.

1578 Marriage negotiations renewed with the Duc d'Alençon, now Duc d'Anjou.

1580 Drake completed circumnavigation of the world. Foundation of the Levant Company. Spanish landing party landed at Smerwick, Ireland.

1582 The Ruthven raid. James VI seized.

1583 Throckmorton Plot revealed. Desmond Plot suppressed. Whitgift installed as Archbishop of Canterbury.

1585 Leicester led expedition to the Netherlands. Spain seized English ships and began invasion plans. Drake carried out explorations and raids in the New World.

1586 Babington Plot revealed. Sidney killed at Zutphen. Marlowe wrote *Tamburlaine* around this time. Camden wrote *Britannia*.

1587 Mary, Queen of Scots executed. Leicester recalled. Drake singed Philip's beard at Cadiz.

1588 Spanish Armada defeated.

1589 Henry IV became king of France. Hakluyt's *Principal Navigations, Voyages and Discoveries* published.

1590 Spenser published first part of *Faerie Queene*.

1591 Grenville sacrificed the *Revenge* and himself.

1592 Beginning of publication of Shakespeare plays (→1616).

1595 O'Neill Revolt started in Ulster. Ben Jonson's *Volpone* published.

1596 Robert Cecil became Secretary of State. Howard and Essex sacked Cadiz.

1598 Death of Burghley (formerly Cecil). France abandoned alliance with England. Anglo-Dutch alliance against Spain. Edict of Nantes.

1599 Essex imprisoned by Elizabeth on his return from Ireland.

1600 East India Company incorporated. Essex released.

1601 Essex executed. Poor Law Act passed. Spanish troops landed at Kinsale in Ireland.

1603 O'Neill Revolt suppressed. Queen Elizabeth died and was succeeded by James VI of Scotland. End of the Tudor era.

The reports were true. On the Continent, Elizabeth's aims were to try to persuade
Philip to grant the Dutch civic and religious rights, which at the same time would
ensure that their country could not be used as a base for an attack upon England.

Sir Francis Walsingham, the much-underrated statesman who was never accorded
the honours and rewards commensurate with his offices and distinguished services,
headed Elizabeth's secret service. It was he who was to expose the Babington Plot, and
to become one of the commissioners at the trial of Mary, Queen of Scots. It was he too
who first discovered the details of the Armada plan. Now, in 1585, before all these
fateful events took place, he had drawn up a plan for 'annoying the king of Spain'.

Fundamental to his plan was the questioning and testing of the Spanish century-old
claim of sovereignty of the seas in the west, and her right to hitherto undiscovered
countries. Queen Elizabeth had warned Philip II of her intentions some years
previously, after she had knighted Drake, in a letter of declaration, a document of
historical maritime importance: 'The use of the sea and air', she asserted, 'is common
to all, and neither Nature, nor use nor custom permit any possession thereof.'

Philip's brooding resentment at this declaration found relief in branding Drake a
pirate and offering a huge reward for his capture dead or alive.

Elizabeth had gone far in checking Philip. In 1585, four years later, Walsingham
proposed dispatching a fleet to the West Indies on a scale far more ambitious than ever
attempted before. The fleet's commander would be Sir Francis Drake.

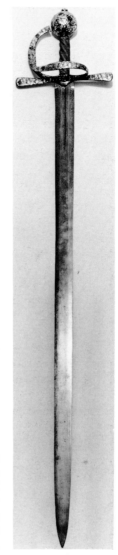

Elizabeth regarded Drake's
plundering of Spanish ships more
tolerantly than did Philip, and
knighted him with this sword after
his circumnavigation of the world. It
is on loan to HMS *Drake* at
Devonport.

3. King and Queen: principals and players

KING PHILIP II, His Catholic Majesty the King of Spain, assumed power with the ease of donning a cloak. He was the most powerful political figure of his time, and although curiously reclusive, he wielded his power autocratically. His rule extended over Spain, Naples and Sicily, over the 'Isles and Continents of the Ocean', over the Low Countries, Mexico, Portugal (from 1580) and much of Italy; over faraway Peru and, apart from Brazil, over all the Americas, discovered and yet to be discovered, and over the rich Portuguese possessions in the East. He was Archduke of Austria, Duke of Burgundy, Brabant and Milan. He ruled from his sparse, windowless study, one of thousands of rooms in the vast, sprawling monastic fortress of a palace at El Escorial, thirty-one miles from Madrid.

Much of Philip's territorial acquisition dated from the late fifteenth century, when the two trading nations of Spain and Portugal had agreed the broad principle that possessions in the East should belong to Portugal and those of the New World in the West should be the prerogative of the Spanish explorers and conquistadors who had opened up these territories to trade. This gentlemanly agreement found utterance in the Papal Line of Demarcation (and the later Treaty of Tordesillas, 1494) which cut the global cake in two: the Spanish West and the Portuguese East, leaving crumbs for the rest.

The Spanish annexation of Portugal in 1580 and Philip's resulting acquisition of the Portuguese crown married the two empires into one vast inheritance.

Mighty though he was in temporal terms, he also commanded great influence and power in Western Europe in religious matters. He spoke with pride of his title 'Most Catholic Majesty' and he made no secret of his almost monastic life, hours of which (some say four to five) were spent every day in prayer upon knees which increasingly degenerated into an arthritic condition. He believed with a profound conviction that it was his duty to eradicate Protestantism from Germany, England, the Low Countries and elsewhere in Europe, enlisting on his side a sometimes reluctant Pope, and no less an ally than Almighty God.

Philip's impulsion to convert or kill heretics was compulsive, and this may have been nurtured by his experience when — perhaps partly to please him, her young King Consort — the Catholic Mary Tudor had burnt English heretics, both lowly and exalted. Even Archbishop Cranmer was not spared the ghastly death of burning at the stake.

Nor would the greatest heretic of them all, Queen Elizabeth of England, have been spared if she had been captured, for she was abominated by Europe's Catholics, and by Philip in particular. But the young, auburn-haired Elizabeth, a bastard of heretical parents, could, Philip once believed, be won over, converted rather than sacrificed.

Philip was four times married, and all marriages were conducted on a political level — 'conquest by marriage', Philip called it. The first was to his cousin Maria, a

This bronze sculpture in the Tate Gallery, *A Royal Game* by Sir William Reynolds-Stephens (1862–1943), splendidly captures the setting of the Armada campaign, with the two protagonists moving models of their ships as chessmen.

Portuguese princess. Then after her death, as we have seen, there came Mary Tudor, and in a sense Philip became King of England before he became King of Spain. More properly, of course, he was King Consort, and he never enjoyed the confidence of the English court, let alone the people. They had their own way — and Mary adopted it too — of keeping him at arm's length, subtly yet surely.

When Mary Tudor came near to her end, having neither produced a male heir nor solved her religious problems, Philip was already casting an eye over the fifteen-year-old Scottish Mary, but before he was free to marry she had consented to become the wife of the backward young Dauphin of France: Scotland and France became strange bedfellows.

Philip saw a greater attraction in young Mary's cousin, the Princess Elizabeth. If he could gain her hand it would also give him the titular crown of England again. When this failed, he married Isabella (Elizabeth) of France, daughter of Henry II, in 1559. A fourth alliance was formed in 1570 after the death of Isabella. He married Anne of Austria, daughter of the Emperor Maximilian II. In no case had he met his future wife before the marriage.

It is said that of all his wives he loved only one. Certainly he doted on his children — except the eldest, Don Carlos, too warped in mind and body to be loved by anyone. Beyond this, Philip was a man lacking in love. Nor did he know the meaning of the word pity. He was truly pitiless, and this was largely brought about — strangely — by his profound religious faith in the Catholic Church and his own belief in God.

The Church and God were all-dominant. They demanded unswerving allegiance, service and worship. As he demanded of himself absolute service, so too did he demand it of others. Any failure or deviation merited cruel and terrible punishment.

This then was the man who contemplated marriage to the young Lady Elizabeth even before his Mary Tudor was dead. When Elizabeth came to her inheritance as Queen of England, Philip made formal proposals of marriage, but Elizabeth declined his offers, kept him at bay till boredom or politics or both drove his interests elsewhere.

Elizabeth ruled England for forty-five years, earned the love of her people, loved with sincerity the country of her birth and gave her name to a proud period of her country's history. Philip never fathomed her mind, and as the years passed she became more skilled in the art of handling kings, monarchs, ambassadors, courtiers, the gentlemen of her Court and Council. Men loved her, would die for her, Cumberland wore her diamond-studded glove in his hat, but she would not give her heart in return. These were reserved for her greatest and most enduring love — for England.

The execution of Mary, Queen of Scots, caused Elizabeth months of wretchedness. In similar circumstances Philip would not have raised an eyebrow. And these reactions differentiate the antagonists of the Armada: a Queen whose heart was given to her country, and a merciless King who drove his country to defeat in the name of God.

PRINCIPALS AND PLAYERS

Elizabeth I, Queen of England (1533–1603) The last of the Tudor dynasty. She was born to Henry VIII and his second wife, Anne Boleyn. Elizabeth never married, although she received many offers including one from Philip II of Spain. She ascended the throne in 1558 to find England torn by religious differences and an empty treasury. Calais — the last English foothold in France — had gone for good, while the King of France held a foothold in Edinburgh. Her title to the throne was even a matter of some dispute. She was learned, wise, scheming, at times wayward, with a sceptical intellect; a moderate Protestant, and quick to anger. Curiously, in a male-dominated world she strengthened the throne considerably during her forty-four years' reign. She displayed a great talent in selecting loyal, gifted adventurers and administrators such as Burghley, Walsingham, Howard, Drake, Raleigh, Hawkins and Leicester.

Her reign was marred by religious strife and Catholic plots, and by the execution of Mary, Queen of Scots, in 1587.

Her years of war with Spain were marked by the attacks on Cadiz in 1587 and 1596, and the defeat of the Armada, 1588. Her reign also saw the beginning of colonization of America and the discovery of new lands. Raleigh's first Virginia colony was founded. Drake circumnavigated the world and returned with untold riches. The great East India Company was formed. Her reign was filled with the riches of scholarship too, in the form of Shakespeare, Spenser, Bacon, Sidney and Marlowe.

Elizabeth left England at her death far stronger and secure, and, in terms of politics and the navy, a first-class power.

*T*HE ARMADA PORTRAIT of Queen Elizabeth depicts two scenes from the campaign in panels behind the Queen.

Elizabeth — the woman — led a gregarious life, in contrast with the almost reclusive existence of Philip II. She found stimulation in company, especially when dancing, playing cards, relaxing in conversation, listening to music — and receiving compliments.

She was not only fascinated by fashion, she led it. She loved clothes and jewellery and heaped them upon herself with outrageous flamboyance. It was once recorded that she could choose from '125 petticoats, 67 round gowns, hundreds of kirtles, mantles, safeguards, foreparts, veils and French gowns'. Her 'colours' were black and white, though she used colours to enhance her reddish-gold hair — russet, tawny, orange, marigold, peach — and rarely used blue, green and yellow.

Her eyes were small and black, but pleasant. Her nose was slightly hooked, and she had a good sense of smell, so she enjoyed gardens and flowers and often wore a small posy in her bodice, and perfume on her body. She had an aversion to bad smells: 'Tush, man,' she admonished a poor courtier, 'your boots stink.'

Her teeth were her worst feature, described sometimes as yellow and at others as black, attributed to taking too much sugar. As she got older the gaps in her teeth increased, and when she spoke quickly it was difficult to understand her. She resorted to regular sweet-smelling mouth washes.

Her sharp intelligence led to her being quick to reprove or reprimand, for she demanded high standards in everything about her, and it found expression in conversation in Latin, Italian, Spanish and French, in which languages she was able to compose verses and prayers, such as the hymn of thanksgiving sung at St Paul's Cathedral after the defeat of the Spanish Armada.

Beeston, Sir George (1499–1601) Naval commander. Born of a Cheshire family. He commanded the *Dreadnought* at the age of eighty-nine during the Armada campaign: he was knighted by Howard of Effingham aboard the Lord High Admiral's flagship off the Isle of Wight along with several other commanders. He died in 1601 at the age of a hundred and two. There is a memorial window in Bunbury church where it is recorded he ended 'his life of honour'.

Blount, Sir Charles, later **Earl of Devonshire** and **eighth Lord Mountjoy** (1563–1606) Scholar and courtier. Oxford MA in 1589. Fought a duel with the Earl of Essex, but they later became good friends. He was described as 'Tall of stature, of comely proportions; his skin fair, he had very little hair on his body, it was nearly black, thin on the head where he wore it short, except a lock under the left ear which he nourished and being woven up, hid it in his neck under his ruff'. Fought in the Low Countries and was wounded in the thigh. Knighted by Leicester in 1587. During the Armada campaign he joined Lord Henry Seymour's flagship, the *Rainbow*, at Dover and fought at Gravelines. Succeeded to the barony as Lord Mountjoy in 1594. Appointed Lord Deputy of Ireland in 1599. Master of Ordnance 1603.

Borough, William (1536–99) Admiral, navigator and author. Devon-born. Went to sea to Russia in 1553 as an ordinary seaman, and again three years later when Novaya Zemlya was discovered. Sailed annually on the Muscovy Company's voyages to Russia. Agent in Russia, 1574–5. Appointed Clerk of the Ships, 1582 after publishing a cartographic book.

He was appointed second-in-command to Drake in 1587 on the Cadiz expedition. Borough was not a courageous or a particularly good naval commander. His crew in the *Golden Lion* mutinied. Drake court-martialled Borough and sentenced him to death, but Lord Howard considered the sentence unjust and quashed it. Borough was restored to his seat on the Navy Board. During the Armada campaign he commanded the galley *Bonavolia* and the Thames supply ships.

His last ten years are obscure.

Some of his charts are preserved in the British Museum, the PRO and NMM.

Burghley (Burleigh), William Cecil, first Baron (1520–98) Secretary of State and Lord High Treasurer. Born at Bourne, Lincolnshire, the eldest son of Richard, a yeoman of the wardrobe, and Jane Heckington. At fourteen he entered St John's College, Cambridge and quickly mastered Greek. There he met Roger Ascham and John Cheke. In 1541 he married Cheke's sister, Mary, and had one child, a son Thomas destined to become the Earl of Exeter. Mary died in 1544 and he was married again the following year, to a daughter of Sir Anthony Cooke. Ascham regarded her and Lady Jane Grey as the two most erudite women of the age. By this second marriage he had a son, Robert, destined to be the first Earl of Salisbury and James I's Chief Minister.

Cecil entered parliament in 1543, and about five years later became secretary to the Protector Somerset. He was sent to the Tower in 1549, but was released on parole. He became a secretary to the Earl of Warwick (later Duke of Northumberland), and was knighted in 1551.

He was a civil servant of the highest calibre, and established a rapport with Elizabeth which gave her the protection of his masterly political acumen.

He survived years of intrigue and political and religious manoeuvrings. He was Master of the Court of Wards, Chancellor of Cambridge University, created Baron of Burghley in 1571 and in the following year he was made Knight of the Garter and Lord High Treasurer.

Camden, William (1551–1623) One of the greatest historians of the Elizabethan age. His *Annales* is the most important source of the contemporary history of Elizabethan England, published in two volumes in 1615 and 1619.

Clifford, George, third Earl of Cumberland (1558–1605) Naval commander, courtier and adventurer. Awarded MA degree at Trinity College, Cambridge, 1576. In 1577 he married his cousin, Lady Margaret ('Sweet Meg') Russell. He turned to a naval life in 1586, hoping to make good much of the inheritance he had squandered. He fitted out ten expeditions at his own expense between 1586 and 1598. In the Armada campaign he commanded the Queen's ship *Elizabeth Bonaventure*, and carried the news of the Gravelines success to the Queen. She admired his invincible courage, his great vitality. He died penniless at the age of forty-seven.

George Clifford, Earl of Cumberland, served throughout the campaign aboard the *Elizabeth Bonaventure*. Note one of the Queen's jewel-studded gloves in his hat.

Cumberland *see* **Clifford**

Davis (Davys) Captain John (*c*.1550–1606) Navigator and explorer. Born at Sandridge near Dartmouth. He was a tough, enduring seaman who sought the NW Passage, explored Greenland, the East Indies and reached the farthest north up to that time — 72°12'N. He possessed an inventive genius and a scientific knowledge beyond his contemporaries' understanding. He commanded the pinnace *Black Dog* in the Armada battles, served off the Azores in 1589 and discovered the Falkland Islands in 1593. He was murdered at sea by Japanese pirates in 1605.

Drake, Sir Francis (*c*.1542–96) Greatest of the Elizabethan seamen. Born at Crowndale near Tavistock. Drake was related to the Hawkinses: Francis and John were cousins. In 1572 he equipped two ships to Nombre de Dios where he was wounded, and for the rest of his life he limped and used a stick. He sacked Porto Bello in 1573 and destroyed many Spanish ships.

Drake's coat of arms painted above a fireplace in his home at Buckland Abbey, Devon; but there is very little evidence that he ever used them.

In 1577 he fitted out the *Pelican* (100 tons), *Elizabeth* (80 tons), *Marigold* and two other smaller vessels. In August 1578 his squadron, reduced by two, entered the Straits of Magellan. He changed the *Pelican*'s name to *Golden Hind*. For 52 days stormy weather beat the ships: *Elizabeth* returned home and *Marigold* foundered with all hands. Drake reached Valparaiso and captured several rich prizes. He headed north as far as about 48°N, then sailed west across the Pacific, seeing nothing of land for 68 days. He landed at Java, crossed the Indian Ocean to the Cape of Good Hope and reached England on 26 September 1580. The Queen knighted him at Deptford in April 1581 for his circumnavigation.

In 1585 he commanded a squadron of 25 ships on a marauding expedition against the Spanish West Indies — Hispaniola, Cartagena and Florida. He singed King Philip's beard at Cadiz in 1587, then captured a Portuguese treasure carrack in the Azores worth about £114,000.

Drake's tactical skills in seamanship, audacious bravery and basic good fortune won him fresh laurels in the Armada campaign of 1588, where he commanded a squadron as a vice admiral of the English fleet. He captured the Spanish Valdes's flagship *Rosario* off Portland.

Drake's name struck terror in the hearts of Spaniards. He was 'El Draque, the vile corsair'. Elizabeth spoke of him affectionately as 'my pirate'. He represented Plymouth as an MP. In 1595 he sailed on an ill-fated expedition: he died of dysentery and was buried at sea off Porto Bello.

Fenner, George Sixteenth-century naval commander of a Sussex family. George was the most notable of the family, but cousin **Thomas** had almost as fine a record: **William** made up a worthy trio. William accompanied Drake and Norris to Corunna, 1589, and died of wounds on the voyage home. George commanded a squadron from Plymouth in 1566 and an expedition to the Indies. For twelve years he was a privateer. During the Armada campaign George distinguished himself in the Channel pursuit, at Gravelines and the North Sea.

Although reported to have died in 1600, in fact he died in Sutton's Hospital on 16 October 1618. He was 'one of the greatest seamen even in the days of Elizabeth'.

Fenner, Thomas (*d.c.* 1590) Native of Chichester, and related to George and William Fenner. It is believed that Sir Julian Corbett in *Drake and the Tudor Navy* attributed the 1566 Azores exploits to Thomas in error for George. Corbett described Thomas as 'one of the most daring and experienced officers of the time'. Fought at Cartagena in 1587 and commanded the *Dreadnought* at Cadiz. In the Armada campaign he commanded the *Nonpareil* in Drake's squadron. Attended Howard's councils of war. Believed to have died c.1590.

Captain Fenner, believed to be Thomas, who commanded the *Nonpareil* throughout the Armada campaign with such distinction.

Fenton, Edward (*fl.* 1577–1603) Naval commander. Came of an old Nottinghamshire family. Brother-in-law to John Hawkins. Commanded the *Gabriel* in Frobisher's second voyage of 1577 and in the following year as Rear Admiral of the *Judith*. Led an expedition in the *Galleon Leicester* to the NW Passage in 1582. At the Armada he commanded the 600-ton *Mary Rose* (but another report gives him captaincy of the *Antelope* in the same Armada year). He died in the spring of 1603 at Deptford 'some days after Queen Elizabeth'. In the church there was erected a memorial: *'To the never-fading memory of Edward Fenton'*.

Fleming (Flemyng) Captain Thomas (*fl.* 1588) West Country sea captain. Alleged by Sir W. Monson to have been a pirate, but State papers contradict this. First to sight the Armada off the Lizard 29 July 1588 in his *Golden Hind* (not Drake's). Through the Gonson family was a connection with the Hawkinses. Frequently mentioned in the ten years following the Armada as captain of Queen's ships and in Cumberland's expeditions.

Frobisher, Sir Martin (c. 1539–94) Distinguished naval commander, pirate, navigator and explorer. Yorkshire-born. As an infant he was sent to his grandfather, Sir John, in London. He was no scholar (he was practically illiterate) and was sent to sea in 1553. He was left as a hostage to a Guinea native chief, captured by the Portuguese, then returned to England in 1559.

For the next fifteen years he was a successful pirate. In 1576 he led three ships in search of the NW Passage, the *Gabriel, Michael* and a pinnace.

He undertook a second and third expedition, heavily financed by city merchants and the Queen herself, to discover gold and explore further the NW Passage region, but they were failures so he returned to his more lucrative piracy. In the Armada campaign he commanded the *Triumph* with distinction, and was knighted by Howard for his excellent tactical fighting. He captured the valuable Spanish carrack *Madre de Dios*, valued at about £150,000, in 1592. In 1594 he was wounded in the hip during a fierce engagement off Brest and died of his wounds on returning to Plymouth.

He was a tough, querulous, brave, ruthless Tudor sea-dog, who lacked the polish of his contemporaries like Drake and Raleigh.

Hakluyt, Richard (1552–1616) Scholar, churchman, indefatigable researcher and traveller. Educated Westminster School and Christ Church. BA 1574 and MA three

THE PRINCIPALL
NAVIGATIONS, VOIA-
GES AND DISCOVERIES OF THE
English nation, made by Sea or ouer Land,
to the most remote and farthest distant Quarters of
the earth at any time within the compasse
of these 1500. yeeres: Deuided into three
seuerall parts, according to the positions of the Regions wherun-
to they were directed:

By *Richard Hakluyt Master of Artes, and Student sometime*
of Christ-church in Oxford.

years later. Read books on travel in Greek, Latin, Italian and Portuguese. Took holy orders: archdeacon of Westminster in 1603. First printed work was *Divers Voyages touching the Discovery of America*, 1582. Inspired by the Armada victory to produce his *Principal Navigations, Voyages and Discoveries of the English Nation*, which appeared in one folio volume in 1589. His great work was reprinted in 1903–5 by the Hakluyt Society founded in his memory.

Hawkins, Sir John (1532–95) Architect of the Elizabethan navy. Son of William Hawkins, a prosperous ship-owner and mayor of Plymouth: he was cousin of Sir Francis Drake. One-time slave trader 1562–8. Married the daughter of Benjamin Gonson, treasurer of the Navy, and became involved in naval administration. In 1577 he succeeded his father-in-law as treasurer, and a dozen years later became comptroller of the Navy, thus holding at the same time the two most influential posts on the Navy Board. He improved the design, building, maintenance and manning of ships, and improved the lot of seamen. Commanded the *Victory* in the Armada campaign, and was knighted during the actual battle by the Lord High Admiral. He always dressed as befitted a wealthy man: he was charming, courteous, but unfathomable. He died off Puerto Rico of dysentery at the age of sixty-three, and was buried at sea.

Hawkins, Sir Richard (*c*.1562–1622) Only son of Sir John Hawkins. Commanded the *Swallow* in the Armada campaign. Attempted a round-the-world voyage in the 300-ton *Dainty*. Rediscovered the Falklands, and attacked Valparaiso. He was imprisoned in Lima 1594, then in Spain and held hostage for £3,000. He was released, then knighted by the Queen. MP for Plymouth. Embarked on an abortive expedition against the Barbary corsairs in 1620. Died, it is said, because of his anger at the delay in paying his men.

Hoby, Sir Edward (1560–1617) Born at Bisham, Berkshire, the eldest son of Sir Thomas Hoby. Educated Eton and Trinity College, Oxford. Nephew and protégé of Lord Burghley. He was knighted, and earned a reputation as a parliamentary speaker. MP for Queenborough, Berkshire, Kent and Rochester between 1586 and 1614. In 1588 he reported to the Queen on preparations for challenging the Armada. Served aboard the *Ark Royal* as secretary to his brother-in-law, the Lord High Admiral. Served at Cadiz in 1596. Keen theologian, and friend of William Camden. He had one son — not by his wife — named Peregrine. Died 1 March 1617.

Sir Edward Hoby, foppish secretary to Lord Howard of Effingham aboard the *Ark* throughout the campaign.

Howard, Charles, second Lord Howard of Effingham and **first Earl of Nottingham** (1536–1624) Lord High Admiral of England. Son of a Lord High Admiral under the Catholic Queen Mary. Grandson of the second Duke of Norfolk, victor of Flodden. Unlike most of the Howards he was a staunch Protestant, and strongly advocated the execution of Mary, Queen of Scots. At the age of twenty-three he was ambassador to France. MP for Surrey 1563–73. Knight of the Garter, Lord Chamberlain of the Household. Although he served at sea for spells, he was primarily a courtier. In

Lord Thomas Howard commanded the *Golden Lion.*

Armada year, when he was fifty-two, the Queen expressed her confidence in her friend and cousin by appointing him 'Lieutenant general and C-in-C of the Navy and army prepared to the seas against Spain'. He was a diligent commander: 'I have been aboard of every ship that goeth out with me.' He was equally attentive to his men: he coped with the administration of a vast fleet such as England had never seen before.

Although much credit for the tactics employed against the Armada goes to Drake, Hawkins and Frobisher, Howard was without doubt one of England's greatest commanders-in-chief of a major fleet in battle. In 1596 he destroyed Spanish shipping at Cadiz, but he continued his administrative duties far too long — till he was eighty-two, when diminishing powers subjected him to a commission of naval administration which found against him.

Howard, Lord Thomas, first Earl of Suffolk and **first Baron Howard de Walden** (1561–1626) Second son of fourth Duke of Norfolk. At the Armada campaign wore his flag in the *Golden Lion*, and was knighted by the Lord High Admiral. Commanded the squadron at the Azores in 1591 when Sir Richard Grenville was killed in the *Revenge*. He was admiral of the 3rd squadron under the Earl of Essex and Lord Howard of Effingham at Cadiz in 1596. The Queen referred to him as 'My good Thomas'. Created Baron in 1597. He sat at the trial of Essex and Southampton. Enjoyed many public appointments. Served James I. Earl of Suffolk in 1603. Helped uncover Gunpowder Plot in 1605. Lord High Treasurer of England in 1614. Disgrace, debt and Star Chamber trial for defrauding the Treasury and the King, but later restored to offices.

Lancaster, Sir James (1555–1618) Commanded *Edward Bonaventure* during the Armada campaign and took her to the East Indies in 1591, but it was a disastrous voyage: sickness, ship-loss, crews killed by natives and marooning. Of 198 men who sailed with him, only 25 returned three years later. Turned to privateering off Pernambuco. In 1601 led the first East India Company expedition. Knighted in 1603 and turned to organizing the affairs of the East India Company. Died in 1618 as a wealthy man: as he had no family he left most of his fortune to the Skinners Company.

ÆTATIS SVÆ 34
AN 1588

AMOR ET VIRTUTE

Sir Walter Raleigh or Ralegh was thirty-four when this portrait was painted, in the year of the Armada.
He is alleged to have served 'as a rear admiral of a squadron' against the Armada but this is not so.
Despite his being one of the finest Elizabethan seamen, there is no evidence that he was at sea at that
time. Earlier, the Queen had appointed him Deputy Lieutenant for the West Country, responsible for
repelling invaders and mustering militiamen.

Mary Stuart, Queen of Scots (1542–87) Born at Linlithgow, daughter of James V of Scotland and Marie de Guise, and succeeded to the throne when only a week old. Her life was marked by murder, intrigue, political chicanery, exile, love affairs and imprisonment. She laid claim to the throne of England. Gave birth to the future James I of England at Stirling Castle in 1566. Her husbands were the Dauphin of France (d. 1560), Lord Darnley (murdered 1567) and James Hepburn, fourth Earl of Bothwell (divorced 1570). Imprisoned in England by Elizabeth. Her execution at Fotheringhay Castle in 1587 precipitated war between Spain and England.

Mary I (Mary Tudor), Queen of England (1516–58) The daughter of Catherine of Aragon and Henry VIII. Suffered neglect, persecution and ill-health. Ascended the throne on the death of her half-brother Edward VI (after Lady Jane Grey's nine-day *coup*) in 1553. She was a devout Catholic. She married the future King Philip II of Spain at Winchester in 1554, but Philip returned to Spain after fourteen months. Mary came to be dubbed 'Bloody Mary' through her religious intolerance, which resulted in the burning of hundreds of Protestants. Calais, British since 1347, was lost to France in 1558. Mary died in 1558 at Lambeth Palace and was succeeded by Elizabeth I.

Ubaldini, Petruccio (?1524–?1600) An Anglophile scholar from Florence who settled in England and wrote at Lord Howard's direction the narrative of the defeat of the Spanish Armada in 1588, and a year later added an original memoir inspired by Drake. These two works are in the British Museum. Augustine Ryther freely translated the first of them with the title *A Discourse Concerning the Spanish Fleet*. The English original has been edited by Professor Sir John K. Laughton in *State Papers Relating to the Defeat of the Spanish Armada*, published by the Navy Records Society.

Walsingham, Sir Francis (c.1530–90) English statesman. Born at Chislehurst in Kent. Studied at King's College, Cambridge. Entered diplomatic service under Burghley. Principal secretary of state to the Queen. Sworn into the privy council and knighted. From 1578 to 1583 on embassy to the Netherlands, France and Scotland.

He established a system of espionage at home and abroad, heading an intelligence and secret service for the Queen. In 1586 he exposed the Babington Plot to kill the Queen and free Mary from imprisonment. He first discovered details of the Armada plan to invade England and was one of the commissioners to try Mary.

Elizabeth acknowledged his genius, his intellectual attainments and his loyal service, but failed to reward him as she did his contemporaries. He was kept poor and unhonoured. He retired to religious meditation and died penniless.

His daughter Frances became, in succession, the wife of Sir Philip Sidney, of the second Earl of Essex and of Richard de Burgh, fourth Earl of Clanricarde.

Wynter (Winter), Sir William (d.1589) From an old Brecknock family. Eldest son of a Bristol merchant-sea captain and one-time Treasurer of the Navy. In 1544 he took part in sacking Leith and Edinburgh. Surveyor of the Navy, 1549. Commanded the *Minion*, 1552. Master of Ordnance, 1557. Commanded a fleet in the Forth in 1559 to prevent a French landing in Scotland. Knighted 1573. Captained *Vanguard* at the Armada campaign, serving under Lord Seymour, with whom he enjoyed the same relationship as did Drake with Howard, that of seaman to aristocrat. He played a distinguished part in the battle of Gravelines. Drake wrote to Lord Seymour: 'I do salute Sir William Wynter . . . and all the rest of these honourable gents'.

Continental Biographies

Philip II, King of Spain (1527–98) Only son of the Holy Roman Emperor Charles V (Charles I of Spain), born at Valladolid. In 1543 he married Maria, daughter of King John III of Portugal, but she died after giving birth to the ill-fated Don Carlos in 1546. His second wife was Mary Tudor, Queen of England: as a dapper 27-year-old he married the 38-year-old spinster at Winchester in 1554 in a 'marriage of policy', but Mary died at the age of forty-two. Philip ascended Spain's throne on the abdication of his father in 1556, and inherited the largest empire since the days of Rome.

Philip tried unsuccessfully to persuade Elizabeth I to marry him. He turned instead to Isabella of France, daughter of Henry II, and married her in 1559. But she too died — in 1568. Philip took as his last consort Anne, daughter of Emperor Maximilian II, who was his cousin. This marriage was in 1570.

Profoundly pious, Philip put himself at the head of the Catholics in Europe and wielded enormous religious power. He set up the Inquisition and extracted enormous sums of money by taxation. In 1580 he annexed Portugal and claimed the throne.

He was provoked to invade England by acts of English piracy, the sacking of Cadiz and the execution of Mary Queen of Scots. However, the 1588 Armada proved disastrous. He made more half-hearted attempts, but none so bold as the first.

To his family he was tender and affectionate, but he lacked pity, political wisdom and breadth of vision; his oppressive taxation policies ruined Spain's commerce.

Aramburu, Marcos Naval commander. Served throughout the Armada campaign aboard the *San Juan Bautista*, the *almirante* of the Castilian Squadron, of whom he was Supervisor and Paymaster. His log detailing his experiences is preserved in the Simancas Archives in northern Spain. He survived the campaign and served with distinction in the Indian Guard until the beginning of the seventeenth century. He played a leading part in the taking of the *Revenge* off the Azores in 1591.

Ascoli, Prince Antonio Luis de Leiva (*fl.*1588) Italian princeling said to be the illegitimate son of Philip II. Served as a member of Sidonia's staff aboard the flagship *San Martin*. He left the ship at Calais on a mission to the Duke of Parma and was ashore when the fireship attack took place. Parma refused to let him attempt to rejoin the Armada, now fleeing northward. Forlornly, he wrote to Philip explaining his predicament. He is believed to have lived long after the campaign, spending much of his time in Italy and Flanders.

Bertendona, Martin Jimenez de (*d.*1607) Soldier and naval commander. His father, also Don Martin, commanded the Biscayan ship which brought Philip to England in 1554 to marry Mary. The younger Martin saw much active service in the Mediterranean, off the Portuguese and Galician coasts. As a gifted young officer he commanded the Levantine Squadron during the Armada campaign. The following year he defended Cadiz against Drake, and in 1591 took the leading part in the great fight off the Azores with Sir Richard Grenville in the *Revenge*. He is the only Spanish officer to have commanded a squadron in all three Spanish armadas of 1588, 1596 and 1597.

Leiva, Alonso de (*c.*1564–88) Distinguished young soldier who would have achieved greater honours but for his early death. Knight of the Order of Santiago. He was tall, slim and handsome, and has been likened as a courtier to the Earl of Essex. He too was dashing and hot-headed. He served in the Low Countries, became Captain-general of Sicilian galleys, then of the Milanese cavalry. Despite his youth, he was to lead the army to invade England. He carried secret despatches from Philip during the Armada campaign nominating him as C-in-C in case of Sidonia's death. He was rescued from the wrecked *Rata Encoronada*, but finally perished with about 1,300 others when the *Girona* foundered on the coast of Ireland.

Oquendo, Miguel de (*d.*1588) Famous mariner from a maritime family. Probably born in San Sebastian. Captain-General of the Guipuzcoan fleet in 1582, when he took part in the battle of Terceira, saving Santa Cruz's flagship from destruction by running his own ship between two of the enemy and capturing the French flagship. He was a proud old officer nicknamed 'The Glory of the Fleet' and regarded as the terror of the Turks in the Mediterranean. He commanded the Guipuzcoan Squadron in the *Santa Ana* during the Armada campaign, when he handled his ship with the skill and dash of a cavalryman. He advocated taking advantage of the English fleet when it was still in Plymouth. He and his ship reached the safety of San Sebastian after the Armada defeat, but he died within a few days of landing. Moreover, soon after his flagship anchored it blew up and sank, with about 100 men aboard.

Don Miguel de Oquendo was a tough, experienced naval commander who handled ships 'like light cavalry.' He died within days of reaching the safety of San Sebastian, where his flagship blew up with heavy loss of life.

Parma, Alexander Farnese, Duke of (1545–92) Distinguished soldier, regarded as the finest general of his time, with a profound political awareness. Educated University of Alcala, near Madrid. Studied with Don John of Austria and Don Carlos. In 1565 he married the Portuguese princess Maria, grand-daughter of King Manuel I, the Fortunate.

Fought at Lepanto in 1571. While he was campaigning in Flanders in 1586 his father died, and he inherited the dukedoms of Parma and Plasencia (or Piacenza). Philip II charged him with marshalling an army to invade England, a commission he accepted once he had occupied the Low Countries and warded off the Dutch Sea Beggars. After the defeat of the Armada he continued campaigning in Europe. He captured Paris, was wounded in 1592 and died in that same year in Arras. He had dedicated his military genius to Spain but Philip never befriended him, distrusting his military genius.

Pimentel, Diego (*fl*.16th & 17th cent). Distinguished soldier, son of the Marquis of Tavara. He commanded cavalry in Italy and Sicily, and during the 1580 campaign to annex Portugal. *Maestro de campo* aboard Hugo Moncada's flagship the *San Mateo* in the first Armada, 1588. He was captured when she foundered on the beach at Calais, but was ransomed and released. Later became Spanish ambassador to Germany. Captain-General of the Andalusian coast. Returned to Italy in 1601. In 1614 Philip III appointed him Captain-General of Aragon and in 1621 of Mexico.

Recalde, Juan Martinez de (*c*.1526–88) Distinguished admiral and Knight of Santiago. Probably born in Bilbao. Saw much active service in the East Indies and the Low Countries. Superintendent of Royal Dockyards and headed the Indian Guard. In 1579 he commanded the landing of 1,000 men in Ireland. Served under Santa Cruz at the battle of Terceira in 1582. In the Armada campaign he gave strong support to Sidonia, although he advocated attacking Howard's fleet in Plymouth. Sailed in the vice flagship of the Duke's squadron, the *San Juan de Portugal*. He was a strong, lion-hearted nobleman and a skilled professional seaman.

Santa Cruz, Alvaro de Bazan, first Marquis (1526–88) Spain's greatest admiral, holder of the Knight of Santiago, and created mayor for life of Gibraltar. Started naval career very young. Saw action off Galicia when he was sixteen. In 1544 served with his father, who was Captain-General of the Spanish fleet. With this privileged background he rose to high command. In 1554 he commanded a squadron against pirates, and for the next ten years saw much active service in the Mediterranean and off Gibraltar.

In 1566 he commanded the Naples fleet. In 1569 he became the first Marquis of Santa Cruz, and two years later at the battle of Lepanto earned renown for his masterly handling of the Spanish ships of the reserve fleet. In 1580 he served in the campaign to conquer Portugal, and in 1582 defeated the French fleet under Strozzi at Terceira off the Azores. Another French squadron was defeated the following year. He was honoured with the title Captain-General of the Ocean Seas.

He became obsessed with invading England, and this occupied his mind for years while he engaged in preparations for the enterprise. He died in February 1588 — worn out, it is said, by the King's constant admonishing.

Sidonia, Alonso Perez de Guzman ('El Bueno'), Duke of Medina Sidonia (?1550–1619) Spanish nobleman and naval commander-in-chief. A member of the illustrious and noble house of Guzman. Became seventh Duke in 1555 on the death of his father. He inherited one of the greatest fortunes and estates in Europe on the death of his grandfather in 1559. He became a great favourite of Philip II's, who appointed him Captain-General of the coast of Andalusia in 1588.

In the previous year he had achieved relatively little while attempting to defend Cadiz against Drake's attack, but he was appointed to command the Armada in February 1588 on the death of Santa Cruz. The ensuing campaign was disastrous for him and for Spain, to which his own ineptitude and lack of seamanship contributed. Despite this, the royal favour was not withdrawn. He was appointed Captain-General of the Ocean Seas in 1595, and remained in practical control of the Spanish navy under Philip III despite further humiliations like the sacking of Cadiz in 1596 and the destruction of a squadron by the Dutch off Gibraltar in 1606. He died at his family home at Sanlucar in 1619 (some sources quote 1615).

Valdes, Diego Flores de (*fl.*1588) Naval commander of twenty years' experience commanding the Indian Guard, the King's ships guarding the treasure ships of the Indies. In 1581 he led an unsuccessful expedition to the Straits of Magellan. Described as narrow-minded, acrimonious and one of the most unpopular commanders in the fleet. He was a professional seaman, expert on tides, currents, ships and the seas. In 1588 when commanding the galleons of Castile he was nominated by the King as second-in-command of the Armada — a curious choice, because he quarrelled with all his brother-officers and had a permanent feud with his cousin Pedro de Valdes.

Valdes, Pedro de (*d.*1614) Naval commander. Born at Gijon. A seaman of long experience, he saw service against the French and Portuguese and was seriously wounded in a fight with two English ships off Ferrol in 1580. The King imprisoned him in 1582 for failing to take the Azores and for the heavy loss of life among the soldiers. He commanded the Andalusian Squadron of the Armada in the *Rosario*, which he surrendered to Drake; he was a prisoner at large for three years till his ransom of about £3,000 was paid. From 1602–8 he was Governor of Cuba. He built the castle of Morro to defend Havana. He retired to Gijon.

Coinage and currency

*T*HE VALUE of Spanish coins at the time of the Armada is an intricate subject which defies simplification, and to try to attribute indexed figures at today's values in order to give a relevant comparative is virtually impossible. Nevertheless, some simple guidelines can be offered. The Spanish coins of Castile are the most important — and the gold ones the most valuable.

A *mark* of gold weighed 8 ounces, or 4,608 grains. A *ducat* (from the time of Ferdinand (1452–1516) and Isabella) consisted of nearly 375 *maravedis*. And 65.3 ducats amounted to one *mark* of gold.

In due time the *ducat* became a mere unit of accounting, and its value stabilized at 375 *maravedis*.

Later in the seventeenth century coins known as doblons de a dos (2), *de a quatro* (4) and *de a ocho* (8) worth two, four and eight escudos came into use. The latter became the celebrated coins of film and fiction, the Spanish doubloon or 'pieces of eight'.

Sources cannot agree on index linking in order to relate 1588's values to those of today. Suggestions vary between 80 and 120 times, with most authoritative sources quoting 80. For practical purposes, a factor of 100 is probably as acceptably near as we can get.

The value of a *ducat* at the time was about 5s. 6d. (27½ p), but for rough calculating purposes it is reasonable to allow 4 *ducats* to the pound sterling. For example, a Spanish treasure ship worth 40,000 *ducats* equated to about £10,000. (Today's value = £1 million.)

4. Cadiz and Philip's Beard

KING PHILIP II was incensed when he learned that Queen Elizabeth had knighted Francis Drake for his circumnavigation of the world. The voyage was seen by him as nothing less than a buccaneering and plundering raid of enormous proportions mounted against Spanish possessions and interests throughout the world. Elizabeth was hard put to explain away her knighting of Drake aboard his ship at Deptford in 1581: neither Philip nor his ambassador believed her. Perhaps the few months' delay in carrying out the ceremony was an excuse; whether this was so or not, she got away with it, but the act rankled with the Spaniards.

Four years or so later another act of Drake's infuriated the Spanish, which was exactly what it was designed to do. This was Walsingham's intention — 'annoying the king of Spain'. It was an act as provocative as the beheading of Mary, Queen of Scots — perhaps even more so, because it was a positive act of aggression directed specifically at the forces of the kingdom of Spain on their own territory; in their own back-yard, you might say. The attack on Cadiz was a deliberate, pre-emptive strike which had formidable consequences that no one could ignore, least of all Philip: to him it must have been as treacherous as a Pearl Harbour strike.

*   *   *

Philip had already dispatched orders for the assembling of the first Armada in Lisbon, and one of the intermediate staging ports for this operation was Cadiz, a major port of southern Spain.

Early in 1587 Cadiz was crammed with shipping, and at the end of April there were perhaps sixty ships anchored or moored in the roadstead, ships of every possible description. There were hulks filled with casks of wine from nearby Jerez; others loaded with cargoes from the Mediterranean, France and Germany; a large Biscayan was ready to sail with ironmongery to the West Indies, as was a Levantine with hides, wool and timber. Requisitioned vessels for the Armada rode at anchor, and there was a variety of naval vessels, including a newly built galleon from a Biscay shipyard.

At about four o'clock on Wednesday afternoon 29 April 1587 a line of ships was sighted standing in towards the harbour from the north-western horizon. There were no means of identifying them, so as a precaution six galleys were ordered out.

*   *   *

When Drake first heard of the ships assembling in Spanish and Portuguese ports he implored the Queen to allow him to 'smoke the wasps out of their nests'. She not only consented, she invested quite substantially in an enterprise which blended naval operations with undisguised privateering.

By 12 April Drake had assembled in Plymouth a fleet of about two dozen vessels, four of them Queen's galleons, another galleon of Drake's, some pinnaces of his own and of the Lord High Admiral, seven armed merchantmen from London's commercial interests, and other commercial privateers. They were all watered and provisioned at a rush, for Drake was anxious to weigh anchor: 'the wind commands me away,' he had written to Walsingham, and signed the letter 'Haste! From aboard her Majesty's good ship the *Elizabeth Bonaventure.'*

Well might he hurry to be off! The Queen, as so often, had second thoughts about the enterprise and dispatched orders to Drake forbidding him to enter a Spanish harbour or land on Spanish soil. Drake got away by the skin of his teeth, the pinnace bearing the orders sent in pursuit failing to catch up.

Drake pressed on at speed, not waiting for laggards to keep up, so that on Wednesday 29 April he led only a small squadron of his fastest ships — the galleons — with the other ships hull down to the rear.

Drake summoned the captains of this vanguard force to a council which he handled in his usual autocratic manner. He *imposed* his plans rather than debating them. He was right, of course; the conditions were in their favour — surprise, unpreparedness in the harbour, the wind and the lowering sun astern. Cadiz could be theirs by nightfall! In they would go!

Vice admiral William Borough, a cartographer of great skill, was Drake's second-in-command. He was methodical, meticulous, used to applying the rules, playing it by the book, and he was appalled at Drake's attitude. He returned to his *Golden Lion* affronted by his admiral's easy-going manner, his lack of detailed planning, his risk-taking in entering a defended harbour.

An engraving of Cadiz just before Drake's Raid in 1587.

Royal commission for the attack on Cadiz

DRAKE LED an audacious raid by a squadron of English ships upon a harbour full of Spanish ships in Cadiz. He sank or captured thirty-three of them and brought away four laden with plundered provisions. The raid postponed the launching of the Armada against England by a year, and humiliated the King of Spain, whose beard was claimed to have been singed. The Queen's Royal Commission gave Drake royal authority to carry out a raid which in modern terms would be described as a pre-emptive strike against a country with which one was not at war.

The Royal Letters Patent to Sir Francis Drake committed to him charge of the fleet to set sail 'for the honour and safetie of our Realms and Domynions . . . We doe of our authoritie royall and of our certaine knowledge give full poer and jurisdiction to you to punish and correct with all severite . . .'

As Drake led his squadron for the harbour entrance six slender galleys pulled out rhythmically to meet him. He turned his cannons upon them and dealt them a shattering blast: galleys versus galleons in these conditions was hardly a fair contest, and the galleys broke off the action and pulled away to safety.

The gunfire alerted the ships and defences of Cadiz, but they were at a tremendous disadvantage. Understandably, ships were unprepared for a surprise attack like this. They were only partly manned, not on a war footing (England and Spain were not at war), sails were furled, boats and pinnaces plying in the late afternoon sun, urcas (see below) being provisioned and cargoes stored.

Drake saw the harbour packed with shipping, and he saw the panic and pandemonium as some ships' cables were cut to allow them to get under way; others collided, some ran aground, yet others found safety in small inlets. A huge Levantine (see below) armed with 40 brass guns got away many shots until pounded into silence by the Queen's ships, and later in the evening she sank at her anchorage. Otherwise the opposition was minor. Gun-shots from the fort and shore batteries barely reached the English ships: they were quite ineffectual.

The English settled down to hours of methodical plundering once resistance had been overcome; far into the night it went, transferring cargoes, disposing of damaged and unwanted vessels, applying prize crews, so that by dawn the magnitude of the victory could be seen.

Then Drake saw a galleon in the shallow upper bay still afloat and undamaged. He anchored his *Elizabeth Bonaventure* in the main harbour, the rest of his squadron conforming, boarded his admiral's barge and led a small flotilla of pinnaces to attack the Spaniard and set her ablaze.

Meanwhile William Borough was agitated by the situation. He visited the flagship to find Drake gone, and then returned to his *Golden Lion*, by which time a Spanish culverin ashore had got the range of his ship. A shot holed the *Lion* at the waterline and the master gunner had a leg sheared off. The *Lion*'s master began to warp the ship out of range, only to expose herself to the damaged six galleys, now anxious to get at the single, distressed English galleon. Drake saw the situation and sent reinforcements to safeguard his vice admiral's ship. The wind fell away, and Borough's ship lay becalmed near the harbour entrance while Drake's drifted without steerageway in the main harbour.

In the next twelve hours the Cadiz defenders worked tirelessly to assemble more cannons and the Duke of Medina Sidonia arrived with more than 3,000 troops. The galleys attempted to attack the drifting English ships, but each time they were repulsed by accurate gunfire. An attempt to launch fireships failed. The sum total of all the Spanish efforts was the one casualty — the master gunner losing his leg — and the waterline damage to the *Golden Lion*. It was little short of miraculous for the English.

When a land breeze got up at about midnight Drake led his squadron with its flotilla of prizes from Cadiz harbour. He claimed to have sunk or captured 37 ships. Perhaps the claim was high — King Philip only admitted to the loss of 24 ships destroyed, with a total value of 172,000 ducats. 'The loss was not very great,' he declared, 'but the daring of the attempt was very great indeed.'

Drake claimed, with understandable pride in this brilliantly audacious exploit, to have 'singed the King of Spain's beard'. He went on to singe it further in six weeks of plundering and blockading of Spanish and Portuguese ports, in the course of which he

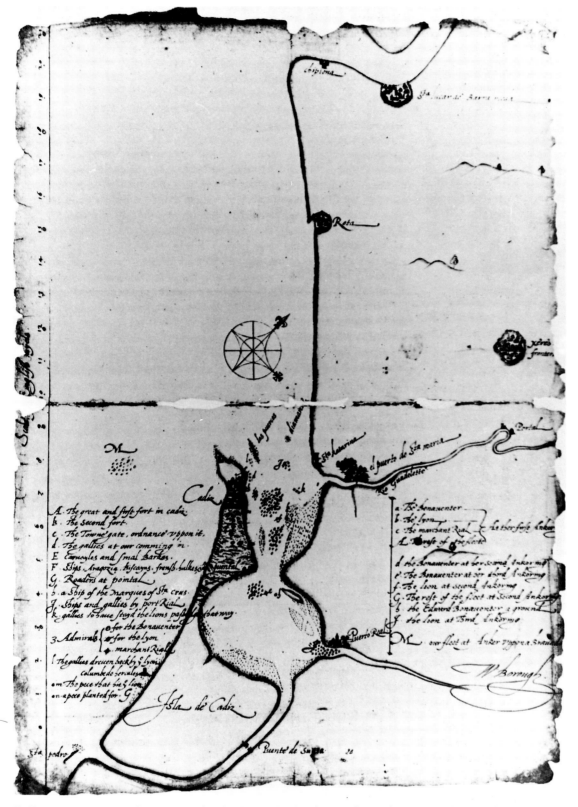

William Borough, second-in-command to Sir Francis Drake, drew and signed this chart of the Raid on Cadiz, 1587, and used it so often it became creased and worn. He compiled the two tabulations which position all the English ships — his own, the *Golden Lion* (designated by the letter 'f' in the outer harbour), was hit by the gun (keyed to the letter 'm') on the eastern shore of the peninsula. The raid was an outstanding success.

Buckland Abbey, Drake's home near Plymouth, is a far cry from the humble cottage where he was born near Tavistock. His round-the-world voyage and his plunderings at Vigo, Cadiz and the Azores made him a wealthy man.

In the Great Hall Drake's drum is displayed together with the oaken table over which he discussed charts with his captains.

Ships of the Sixteenth Century

Carrack: the biggest and most important merchant ship of the 14th-17th centuries in the Mediterranean, which readily doubled as a warship. Carracks often carried three decks, were heavily built with lofty overhanging bow and stern castles and with deep holds.

Caravel: a lighter and more seaworthy version of the carrack: three-masted and among the most manoeuvrable of ships.

Fly-boat: small fast sailing vessel of shallow draught for the shoal waters off Flanders and the Netherlands. Popular with pirates and sea-robbers. Cargo capacity 40–140 tons.

Galleasse: this ship demonstrated the transitional design from oared galley to sailing merchant ship, combining the best of both worlds, the speed of the galley and the firepower and seaworthiness of the galleon. She was a formidable warship, regarded as equivalent to five galleys in battle. The Naples galleasses of the Armada each mounted 50 sizeable guns: they carried 25–30 oars on either side, each manned by 5–8 convict rowers. They were 40–50 m long, had an iron-capped battering ram and carried 200–300 soldiers.

Galleon: a large sailing vessel, precursor of the ship of the line: the standard fighting ship of the Atlantic. She had two or more decks from stem to stern with main batteries in broadsides. Castles fore and aft bristled with lighter quick-firing guns. A galleon could displace 2,000 tons but the English lighter versions were 500–600 tons and about 50–60m long. They were also better rigged and faster sailing and were known as 'race-built' galleons.

Galley: a long, manœuvrable oared vessel — successor to the ancient trireme — used from earliest times till the eighteenth century. It could cram aboard 240 oarsmen to give maximum rowing power. The great clumsy oars weighed 300 kg and were 12m long; at full speed five men per oar at 22 strokes per minute (with quick bursts of 26 strokes) gave over 4 knots. The ship was long and narrow with a low freeboard. When other ships were becalmed the galleys had a significant advantage. The galley is probably the most notorious ship ever built. (*See illus.*).

Great ship: a term applied to an armed merchant ship which supplemented galleons in battle: she was usually over 300 tons. The most formidable Elizabethan-period great ships were those of the Levantine Company, armed with culverins and demi-cannons. These English ships were built for speed and manœuvrability for fighting Mediterranean corsairs.

Hulk: (a) a stripped hulk of a sailing ship, minus her masts and rigging and used as customs guardship, prison, hospital, coal and provisions store, arsenal, barracks. A sheer hulk was a hulk fitted with sheer legs. (b) the urca, a north European, Baltic trade, sailing ship, flattish bottomed, without a keel, slow and clumsy but seaworthy. She had a ratio of ship's length to beam of 3:1.

Levantine: see Great ship.

Patache (patajes or patax): see Zabras.

Pinnace: (a) a rowing boat, usually built of spruce (Pinus), smaller than an officer's barge. (b) a small three-masted ship of about 35m long, fitted with about 18 small guns, later versions carrying up to 30, making her like a small frigate.

Urca: see Hulk.

Zabras, fregatas, pataches: these were the names given to Spanish vessels approximating to the English pinnace. They are listed in descending order of size. They were all handy, fast and lightly armed. Pataches were the 60–70 ton ships of the Armada.

captured or destroyed 100 small ships. The principal cargo he captured and burnt was 1,700 tons of hoops and seasoned barrel staves intended for casks and pipes. This had the effect a year later of coopers having to use 'green' staves for barrels, contributing to the leaking of water and the spoiling of provisions months later.

Drake continued to seek bases to attack or blockade. When he received intelligence of a large East India carrack due to arrive in the Azores it was there he headed. A southerly gale roared for forty-eight hours, dispersing many ships, including Borough's *Golden Lion*, which sailed to England. Drake was furious, regarding it as desertion. He convened a court martial and found Borough guilty, in his absence, of treason and mutiny — a harsh verdict, but the sentence was never carried out. Borough had influential friends in London, and perhaps the later events and ensuing euphoria put such matters into a true perspective.

Drake captured the enormous Portuguese carrack *San Felipe* of 1,400 tons, laden with a rich cargo to the tune of £114,000: this one ship and her cargo was worth more than three times all the plunder from Cadiz. The Queen's share amounted to £40,000 and Drake's to £17,000. He sailed for home to regal acclaim and to enjoy untold riches.

In his audacious Cadiz Raid Drake had effectively postponed the launching of the Armada upon England for a year. What he had also done was to ensure — with absolute certainty — that the Enterprise of England would now be launched. There was no question of it: it was only a question of when.

Nor did it please the King to learn from the Venetian Ambassador that the Pope had been impressed by Drake's successes, and thought Philip ought to hurry along with effective counter-measures.

5. *The invasion plans*

KING PHILIP II needed no prodding from the tactless Pope Sixtus V about planning counter-measures against England. He had every intention of hurrying along with retaliatory action after the Cadiz raid. But as with all his major decisions, the King spent weeks of detached thinking and quiet deliberation seated at his desk in the Escorial. He turned to the various plans at his disposal for dealing with Elizabeth and England. There were plenty for him to choose from.

The Marquis of Santa Cruz had urged upon the King the need for an invasion plan against England several years earlier, while he himself was still bathing in the glory of his victory off the Azores in 1582. He had written to the King: 'For a long while your Majesty has cherished an idea of undertaking something against England . . .' Santa Cruz pointedly drew Philip's attention to the heretical sovereign of England and her plundering of Philip's colonial domain in the West Indies, and recommended his Majesty to adopt an equally offensive spirit.

Further, he proposed that his present fleet should be retained to form the nucleus of 'the Enterprise of England'. Philip was, of course, interested in the proposals, but the time was not propitious for such an undertaking. The King needed further convincing, and he resorted to the bureaucratic delaying tactic of requesting fully costed details of the admiral's proposals. This Santa Cruz did — down to the last ducat.

The facts and figures he presented leave one gasping. Philip must have found them utterly bewildering and totally impracticable. For example, Santa Cruz concluded that the size of the mighty seaborne invasion force should be 556 ships, in addition to which he calculated there would need to be another 20 *fregatas*, 20 *faluas* and 200 flat-bottomed barges, all of these 240 vessels to be hoisted aboard larger ships like the ship-borne landing-craft of the twentieth century. This meant a grand total of 796 vessels.

Santa Cruz went on to define these in some detail. 196 of them were to be, in modern terminology, 'capital ships'. Of these, 150 were to be large sailing-ships, 40 oared galleys and 6 galleasses. Of the 196 ships, Santa Cruz considered 71 were to be 'King's ships', the property of the Crown. He defined these as the 40 galleys, 15 royal Portuguese galleons, 10 Spanish galleons and the 6 galleasses.

The total number of seamen and soldiers to be transported in this mighty fleet he had calculated with incredible precision to be 94,222. In round figures these can be grouped as follows: 65,000 soldiers and 30,000 mariners.

When it came to the sheer logistics of supplying such a mighty Armada with its requirements of victuals, drink, armaments, the thousand and one items needed to keep a 'modern' fleet with a manning establishment not far short of 100,000 men at sea on a war footing for several weeks, then Santa Cruz seems to have been transported into the realms of fantasy. Nothing daunted, he pressed on with his calculations. He

Philip II ruled his vast Spanish possessions from a private suite in the Escorial Palace near Madrid. It comprised a study, bedroom and a private chapel. Here he received Ministers and officials, worked and prayed and administered his empire. In this worn chair he planned the invasion of England and dispatched the mighty Armada.

listed the following victuals for a voyage of unknown duration but certainly for not less than 6 months and probably as long as 8 months: 373,337 cwt biscuits; 22,800 cwt bacon; 21,500 cwt cheese; 23,200 barrels tunny fish; 16,040 cwt salt beef; 11,200 gallons of vinegar; 22,000 pipes* of water and 46,800 pipes of wine.

* A 'pipe' was a large cask equivalent to two hogsheads = 110 gallons. Thus the total wine provision amounted to over 5 million gallons. The water content of nearly 2½ million gallons was listed in Santa Cruz's estimates under the provision for horses and mules, and it is presumed the men were not expected to drink it, although it would have been required for cooking.

Seamen's victuals

*I*N THE YEAR before the Armada campaign the allowance paid to an English contractor was raised to 6½d. per man per day in harbour and 7d. at sea. A further allowance for 'purser's necessaries' was set at 4d. per man per month while at sea and 8d. in harbour. These costs were intended to cover the contractor for supplying the food, its storage, custody, conveyance, etc.

The victuals allowed to the seamen of both countries were generous in quantity but of appalling quality. Two sources for the amount of the English victuals are quoted, giving daily and weekly figures, and both are well documented.

ENGLISH

1 gallon Beer per day
1 lb Biscuit per day
1 lb Salt Beef on Sunday, Tuesday and Thursday
¼ of a stockfish or part of a ling on Wednesday, Friday and Saturday, plus
Cheese and butter
1 lb Salt Pork with peas on Monday.

A Weekly Allowance is quoted:
8 lb Beef
7 lb Biscuit
9 lb Salted Fish
¾ lb Cheese
¾ lb Butter
7 Gallons Beer
Purser's necessaries: oatmeal, pepper, mustard, vinegar.

SPANISH

1½ lb Biscuit per day or
2 lb Fresh Bread
6 oz Salt Pork and
2 oz Rice on Sunday and Thursday
6 oz Cheese and
3 oz Beans or Chick Peas on Monday and Thursday
6 oz Dried Tunny, Cod, Squid or
5 Sardines with
3 oz Beans or Chick Peas with
1½ oz Oil and
¼ pint Vinegar on Wednesday, Friday and Saturday
Wine allowance: roughly equivalent to a modern bottle a day, or a pint of stronger wine such as Candia.
3 pints of water a day for cooking, drinking and washing.

Modern dieticians would condemn these diets on many counts. The English diet is specially deficient in vitamin C because of the lack of fresh fruit and vegetables, and this was a direct cause of scurvy. The exceptionally high meat content would have provided adequate amounts of protein, fat and minerals, and of vitamin B, and the latter — also, incidentally, found in beer — helped to utilize the carbohydrate. But fatty meat, together with cheese and butter, would have been high in cholesterol, leading to an increased risk of heart disease.

The daily alcohol allocation is excessive: today's medical knowledge would recommend a daily limit of one *pint* a day. Presumably the beer helped counteract the heavy salt content of the diet. The lack of calcium would have helped keep the mariners short in stature, and they would have suffered from constipation because of the low fibre content of their food — unless the biscuits were wholemeal.

Higher marks would go to the more varied Spanish diet. It still lacked vitamin C, but the beans, chick peas and biscuit gave a better fibre content. There was little to choose between the often impure water on the Spanish list and the often sour English beer. Perhaps the Spanish wine was a better choice, if only because it led to a smaller alcohol intake.

Toothache would have been common to both English and Spanish mariners: loose teeth and diseased gums were symptoms of scurvy, and eating tough meat would have been painful and difficult.

A musketeer typical of the
Armada period, showing
the U-topped crock on
which he rested the barrel of
his musket.

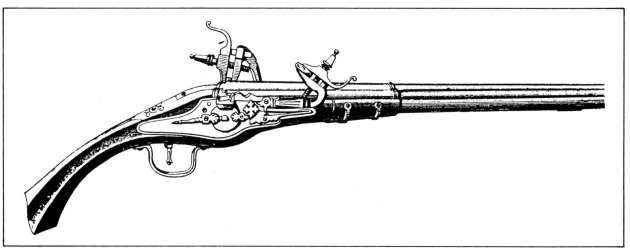

A sixteenth-century wheel-lock arquebus.

The list seems endless: we have not touched upon the shot and powder required, the countless items of equipment for the ships, their sails and yards and rigging, their artillery and weaponry, the hospital stores, the cordage and other chandlery; oil, animal feed . . . The King must have sighed in bewilderment at the estimate.

He must have realized when he reached the 'bottom line' the total impracticability of the plan simply on a cost basis. Santa Cruz himself — veteran seaman, grandest admiral of his time, skilled naval administrator — must have realized the absurdity of his own proposals long before he arrived at the estimated cost of the plans. The figure was astronomical — 1,526,425,498 maravedis, equivalent to something over 4 million ducats. This sum equalled all the riches Philip could expect to acquire from the annual treasure of the New World — three times over.

The plan required the commitment of the combined maritime strength of Spain and Portugal and an extensive new construction and refitting programme. It was altogether too much for the prudent Philip. He let matters proceed without sanctioning anything of any consequence. He reasoned with himself and derived comfort from the belief — fundamental to almost everything he did or contemplated — that, come what may, God would be on his side, on the side of the Catholics.

Other plans had been submitted to Philip over the years: Don John of Austria had been obsessed with a dash across the Channel to rescue the Queen of Scots, a triumphal march on London to dethrone Elizabeth and re-establish the Catholic faith. Alexander Farnese, the Duke of Parma and the finest soldier of his generation, proposed an altogether different plan to invade Kent.

The plan set before the King by the young Duke of Parma, the leading army strategist and tactician on the continent of Europe, bore all the freshness and signs of common sense, reasonableness and, most exhilarating of all, promise of victory. Parma's plan embodied the best elements from both Santa Cruz's and Don John's. The army, he agreed, should be transported — but *swiftly* — across the Channel in flat-bottomed boats *in a single night*. He believed that an army as large as 30,000 men with 500 cavalry could be hustled across the Channel like an endless train of ferries to land on the coast of either Kent or Essex in a period of eight to ten hours.

Curiously, Parma's invasion plan foreshadowed the appreciations of Napoleon and Hitler for their own assaults on England centuries later. It is interesting to observe that all of the plans foundered on insufficient consideration being given to the question of command of the sea. Parma, Napoleon and Hitler, military geniuses of their eras, gravely overestimated the ability of the military to cross the Channel with relative ease.

Parma's enterprise sensibly stressed the element of surprise: before the English could muster strength ashore to repel the assault the invaders would have secured a strong foothold — and victory would be within the army's grasp. Virtually nothing could stop his army of 30,000 disciplined men, battle-trained in the Low Countries. It was an army comprising men devoted to living and dying as soldiers; their brutalized conditions of soldiering toughened them into fighting men of considerable ability. They were officered by noblemen brought up to believe that soldiering even in the infantry was a respectable and perfectly honourable profession. The result was an army rarely seen in Europe since the Roman legions fifteen centuries before.

But the sea: therein lay the secret — and Philip knew it. Parma's plan displayed a weakness, and Philip could see it. Parma reckoned that a force of 25 warships — only 25 — would effectively guard the narrows and safeguard the flat-bottomed flotillas.

Philip detected another flaw in Parma's plan, and he put his finger on it quite unerringly. The element of surprise simply was not a possibility. Philip annotated to this effect in the margin. Once he wrote *Disparo* (nonsense!) against the statement that it would be easy to invade England.

Early in 1587 Philip began to favour the combined operation of employing some 17,000 men from Flanders to be transported across the Channel together with an armada from Lisbon to sail up Channel, rendezvous with the army in Flanders and escort it to the beaches in Kent.

Once a foothold had been established ashore the targets would be readily achievable: the occupation of Kent, possibly a battle in the Canterbury region, then, counting on a gathering momentum, taking London by storm, possibly with a flying column of well-trained professionals, capturing Elizabeth, her Court and Ministers.

Philip's reasoning was probably right. Queen Elizabeth had few soldiers and officers as well trained, experienced and skilled as Parma's men. What troops were available would be thinly spread over several counties along hundreds of miles of coastline to answer a call to catch the enemy 'at the sea side'. No defence strategy existed of a concerted or concentrated nature. Some strategists supported the plan of withdrawing all troops inland to make a stand (such as at Canterbury) and 'staye the enemy from speedy passage to London or the harte of the realme'.

Seven workmen in this Low Countries gun foundry in the sixteenth century illustrate the stages in gun-founding. One works a treadmill, two more chip away residues on castings, another shovels scrap into the furnace, while three more watch the molten bronze flowing into the mould of a gun placed vertically, breech end down, in the earthen floor.

The King endorsed this revised plan, and authorized Santa Cruz to implement it. Philip and his advisers reckoned that Catholic friends and sympathizers in the north and west of England and in Ireland would rise in rebellion, contributing to the rapid conquest of the whole of the island. Such was the thinking.

Philip noted in September 1587 that 'although the forces we now have both there and here are insufficient on their own, together — if we can get them together — they will win'.

It was in this same month that the King instructed Santa Cruz that as soon as the galleasses of Naples and the victuallers of Andalusia had joined the assembling fleet at Lisbon, the Marquis was to sail for 'the cape of Margate' with whatever forces he could muster. Santa Cruz pleaded unpreparedness of the ships, necessity of urgent repairs and the need for more weeks' delay.

In fact, for over two years Santa Cruz had been parrying similar exhortations from his King. Philip had kept up a never-ending stream of messengers visiting the Marquis daily, even hourly, with a constant stream of nagging messages which sought, cajoled, exhorted, demanded more and more from the wearying and now ageing admiral.

In December 1587 the King instructed him to dispatch a fleet — even if it only comprised a fleet of 35 vessels — even if it was not commanded by Santa Cruz himself — to support Parma's cross-Channel intention.

The sudden mobilization of the English fleet enabled Santa Cruz to warn and persuade the King that a fleet of 35 ships would probably be totally inadequate and therefore at great risk. He earned a further stay of dispatch. But Philip insisted that a date of 15 February should be set as the target date for the departure once and for all of the Armada from Lisbon — and he sent along as his personal representative Count Fuentes to keep jollying along the reluctant Marquis.

One can sympathize with Santa Cruz, the professional adviser constantly at odds with his King, arguing and disagreeing, writing interminable reports, while all the time the King demanded action, guided often by God rather than by military reason. The Marquis did not need the reassurance of God's will. He knew, even before the phrase came into use centuries later, the meaning of the maxim that victory went to the side with the heavy battalions.

He sought a minimum of 50 galleons in the Armada in order to be sure of beating the English. Unfortunately, he only mustered 13, one so rotten and old that she might founder. In addition, he sought another 100 vessels — armed great ships, 40 hulks or urcas for victuals and as a fleet train, six galleasses, 40 galleys and probably 150 small craft.

In the event, at the end of January he could count his 13 galleons, 4 galleasses, perhaps 60–70 ships hired or commandeered, ships of great variety, many of them ill prepared for a warlike venture — and the shortage of auxiliary small craft was deplorable.

With only one week to go before the 15 February deadline the enormous demands on the grizzled old admiral's health and resources proved too great. He was weighed down with the endless worries of the giant undertaking in which it is quite possible he no longer believed.

He was in his sixty-third year, and past his peak. On 9 February of Armada year he gave up the ghost and died peacefully at Lisbon. Some said that with his death there died the hopes of the Armada.

Philip bore the heavy blow with apparent equanimity. He was disturbed and dismayed, of course, at the further enforced delay, but he drew comfort from what might have been a worse situation: 'God has shown me a favour,' he confided a week after the death, 'by removing the Marquis now rather than when the Armada is at sea'.

Philip had already decided upon a successor. The great admiral was to be replaced by a greater grandee, a nobleman of higher status than Santa Cruz, higher than a marquis; a duke, no less.

Bold though this decision was, it was a desperately unfortunate choice.

*   *   *

The Duke of Medina Sidonia was no great man of war, let alone a sailor. By all contemporary accounts he was a gentle man, peaceful, polite, courteous and considerate: colourless, it is true, deeply religious, lacking in ambition — what more could he want in materialistic terms? He was a man of honour, as one might expect of a well-born courtly aristocrat of the Spanish establishment.

It took exceptional circumstances to rouse him to anger, for he disliked violence. His dislike of everything military and violent was strangely out of character with a rich warrior background to his family ancestry. Soldiering was more than a thread in the tapestry of his family: it was the very fabric on which the threads were painstakingly stitched.

He could raise an army of thousands at the will of the King — he did so for the annexation of Portugal in 1580. Most recently in 1587 he had arrived in time to prevent the devastation of Cadiz by Drake, and over the years had kept peace over the countryside of Andalusia.

What the Duke of Medina Sidonia did possess in abundance was noble standing. He was one of Spain's grandest aristocrats at a time in Spanish and English history when power and position rested in the hands of the influential few. He was wealthy, immensely, immeasurably wealthy, his duchy the most ancient in Spain and one of the greatest private estates in Europe.

No naval or military officer, however noble, could be offended by being asked to serve under a grandee of such dazzling eminence. From that standpoint, his appointment was at first glance a shrewd one.

Medina Sidonia has survived in portrait form in only one picture, painted when he was an old man, years after his dreadful experience of defeat with the Armada. It is hard to discern from this the true likeness of a man who was only in his late thirties at the time of the Armada, but his intelligence comes through, as does the sensitivity of his high forehead, his brooding, melancholy face. One senses that here was a man to respect, though possibly not a strong leader: there is no gleam of ambition in his eyes, they are not the eyes to inspire men to fight and die for you. Some said, unkindly, that he always conducted himself with dignity except at time of great stress, when he inclined to panic.

The letter inviting Medina Sidonia to succeed Santa Cruz came to him from the King's secretary, and Sidonia's reply of abject wretchedness as he attempts to disqualify himself says much about the man. It says much too about the King's ill-judgment in continuing with the appointment in the face of such critical self-denial. But when Medina Sidonia was pressed by the King he readily acquiesced through a sense of loyalty to King and country — *noblesse oblige*.

A sixteenth-century terrestrial globe
now in the National Maritime
Museum.

An astrolabe of about 1580,
typical of many in use by English
seamen at the time of the Armada.
Its diameter is 21·8 cm.

Medina Sidonia declines command of the Armada

*T*HE DUKE REPLIED to Don Juan de Idiaques, Secretary to King Philip II, declining the invitation to command the Armada. The letter was dated 16 February 1588:

My health is not equal to such a voyage, for I know by experience of the little I have been at sea that I am always seasick and always catch cold. My family is burdened with a debt of nine hundred thousand ducats, and I could not spend a real in the King's service. Since I have had no experience either of the sea or of war, I cannot feel that I ought to command so important an enterprise. I know nothing of what the Marquis of Santa Cruz has been doing, or of what intelligence he has of England, so that I feel I should give but a bad account of myself, commanding thus blindly, and being obliged to rely upon the advice of others, without knowing good from bad, or which of my advisers might want to deceive or displace me. The Adelantado Major of Castile is much fitter for this post than I. He is a man of much experience in military and naval matters, and a good Christian, too.

But Philip persisted persuasively and Sidonia was impelled to reply:

Since your Majesty still desires it, after my confession of incompetence, I will try to deserve your confidence.

Medina Sidonia set off for Lisbon with all haste after having made hurried arrangements — despite his pleas of being burdened with debt — to donate a large sum of money to the government exchequer. There he met the real head of the Armada, the man chosen by the King as the professional representative of the naval element. This was the man who would act as Sidonia's chief of staff, Don Diego Flores de Valdes.

6. The Armada sails from Lisbon

A FRESH WIND was blowing in the estuary of the Tagus and the protected anchorages of the splendid harbour of Lisbon on the morning of 9 May 1588, enough wind to whip the waters and give movement to the scores of ships crammed into the bays and creeks and open anchorages. Lisbon, just ten miles from the mouth of the Tagus, was witnessing a historical event of enormous proportions. The place was — and had been for weeks — abounding in movements of men and ships, weaponry and guns, stores and provisions of every imaginable kind, culminating on this day with the final, irrevocable activities of a departing fleet.

Oared boats and pinnaces pulled from ship to shore and ship to ship with last-moment messages and errands. Aboard the ships there was a seeming maelstrom of activity, with the never-ending duties of seamen in securing the last casks of victuals, the huge pipes of wine, checking barrels, stowing tackle, testing lashed anchors, checking rigging, yards, cordage, sails and lashing gun carriages.

A favourable day had been awaited for the past fortnight, for it had been a miserable spring all over Europe and no one was more concerned about the weather than the

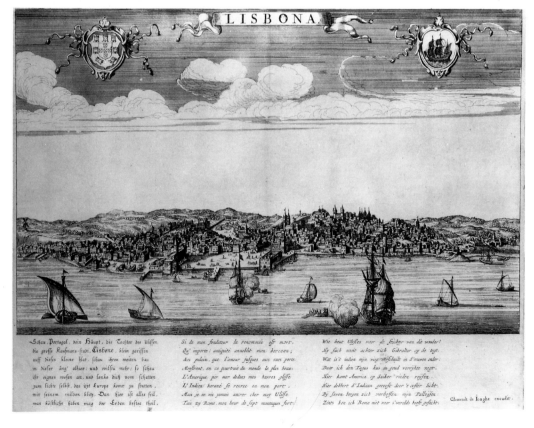

LISBONA

A contemporary engraving of Lisbon harbour, where the Armada assembled before sailing for England.

Duke, waiting impatiently — brooding is perhaps the better word — aboard his flagship. In his almost daily communications with the King he set down his thoughts — usually pessimistically, for unlike his English opponents, he was not by nature an optimist. Heaven knows, the old marquis had made superhuman efforts during the past winter to bring to the disorder of the Armada as much order, control and organization as he could, under the constant prodding of the King. By his death in February the ships were almost ready for sea with water pipes filled with fresh water.

The Duke of Medina Sidonia brought to his task as replacement commander a less zealous approach, and a less dedicated attitude to completing the outfitting of the fleet. This had its effect: without firm direction and prodding, progress in the preparations declined, and dockyards, eased of the pressures, lapsed into carelessness.

By May the ships of the Armada were still stocked with much of the provisions taken aboard before February and many of the casks were now filled with rotting or half-putrid victuals, of foul and foetid water, the presagers of dysentery and death.

But the ships themselves looked in fine fettle. The Armada looked impressive, enormous, intimidating, awesomely invincible.

It had been organized with professional skill into squadrons according to the individual ships' fighting and sailing capabilities.* The main ships of battle were the galleons, formed into two squadrons, the most powerful being the ten galleons of the Portuguese Squadron which included the 1,000-ton flagship of Medina Sidonia, the *San Martin*, known as the *capitana general* or what we would call today the C-in-C's flagship. The *almirante* of the squadron, the *San Juan*, was the second-in-command.

The second squadron of galleons came from Castile, another ten of them, smaller than the Portuguese, and supplemented by four more of the Indian Guard from the

* See Supplement 1 for full details of the ships of the Armada.

A Mediterranean-built merchant ship of the Armada period, typical of the *Nuestra Señora de la Rosa*.

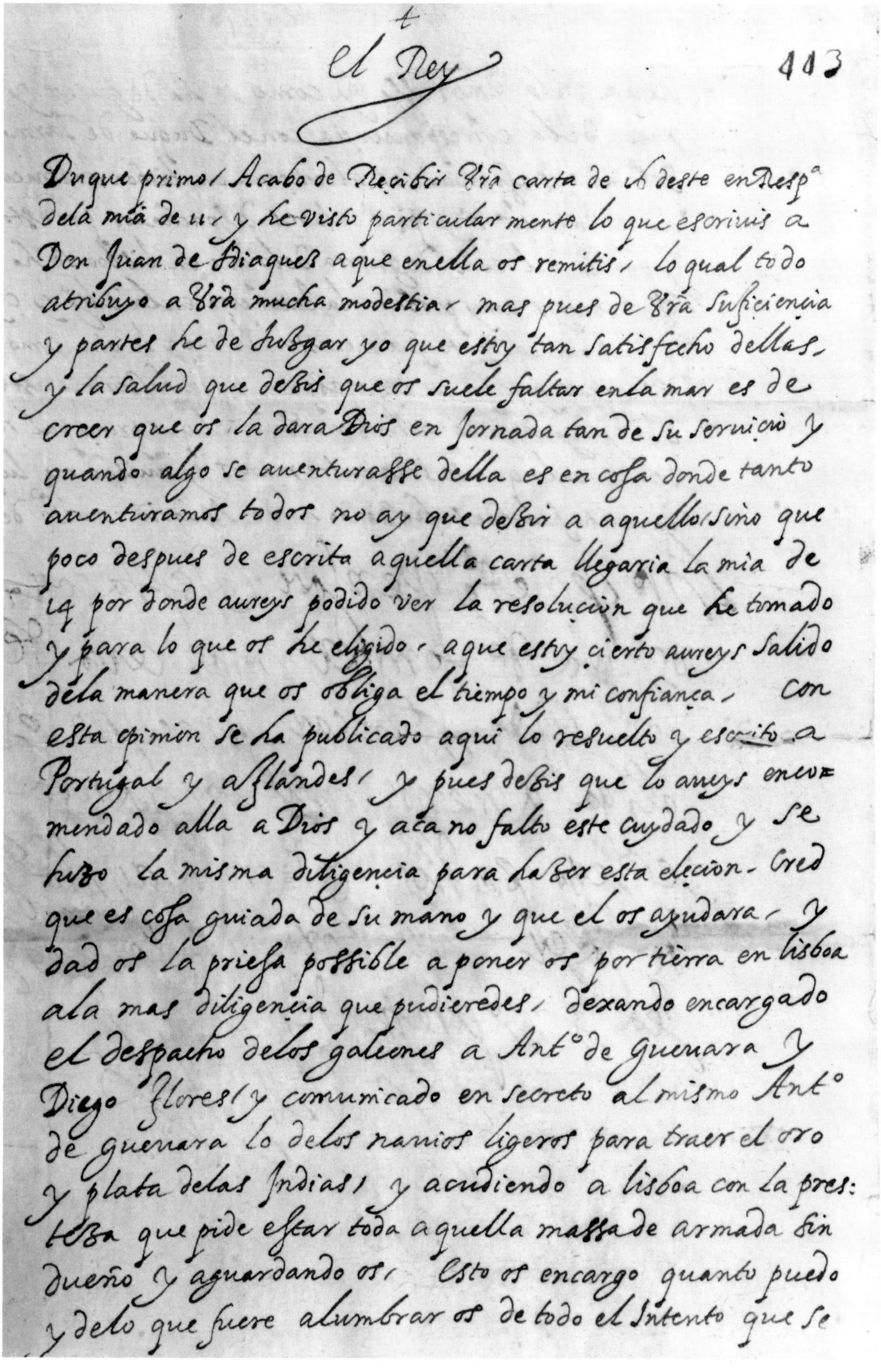

El Rey

413

Duque primo, Acabo de Recibir v̄ra carta de 16 deste en Resp̄a
dela mia de 11, y he visto particular mente lo que escriuis a
Don Juan de Idiaquez aque enella os remitis, lo qual todo
atribuyo a v̄ra mucha modestia, mas pues de v̄ra suficiencia
y partes he de Juzgar yo que estoy tan satisfecho dellas,
y la salud que dezis que os suele faltar enla mar es de
creer que os la dara Dios en Jornada tan de su serui̇çio y
quando algo se auenturasse della es en cosa donde tanto
auenturamos todos no ay que dezir a aquello, sino que
poco despues de escrita aquella carta llegaria la mia de
14 por donde aureys podido ver la resolucion que he tomado
y para lo que os he eligido, aque estoy cierto aureys Salido
dela manera que os obliga el tiempo y mi confiança, Con
esta opinion se ha publicado aqui lo resuelto y escrito a
Portugal y aflandes, y pues dezis que lo aureys encov-
mendado alla a Dios y aca no falto este cuydado y se
hizo la misma diligencia para hazer esta elecion, Cred
que es cosa guiada de su mano y que el os ayudara, Y
dad os la priessa possible a poner os por tierra en lisboa
ala mas diligencia que pudieredes, dexando encargado
el despacho delos galeones a Ant⁰ de gueuara Y
Diego flores, y comunicado en secreto al mismo Ant⁰
de gueuara lo delos nauios ligeros para traer el oro
y plata delas Jndias, y acudiendo a lisboa con la pres:
teza que pide estar toda aquella massa de armada sin
dueño y aguardando os, Esto os encargo quanto puedo
y delo que fuere alumbrar os de todo el Jntento que se

(see caption
overleaf)

[Facsimile of a handwritten letter in Spanish, dated 1588]

Llena en la Empressa y como se ha de guiar y el
modo de la correspondencia con el Duque de Parma mi
Sobrino. os esperara Sas alcançara en Lisboa Instrucion y
aduertimientos muy particulares despachados por esta Via,
y por la del cons de guerra debo que en Lisboa se ha de haber,
Que os teneys muy probada la Intencion en la dilig.a y cuydado
y pues nunca tanto fue menester lo vno y lo otro como agora
disponeos y afinaos como espero para haber me este Servi:
cio y ayudar me a haber a Dios el que principal mente pre
tendo en lo que se trae entre manos y auisad me luego de
quanto hiziere des habiendo: de Madrid a 2.o de hebrero

1588

[Eight lines added in the King's own hand]

No puedo pensar que esta carta no
os aya de tomar mas cerca de Lis
boa que de S. Lucar. pues no os o
bliga a menos mi confiança y
espero en Dios Q con su ayuda se ha
de haçer por vra mano lo Q se de
sea y pretende
Yo el Rey

In this letter from the King (written by a secretary) to the Duke of Medina Sidonia dated 20 February 1588 the King has added eight lines in his own hand: 'I can only think this letter will find you nearer Lisbon than San Lucar, since the trust I place in you obliges you to do no less. I trust in God that with His aid, through you, the task which we desire and propose to do will be accomplished.
I, the King.'

West Indies. This squadron's *capitana* was Sidonia's chief of staff, Don Diego Flores de Valdes, but he spent all his time aboard the *San Martin* with the Duke.

Also regarded as battle-line ships were the four galleasses from Naples commanded by Don Hugo de Moncada; fast, heavily armed hybrid ships with sails and oars, highly versatile ships.

Four squadrons of merchantmen, the largest of them heavily armed, formed the second line of attack, each squadron comprising ten ships: those of the Biscayan Squadron commanded by the noble Juan Martinez de Recalde in the *Santa Ana*; the Andalusian Squadron commanded by Don Pedro de Valdes — cousin to Diego Flores de Valdes — with his flag in the *Nuestra Señora del Rosario*; the Guipuzcoan Squadron (from the region of San Sebastian) was commanded by the hot-headed Don Miguel de

The Duke of Medina Sidonia's fleet train

KING PHILIP II took the unprecedented step of publishing details of the logistics of his Armada. Almost within days — but certainly within weeks — copies of his pamphlet had reached Walsingham, and England was in possession of invaluable intelligence of the enemy's strength: it is evident that this was Philip's intention. If his object was to frighten England by the sheer magnitude of his preparations and of his Armada he failed dismally. His stratagem was counter-productive, and he generated instead a Dunkirk spirit. In the event, almost all of the figures listed below were not accurate, but they are published here as originally promulgated because they give at least some idea of the size of the undertaking:

134 ships of a total burden of 57,868 tons
19,295 soldiers
8,450 mariners
2,088 slaves (more properly they were galley convicts)
2,830 cannons
123,790 cannon balls of all weights
22,000 pounds of great shot
40,000 quintals or cwts of powder
1,000 quintals of lead for bullets
10,000 quintals of match
7,000 muskets and calivers
1,000 partisans and halberds
Mules, horses and asses and their provisions
Racks, thumbscrews, chains, whips, butchering knives and other items of torture

Miscellaneous stores for the army that was to land in England:
5,000 pairs of shoes
11,000 pairs of sandals
8,000 leather bottles
10,000 pikes and half-pikes
7,000 arquebuses
1,000 muskets
21 gun carriages for land artillery and 40 mules to draw them

Food and drink for the Armada
The Armada set out from Lisbon with enough victuals to last six months. The stores taken aboard included:
11,000 pipes of water
11,117 mayors of wine
110,000 quintals of biscuits
6,000 quintals of salt pork
3,000 quintals of cheese
4,000 quintals of rice
6,000 quintals of fish
6,000 fanegas of beans and chick peas
10,000 arrobas of olive oil
21,000 arrobas of vinegar

The logistics problem of ensuring equal distribution of these stores among the 130 ships comprising the Armada had been solved by meticulous planning under the direction of Medina Sidonia and his staff.

Pipe = cask of 110 gallons
Quintal = 101.4 lb
Fanega = 1.5 bushels
Mayor = cask of 56.1 gallons
Arroba = 3.5 gallons

Oquendo, whose *capitana* was another *Santa Ana*; and the fourth, the Levantine Squadron, comprising ships from Venice, Ragusa (today's Dubrovnik), Genoa, Sicily and Barcelona commanded by Don Martin de Bertendona with his flag in *La Regazona*, at 1,249 tons the largest ship in the Armada. Of the four flagships only this last was to survive the campaign.

In addition to these squadrons there was another squadron of twenty-three hulks or urcas, freighters or supply ships, slow and unwieldy vessels which themselves needed protection.

There also came with the Armada four galleys, the infamous oared slave ships, leftovers from the battle of Lepanto seventeen years earlier.

Finally, there were a large number of what the English called pinnaces but which the Spaniards named more precisely as patches, fregatas and zabras. These were all small ships, the largest of which would be about 70 tons. There were about thirty-four such vessels — speedy light craft, ideally suited for scouting duties, dispatch-running and similar fleet duties.

All told, the mighty Armada had marshalled in awesome splendour an impressive fleet of about 130 ships.

Diary of the Enterprise

Monday 30 May: The Armada stood out to sea from Lisbon's river Tagus and immediately encountered gales which drove it southward.

Thursday 2 June: Lord High Admiral Howard arrived at Plymouth to command the combined English fleet. Ceremony of Drake hoisting his vice admiral's flag. Armada still trying to beat north.

Friday 10 June: Armada in a position 40°N., 100 miles farther from Finisterre than when it started eleven days ago.

Friday 17 June: Armada puts in to Corunna for provisioning. Hit by a storm; rested and effected repairs for a month.

Sunday 17 July: Combined fleet sailed from Plymouth to attack the Armada in Corunna, but the plan was aborted when the wind changed.

Friday 22 July: Combined fleet back in Plymouth. On this same day Sidonia sailed the Armada from Corunna on the Enterprise of England.

Tuesday 26 July: Fifth day out, and the Armada was becalmed. At midday a northerly blew, increasingly, until the early hours of Thursday (28th). The four galleys parted company to seek shelter, and the Armada became scattered. The *Santa Ana* (Biscayan Squadron) ran before the storm to La Hogue Bay and took no part in the campaign.

Friday 29 July: Armada re-formed late afternoon off the Scillies, then sighted Land's End. Captain Fleming in the *Golden Hind* brought news of the Armada's approach. Drake probably playing bowls. English fleet prepares to warp out of Plymouth. Beacons probably lit this day.

Saturday 30 July: Armada adopted its crescent formation and began slow passage up-Channel. Decision taken not to attack English in Plymouth. In fact the English fleet had warped out of harbour and was anchored at Rame Head.

Sunday 31 July: Howard gained the weather gage, and the Spaniards lost the chance to catch the English embayed. First action off Plymouth. *Rosario* damaged in collision. *San Salvador* gutted by explosion and fire. Both damaged ships taken by the English during the night and following day.

Monday 1 August: Pedro de Valdes surrendered his *Rosario* to Drake's *Revenge*. No fighting this day. Armada passed through Torbay.

Tuesday 2 August: Action off Portland Bill prevented Sidonia taking Weymouth. Frobisher extricated his *Triumph* from danger. Armada seemingly untroubled by English attacks.

Wednesday 3 August: Skirmish in the evening off the Isle of Wight a few miles south-west of the Needles. *Gran Grifon* severely damaged: 60 killed and 70 wounded. Howard adopted for very first time a squadronal organization, with Drake, Frobisher, Hawkins and himself commanding independent squadrons.

But perhaps what was more impressive than the fleet itself was its provisioning. Sidonia had followed the example set by Santa Cruz and entered into the minutest detail of requirements for his fleet, and the King actually authorized publication of the list of requirements for the fleet throughout Europe.

The morning of 9 May 1588 saw all these ships weighing anchor, shaking out furled sails that billowed to the freshening winds which took them down the Tagus, slipping past Belem, but just inside the bar they cast their anchors again. The freshening wind was blowing hard down the passage and the ships were unable to back against it. It was more like December than May. The ships rolled unhappily to their anchors, but the mood among the mariners and soldiers was one of optimism and happiness: not for nothing had it been named the *Felicissima* Armada, and today it looked every bit Invincible as well.

Aboard every ship a sermon of sorts was read aloud to every soldier and sailor. Its main import was propagandist rather than religious: it was a violent, denigrating recital of all the sins and crimes of Elizabeth of England, tempered with the statement that the heretics of England were really quite few in numbers, that the great majority of people in England were Catholics eagerly awaiting the Armada with open arms.

Thursday 4 August: Battle of the Isle of Wight. Armada carried past the Solent, and Sidonia lost his chance to capture the island. Frobisher again extricated himself from danger and capture. Armada almost wrecked on the Owers. Ammunition on both sides desperately short. Fleets disengaged.

Friday 5 August: No fighting between Beachy Head and Dungeness. Howard knighted several officers aboard his flagship, *Ark Royal*.

Saturday 6 August: Late afternoon the Armada anchored off Calais, Howard's fleet immediately following suit. Lord Seymour's eastern squadron from the Thames/Downs joined company. Sidonia still unable to effect meeting with the Duke of Parma. Invasion fleet not prepared.

Sunday 7 August: English launched fireship attack and scattered the Armada, breaking the week-long disciplined Armada formation.

Monday 8 August: Galleasse *San Lorenzo* beached and Hugo de Moncada killed. Five thousand soldiers begin assembling at Tilbury. At sea the battle of Gravelines fought. Armada almost driven on to shoals. *San Felipe* and *San Mateo* grounded and taken by Justin of Nassau's forces. Armada ships took heavy pounding from English guns.

Tuesday 9 August: Disaster of grounding on the Zeeland Banks averted by change of wind. Armada fled northward into the North Sea, the English in pursuit. London in a state of siege: 10,000 soldiers manned the defences.

Friday 12 August: About 56°N. — with the Firth of Forth abeam — the English fleet abandoned pursuit, satisfied the threat of invasion was gone.

Sunday 14 August: Three great Levant carracks left the Armada to sail east, but were never seen again.

Wednesday 17 August: *Gran Grifon* and several hulks went missing. Armada turned for the Atlantic.

Thursday 18 August: English ships made port along east coast from Harwich to Margate. Elizabeth I set off for Tilbury.

Friday 19 August: Elizabeth's speech at Tilbury: 'Let tyrants fear . . .'

Sunday 21 August: Armada about 58°N. altered course for Spain. Beginning of the Atlantic storms which scattered it.

Saturday 3 September: Sidonia reckoned he was still only 58°N. He took to his bunk, burning with fever.

September: The remnants of the Armada endeavoured to escape the dangers of shipwreck on the Irish coasts or foundering in the Atlantic gales. More than two dozen ships were lost off Ireland.

Friday 23 September: Sidonia's flagship *San Martin* arrived at Santander.

Friday 7 October: One of the last arrivals, Recalde, reached Corunna safely.

Wednesday 26 October: Last ship of the Armada to be wrecked on the Irish coast was the *Girona*.

This sermon-cum-harangue appears to have been the King's belief and testament: he even allowed himself to believe that England would welcome him as King or his daughter as Queen. Rarely has a monarch about to launch a war been so mistaken about his enemy.

The ranting priests declared the expedition upon which they were all outward bound was 'Glorious for our country because God had deigned to make it His instrument for such great ends'. Riches, too, were promised: '. . . because of the plunder and endless riches we shall gather in England, and by favour of God bring gloriously and victoriously back to our homes . . . God, in whose sacred cause we go, will lead us. With such a captain we need have no fear.'

Two more documents repeating orders from the King to Medina Sidonia call for comment. Both were issued to every ship, the first addressed to all ships' masters, incredibly enough going into the minutest detail of every man's daily allocation of food and wine. The King was most specific about the daily wine allocation. Each day's issue, it has been calculated, was equal to a modern bottle. Condad, Lisbon wines, Lemego, Monzan wines and Sherry were to be issued in that order, he instructed. Candia was the strongest, it lasted the longest and therefore should be issued last — and at a rate of only a pint a day because of its strength . . . 'it would bear,' he considered, 'a double quantity of water.'

The water ration was to be three pints a day for all purposes, cooking, drinking (few could stomach the foul taste), personal washing and laundering, both rarely performed at sea.

The King's orders underlined the egalitarian intention: 'you must not service out more than the ordinary ration to any captain, ensign, sergeant, corporal or other official; nor to any drummer, fifer or other without my order.'

The second document was the Duke's general orders, translated into *Orders Set downe by the Duke of Medina, Lord general of the King's Fleet, to be observed in the voyage toward England.* Ships' captains throughout the fleet read the document for the first time as their ships lay at anchor at the mouth of the Tagus. The first of his orders came directly from an instruction from the King in a letter to the Duke in April. It began loftily:

> In the first place, as all victories are the gift of God Almighty, and the cause we champion is so exclusively His, we may fairly look for His aid and favour, unless by our sins we render ourselves unworthy. You must therefore exercise special care that such cause of offence shall be avoided in the Armada, and especially that there shall be no sort of blasphemy. This must be severely enforced, with heavy penalties.

In modern terms, it seems quite incredible that a sovereign and technically the C-in-C of the Navy should have to concern himself with such minutiae as blasphemy among his sailors and the issuing of the daily wine ration. But this was typical of the outpourings of a King who has often been described as a bureaucrat *par excellence*. He liked everything in meticulous order, he liked to cover every situation with a set of rules or guidelines. He worked tirelessly. He would have made a painstaking chief secretary of a Whitehall department today.

The Duke's orders went on to exhort all ranks to be confessed and absolved of their sins before sailing. The puritan streak showed through:

I also enjoin you to take particular care that no soldier, sailor or other person in the Armada shall blaspheme, or deny Our Lord, Our Lady or the Saints, under very severe punishment to be inflicted at our discretion. With regard to other less serious oaths, the officers of the ships will do their best to repress their use, and will punish offenders by docking their wine ration, or in some way at their discretion. As these disorders usually arise from gambling, you will endeavour to repress this as much as possible, especially the prohibited games, and allow no play at night on this account.

Nor would the Duke allow any heterosexual activity aboard the ships: women were barred. 'I order that none shall be taken on board. If any attempt be made to embark women, I authorize the captains and masters of ships to prevent it, and if it is done surreptitiously the offenders must be severely punished.'

Religious ceremonies started every morning at day-break with the ships' boys saying 'their *Good Morrow* at the foot of the mainmast, and at sunset the *Ave Maria*. Some days, and at least every Saturday, they shall say the Salve with the Litany.' Later in the Orders, the Duke introduced a watchword for each day of the week: Sunday's was *Jesus*; Monday's the *Holy Ghost*; Tuesday's *Most Holy Trinity*; Wednesday's *Santiago*; Thursday's *the Angels*; Friday's *All Saints*; and Saturday's *Our Lady*.

The Orders, it was evident, were endorsing the King's view that the Armada campaign had taken on the mantle of a religious crusade.

Eventually he came to the burden of his Orders:

If any ship be forced off course by storms before reaching Cape Finisterre, they will make directly for that point, where they will find orders from me: but if no such orders await them they will make for Corunna. Any infraction of this order will be punished by death and forfeiture. On leaving Cape Finisterre, the course will be to the Scilly Islands, and ships must try to sight the island from the south, taking great care to look to their soundings. Ships are not to return to Spain on any account. If on their arrival at the Scillies the Armada is behind them, they will cruise off the place keeping up to windward, until the Armada appears or until they satisfied themselves that it has passed them, in which case they will make for Mount's Bay between Land's End and the Lizard, where instructions will await them if the Armada is not there.

*   *   *

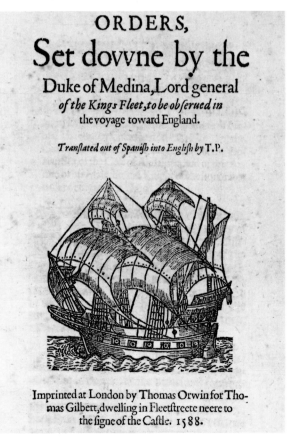

ORDERS,
Set dovvne by the
Duke of Medina, Lord general
of the Kings Fleet, to be obſerued in
the voyage toward England.

Tranſlated out of Spaniſh into Engliſh by T.P.

Imprinted at London by Thomas Orwin for Thomas Gilbert, dwelling in Fleetſtreete neere to
the ſigne of the Caſtle. 1588.

Soon after the Armada left Lisbon the Duke's *Orders* were published in London as a fourteen-page booklet with this title page. It was thought that the magnitude of the enterprise described in these orders would intimidate and frighten the English into seeking a settlement of some sort with Spain.

The Invincible Armada

THE WORD ARMADA simply means fleet. The name 'Invincible' so commonly applied to the Armada was not an official title. King Philip II, the Duke of Medina Sidonia and all contemporary chroniclers wrote of it as the 'Grand Fleet'. In an elaborate, semi-official publication printed in Lisbon in 1588 the title became *La Felicissima*

Armada — the Most Fortunate or Happy Fleet. The booklet's frontispiece is reproduced here, together with a summary of the inventory which makes fascinating reading. Because of the awesome strength of the Armada which assembled in Lisbon it is thought that the Spaniards probably came to adopt the word 'Invincible' as an act of braggadocio.

SSVMARIO
GENERAL DE TODA
EL ARMADA.

	Numero d'Navios	Toneladas	Géte d'guerra	Géte d'mar	Numero d'todos.	Pieças de artilleria.	Peloteria.	Poluora	Plomo quintales.	Cuerda quintales.
¶ Armada de Galeones de Portugal.	12.	7.737.	3330.	1293.	4623.	347.	18450.	789.	186.	150
¶ Armada de Vizcaya, de que es General Iuan Martinez de Ricalde.	14	6567.	1.937.	863.	2800.	238.	11.900.	477.	140.	87
¶ Galeones de la Armada de Castilla.	16	8714.	2.458.	1.719.	4171.	384.	23.040.	710.	290.	309
¶ Armada de naues del Andaluzia.	11.	8.762.	2.325.	780.	3.105.	240	10.200.	415.	63.	119
¶ Armada de naos de la Prouincia de Guipuscua.	14	6.991.	1992.	616.	2.608.	247.	12.150.	518.	139.	109
¶ Armada de naos le uantiscas.	10.	7.705.	2.780.	767.	3523.	280.	14.000.	584.	177.	141
¶ Armada de Vrcas.	23.	10271.	3.121.	608.	3729.	384	19.200.	258.	142.	215
¶ Pataches y zabras.	22.	1.221.	479.	574.	1.093.	91.	4550.	66.	20.	13
¶ Galeaças de Napoles.	4.		873.	468.	1.341.	200.	10.000.	498.	61.	88
¶ Galeras.	4		362.	362.	20.	1.200.	60.	20.	20.	
	130	57.868.	19295.	8050.	27365.	2.431.	123790.	4575.	1.232.	1.151

Gente de remo.

En las Galeaças.	1.200.
En las Galeras.	888.
	2.088.

De mas de la dicha poluora se lleua de respecto para si se ofreciere alguna bateria 600. qs.   600.

POr manera que ay en la dicha armada, segun parece por este sumario, ciento y treynta nauios, que tienen cincuenta y siete mil ochocientas y sessenta y ocho toneladas, y deziocho mil dozientos y nouenta y cinco soldados de Infanteria, y ocho mil y cincuenta y dos hombres de mar, que todos hazen, veyntisiete mil trezientas y setenta y cinco personas, y dos mil y ochenta y ocho remeros, y dos mil y quatrocientas y treynta y vna pieças de artilleria, las mil quatrocientas y nouenta y siete de bronze, de todas suertes en que ay muchos cañones, y medios cañones, culebrinas, y medias culebrinas, y cañones pedreros, y las nueuecientas y treynta y quatro restantes de hierro colado de todos caliuos, y ciento y veyntitres mil ciento y nouenta balas para ellas, y cinco mil ciento y setenta y cinco quintales de poluora, y mil y dozientos y treynta y ocho de plomo, y mil ciento y cincuenta y vn quintales de cuerda: y los generos de los nauios son en esta manera.

A 9

On the evening of 30 May a light offshore wind encouraged the Duke to order the fleet to weigh anchor. The Armada came out of the river led by the C-in-C in his flagship, the *San Martin*. She was caparisoned with decorated sails, flags, ensigns and bunting, a beautifully coloured Portuguese galleon which sailed past Castle St Julian, replying in succession to the castle's salutes. By dawn of the next day all ships had cleared the bar, though some of the galleons had to be towed over. The whole Armada stood out to sea close-hauled to a fitful, squally wind from the NNW.

No sooner were all ships heading north on the first leg of their voyage to Finisterre than the wind freshened and the Armada was forced to sail into the teeth of it, standing out to sea for safety's sake, close-hauled on a starboard tack and hoping desperately for a southerly wind.

After forty-eight hours at sea laboriously manœuvring, this vast number of ships — the cumbersome urcas were specially sluggish, and governed the speed of the whole fleet — were nearly back where they started, five miles SSW off the Rock of Lisbon. The total distance made good since clearing the bar was about fifteen miles.

The wind abated and the ships lost steerage-way, sails flapped lazily, ships drifted and rolled sickeningly in the heavy Atlantic swell. But worse was to come. Storms raged for a week and the ships beat back and forth helplessly, losing distance at every tack. Despite all their skilled efforts at seamanship in attempting to sail to windward, the ships were actually making progress to leeward. Some pilots declared that after a few days the Armada had blown off its course so far that it was labouring off Cape St Vincent, but this sounds too extreme.

When the wind veered round to WSW on 10 June — eleven days after leaving Lisbon — the Armada was in latitude 40°N, roughly 100 miles farther from Finisterre than it has been when it left the Tagus. The first attempt of the Armada to put to sea to do battle was, even to the most generous mind, an abysmal failure. It did not augur well.

Armada Supernumeraries

IN ADDITION TO the 19,295 soldiers, 8,450* mariners and 2,088 convicts manning the ships of the Armada, there were probably another 2,700 men accompanying the largest fleet the world had ever seen. These included numerous noblemen and gentlemen with long retinues of servants and attendants. All the following supernumeraries have been documented:

146 gentlemen awarded cots or cabins of their own
138 'unattached' officers, gentlemen adventurers or mercenaries
728 servants which included:
  50 of them attending the Duke of Medina Sidonia
  39 of them attending the young Prince Ascoli
  36 of them attending Don Alonso de Leiva
180 priests, monks or friars
6 surgeons and 6 physicians plus
62 medical orderlies

* Probably as many as 4,000 of these mariners were not Spanish, but Portuguese, German, Italian, Flemings, Dutch and even some English.

In addition, there were officers of justice, paymasters and their considerable staff.

7. Corunna to the Lizard

*T*HE FAIR WIND which came up from the south-west — dead astern for the course to Finisterre — took the Spanish ships along at a rate of about 4 knots, the fastest speed by far that the Armada attained during the whole of the campaign. They sighted the cape at Finisterre after three days.

Then near-disaster of another sort drove Medina Sidonia to seek sanctuary in the spacious sheltered bay at Corunna. Want of fresh water and victuals impelled him to immediate action. Casks of meat, fish and vegetables and pipes of water, stored aboard months previously, had now gone rotten and foetid and men were falling sick with dysentery — what English sailors called 'the flux' — in desperately cramped living quarters, infecting each other in stinking, unhygienic conditions, with all sorts of intestinal diseases.

Sidonia complained as bitterly as he dared in one of his numerous letters to the King. Referring to the victuals, he wrote:

They have gone bad, rotted and spoiled . . . We have had to throw a large part of the food overboard because it was only giving men the plague and making them sick . . . So I must inform your Majesty and humbly beg you to agree to send out to us more provisions to supplement what we have. What we mainly lack is meat and fish, but we need everything else as well . . .

Off Finisterre he hovered around the cape for four days, watching and waiting for the fleet of provision ships and boats. He had also written to the governor of Galicia, the Marquis de Cerralvo, asking him to load all the meat, salt meat, salt pork, cheese, fish and tallow on which he could lay his hands, into ships, barges, fishing-boats — anything which could be found — and to send them out to the Armada.

Water in particular was the latest worry on two counts: firstly, many casks had leaked, and when broached were found empty; others that were full gushed forth green, slimy water, not only undrinkable but unfit even for cooking the salt meat.

While hovering off the cape, Medina Sidonia wrote again to the King, a much more cheerful letter, undoing much of the good that his earlier home truths must have done. In this letter he made no reference to his problems with sickness or provisions: 'The men are well, God be praised,' he wrote at a time when *hundreds* of men lay about in pain and misery, 'and the cool weather is helping to keep us in good health, so I have great hope that His Divine Majesty will bring us in this expedition to a happy and favourable conclusion.'

All the council of war members — Recalde, Oquendo, Pedro de Valdes, Flores de Valdes and Sidonia himself — reported the urgent need for fresh supplies of water. By the fourth day the fleet lay off Corunna harbour. A strong wind got up and Sidonia's flagship was forced to enter harbour — and about forty or more sail followed her in to find an anchorage, but darkness compelled the rest to stand off outside to await daylight. Those left outside were the slow sailers, nearly all the hulks and the Levanters with Recalde's squadron, plus another six or seven galleons, the four galleasses and some smaller craft: they all stood off beyond the headlands.

Sidonia wrote a hurried note to the King:

> I shall stock up with water and put ashore the dangerously sick and then, weather permitting, put to sea again. The wind that takes me out will be the right one for our voyage. So I hope only to stay here a short time.

Poor Sidonia. He seemed fated to attract bad luck. That night the wind backed to the south-west and a storm struck the major part of the Armada still at sea with fearful intensity. The ships ran before the storm. There was nothing else they could do. By morning there was neither sight nor sound of them. Two-thirds of the Armada had scattered. In the sheltered harbour itself one ship had dragged anchor and collided with a galleon. On the following day, when the wind had abated somewhat, Sidonia sent out some pinnaces to search for the scattered ships. Intelligence came in of de Leiva with ten hulks, Levanters and a pinnace being safe in a nearby port, but pinnaces scoured as far as the Scillies to recover some missing ships.

It was to be a month — not two days — before the Armada had regrouped in Corunna, but the stay there had worked wonders for the men and the ships. The fleet was replenished with fresh water and victuals. Galicia was good farming land, and the men fed well during this month and became restored to health and vigour. Ships themselves were repaired.

But a mood of depression persisted with Sidonia and he put his most sombre and darkest thoughts in a letter to the King. It was a long apologia, and asked for the King to judge whether the voyage of the Armada should continue. He pointed out the inadvisability of undertaking such a great task as the Armada was doing with forces even equal to those of the enemy: to do it with an inferior force (as he now judged the Armada to be) would be even more unwise. 'Well, sire,' he posed the question bluntly, 'how do you think we can attack so great a country as England with such a force as ours is now?' Sidonia concluded by suggesting coming to favourable terms with England, and even at this late stage he urged the King that he 'should deeply ponder . . . what you are undertaking . . .'

It must have been with considerable trepidation that the Duke entrusted this letter to the messenger, and the days of expectancy and hope while waiting for a reply must have been unnerving.

The King's reply to Sidonia was anticlimactic. Instead of dismissal, after charges of cowardice and treason, there came but gentle rebuke: the tone was surprisingly mild. The King reiterated his intention to press on with the enterprise despite the feelings of the council and the C-in-C: he was to press forward provided he had recovered the missing ships: he had permission to abandon 12 to 15 ships too damaged to repair, so long as they were gutted, crews and stores being transferred to other ships — and the revitalized Armada was to sail by 12 July.

Even before the King's letter was received matters had changed for the better, and we find Sidonia writing again in more optimistic frame of mind. God, he declared, had been pleased to send into port all the missing ships apart from two Levanters and two urcas.

On 5 July a pinnace commanded by Ensign Esquival came into harbour with a convoy of a dozen ships rounded up off the Scillies, some of them within sight of Cornwall. He captured some English sailors and, curiously, two Irish priests, and from them learned that Drake (he was synonymous with England) had a hundred and eighty ships in three squadrons, one in Plymouth and two to the east of Dover. This young ensign had had the splendid experience of writing a report beginning: 'At dawn on Friday 1 July, we sighted St Michael's Bay and Land's End, five or six leagues distant. We took in all sail and rowed inshore . . .'

On 20 July Sidonia met all the pilots, experienced men of the sea, versed in weather and tides, currents and ship-handling. Yes, they assured him confidently, the weather looked settled for several days and would get the fleet safely clear of Cape Priorio, Corunna's northernmost promontory.

Sidonia, taking the mood of most of his commanders, decided that if they were to sail, the sooner the better: dawn on the following day . . . unless the weather deteriorated. A signal gun announced his decision to the fleet and the ships singled up to one anchor. At midnight the *San Martin* fired another signal gun to order the leading ships to weigh and get clear of the harbour to allow the mass exodus of the next day.

At daybreak another gunshot was the signal for all ships to shake out their sails, but the light south-west breeze barely filled the canvas, and after several hours the fleet had

This painting by Oswald W. Brierly (1817–94) is headed *The Spanish Armada sailing from Ferrol [Corunna] 12 July 1588 Starting for the Conquest of England.* The caption reads:

> The scene as the fleet passed out of the harbour must have been singularly beautiful. It was a treacherous interval of real summer. The early sun was lighting the long chain of the Galician mountains marking with shadows the left defiles and shining softly on the white walls and vineyards of Corunna. The wind was light and falling towards a calm, the great galleons drifted slowly with the tide on the purple water, the long streamers training from the trucks, the red crosses, the emblem of the crusade showing bright upon the hanging sails. The fruit boats were bringing off the last of the supplies and the pinnaces hastening to the ships with the last loiterers on shore. Out of 30,000 men who that morning stood upon the decks of the proud Armada 20,000 were never again to see the hills of Spain.

made good just three miles, and the bulk of it had not cleared the cape. Gradually the breeze strengthened and the fleet got away, leaving the land diminishing astern, never to be seen again by many thousands of the men still gazing at it.

For many days the breeze powered the fleet along at a pedestrian rate, the wretched hulks acting all the time like a sheet anchor on the fleet's progress: the King's ships — and others — were compelled to shorten sail so as not to outdistance the urcas. On Tuesday 26 July even this breeze dropped away and the fleet became becalmed, drifting aimlessly.

*   *   *

Masters aboard the ships strove to find their way on the charts. No longer were they caping or piloting the ships — they were out of sight of land and therefore navigating, and goodness knows there was precious little art and not much skill either in sixteenth-century navigation. Almost every navigational aid was in its infancy — charts, instruments, compasses, astrolabes, cross and back staffs. Leads for depth-finding and masters' notebooks were the two basic items for locating a ship at sea.

Piloting — or caping, as it was called — was literally sailing from cape to cape by sight, following a coastal route, aided by privately compiled notebooks which masters maintained throughout their lives at sea, recording navigational aids of every description.

Drake's astronomical compendium

*T*HIS astronomical Compendium — a type of Elizabethan mini-computer — is reputed to have belonged to Sir Francis Drake. It is inscribed as having been engraved by Humfray Colle in 1569, the chief engraver to Elizabeth's Royal Mint. It is made in gilt-brass with a diameter of only 6.3 cm, and comprises seven layers of instruments bearing a wealth of navigational information.

One layer is inscribed with a table of latitudes of European ports, another with their tide tables. A calculator enabled the pilot to define the ship's position by noon observations of the sun's angle above the horizon. A sight indicator worked for both vertical and horizontal bearings. A sun-dial gave the time of day by the sun casting a shadow on a series of Roman numerals — it also worked on the pole star and a nocturnal dial at night. The perpetual calendar was yet another feature of the instrument, highlighting religious and saints' days.

The compendium was too miniaturized to give great accuracy, but backed up by astrolabe and cross or back staff calculations and other navigational aids of the era it gave a handy rule-of-thumb guide to the mariner.

Navigation and pilotage

OCEAN navigation and inshore pilotage were the two means of finding one's way at sea. For ocean navigation — i.e., when out of sight of land — the cross staff, back staff and astrolabe were employed for observing the elevation of the noonday sun or the pole star at both dusk and dawn, or even the moon when the horizon was visible on clear nights. Navigators had almanacs from which they could convert their readings into estimates of latitude. With care and good visibility, plus a touch of luck, navigators could observe to an accuracy of perhaps half a degree, or about thirty miles. But longitude — that is, east or west of the prime meridian — was of course another matter, since the only means of calculating that was an accurate chronometer, and that would not come along until the eighteenth century.

The compass variation in English waters during the Armada campaign was 17° more easterly than it is now. All courses and wind directions were a point and a half from what would be shown by a chart or compass today.

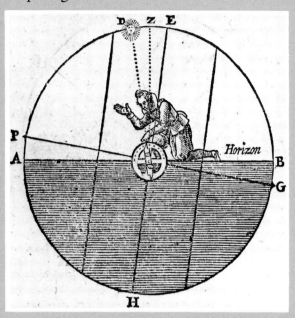

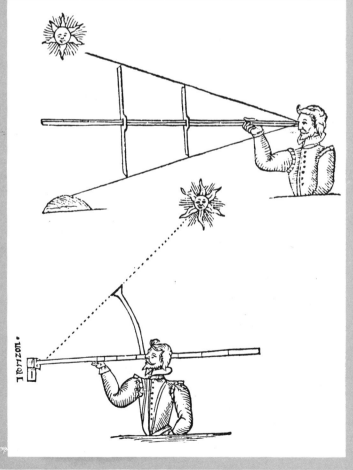

For piloting the ancient lead was a primary tool of trade, and some of these leads were extraordinary. A 14lb lead, known as a dipsie (or deep sea), had a line of an incredible 200 fathoms length — 1,200 ft — and had to be used while the ship was stopped, or from a ship's boat laying off. The more common 7lb lead was used while the ship was under way. Both leads would have a hollow the size of an egg-cup in the base filled with tallow to pick up traces of the sea-bed: thus both the depth and the nature of the sea bottom would be recorded in the notebook — and this notebook became known as a 'rutter' from the French word *routier*.

The private rutter, which was often decorated with sketches or paintings of the view of a harbour from the sea (Drake was adept at this decoration), was frequently handed down from father to son.

The first rutter printed in English appeared in 1528, followed by later editions. Spanish translations would have been available for the ships of the Armada. They were all crude affairs by any standards but they were the best to be had. Compass directions from cape to cape were sound enough, the state of the tides at full and new moon and navigational hazards and beacons were useful, but distances were given in 'kennings', distances at which a mariner might recognize a ken or coast. Thus the Straits of Dover were one ken — though it must have been an incredibly keen-sighted lookout who could discern a recognizable French coast from Dover. The Chops of the Channel (from Ushant to Scilly) was five kennings wide.

The compass, crude though it was, served well enough, even though the needle was not a permanent magnet, so that a lodestone was needed periodically to charge it by induction. The compass card was marked out in the regular thirty-two points, with the north indicated by a decorated device.

Thus, with lead and line, with his own private rutter, with a compass, some landmarks to assist caping, an estimated speed by watching the bubbles surge along the ship's side, and by dead reckoning, a master, pilot or navigator could place his ship reasonably accurately.

There was one other navigational aid in northern pilotage of enormous consequence, like the modern introduction of radar or some similar electronic aid. It was what became known as a Waggoner, a term anglicized (as the Navy would have these things) from the Dutch Wagenaer. Lucas Janszoon Wagenaer published a volume — nothing less than an atlas, manual of navigation, rutter and almanac all rolled into one — from Cadiz to the Zuider Zee in 1584. A second volume appeared in the following year covering the North Sea and the Baltic. A Latin edition came out in 1586, and it is possible that the Spaniards had translated at least relevant parts of the Waggoner for their own purposes by the time of their Armada campaign, or they could have got by with the Latin version.

The volumes were works of art, and for all their limitations and inaccuracies they were of enormous navigational worth. The charts were a delight to behold, elaborately decorated with maritime devices of every description, and any harbour of any consequence was sketched as viewed from seaward and shown on the map disproportionately large for ease of identification. Distances were marked in leagues, not kennings, though it was wise to know that a Spanish league was 3½ nautical miles, a Dutch four, and an English three.

*   *   *

The first 'Waggoner'

*L*UCAS Janszoon Wagenaer (*c.*1534–1605) was a Dutch seaman and cartographer who was born at Enchuysen where he became a pilot and collector of harbour dues. In 1582 he began compiling a sea atlas which was first published in Holland in two parts in 1584–5 under the title *Spieghel Der Zeervaerdt*. It combined a manual of navigation with a collection of naval charts covering the coastal waters of Western Europe from the Baltic in the north to Cadiz in the south. It became the most famous collection of charts in its time, widely used by British seamen for more than a century.

Lord Howard of Effingham was so impressed when he saw a copy that he commissioned Anthony Ashley to produce a translation. This English edition was published in 1588 as *The Mariner's Mirrour*, but the name of its original Dutch compiler soon became corrupted to 'Waggoner', which was the name given to all similar subsequent collections of charts.

Incidentally, *The Mariner's Mirror* today is a quarterly journal of the Society for Nautical Research, and recognized throughout the world as one of the most scholarly of maritime journals.

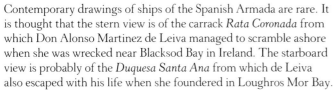

Contemporary drawings of ships of the Spanish Armada are rare. It is thought that the stern view is of the carrack *Rata Coronada* from which Don Alonso Martinez de Leiva managed to scramble ashore when she was wrecked near Blacksod Bay in Ireland. The starboard view is probably of the *Duquesa Santa Ana* from which de Leiva also escaped with his life when she foundered in Loughros Mor Bay.

The becalmed Armada's ill fortune continued, for the breeze which got up brought with it a lowering sky and within hours the storm which was presaged blew up out of the north, accompanied by blinding squalls of rain. The ships bore away to the westward to seek the safety of searoom. The galleys with their low freeboard and narrow beams were poorly suited to a Biscay storm and they began to strain seams. The *Diana* in particular began to leak badly and Sidonia gave her permission to act independently and to seek a friendly port. All four galleys were in danger of being swamped. One did in fact become wrecked, but the others survived, although none of them rejoined the Armada, and they took no further part in the campaign.

Another casualty was more serious for the Spanish — but the mystery surrounding the actions of the *Santa Ana de Juan Martinez* [de Recalde] have never been explained satisfactorily. She was the *capitana* (we would say flagship) of the Biscayan Squadron but the admiral, the brilliant Recalde, was not aboard and had already transferred to the galleon *San Juan de Portugal*. Curiously, in the storm off Corunna the *Santa Ana* had ended up at Santander — two hundred miles away. The excuse given was that she was old, and in need of repairs of a more permanent nature than the make-do-and-mend kind; but these are unconvincing. Now in this storm she ran before it, easterly, on a course which took her up-Channel, at least 90 degrees off course, limping into the bay of La Hogue, then eventually finding sanctuary in Le Havre, never to take part in the rest of the campaign. Once the whole Armada campaign was ended English ships attacked her, but although she was not taken, she never reached home again.

The storm increased in intensity as night fell and the wind hauled round to the north-west. Heavy seas crashed aboard the ships and the conditions became awful. Everything was sodden, water sloshed everywhere and the ships moved with sickening instability. Coldness, wetness, sickness, lack of food, and stench: these accompaniments to the howling wind — the Spaniards called it a *tormenta*, a full gale — made life aboard the wooden ships almost intolerable.

The Spanish seamen and their naval officers were not the fair-weather sailors they have often been depicted: they were men of substance. The English were certainly superior in many ways, but the majority of the Spaniards were tough, seasoned sailors, even though there was the usual sprinkling of peasants and pressed men culled from prisons, hospitals and taverns. Many had served for years in the Atlantic and West Indies; the Biscayans knew the sea well in all its moods, the Levanters and other Mediterranean-serving seamen lacked the storm-experience of the others but they were of good seafaring stock.

However, it is worth recording that the Spaniards on the whole were less experienced than the English in encountering gales at sea, and it is noticeable that they seem to have recorded worse storms and sea conditions than did their adversaries. This storm, for example, has been described in a Spanish log as having 'the sea so high that all the mariners said they had never seen the like in July'. Yet it rates no mention at all in the English reports except for the casual remark by John Hawkins that 'a little flaw took them'.

The ships made what northing they could in the storm, which raged for two days. When it abated and good visibility returned it was for Sidonia to see his fleet scattered yet again: all the Andalusians, various hulks and others, forty ships in all, some in groups, others independent. Pinnaces were dispatched to bring stragglers and lost ships to the rendezvous.

One pinnace returned to report that the bulk of the missing ships were waiting off the Scillies under the command of Pedro de Valdes in the *Rosario*.

On Friday 29 July the Armada assembled south of the Scillies, waiting for the late arrivals, waiting till late Saturday morning, 30 July, while the fleet remained hove-to. The time was put to good use by Don Hugo de Moncada, whose galleasse flagship, the *San Lorenzo*, had a broken rudder. This same trouble was to recur later in much more serious circumstances. 'These craft are really very fragile for heavy seas,' the Duke noted.

At four o'clock in the afternoon of Friday 29 July a lookout in Medina Sidonia's flagship, *San Martin*, yelled to those below and pointed with outstretched arm to land on the port bow. Little did he know at the time that he was indicating the Lizard. The Armada had made an excellent landfall.

Aboard the *San Martin* Medina Sidonia hoisted the royal standard at the fore and the fleet's battle insignia at the mizzenmast top. Other flags by the score were streaming in the breeze. Each squadron wore the flag of its province — the castle of Castile, the dragons and shields of Portugal, the cross and foxes of Biscay — as well as the flags of the noblemen and knights aboard, plus, perhaps, flags of saints to whom the ships had been dedicated.

The huge banner of Christ Crucified with the Virgin Mother and Mary Magdalene depicted on each side of Him was unfurled at the main for all to see; it had been seen last when it had been blessed by the Pope himself. Now it streamed in the wind, signifying the Armada's crusade.

Unknown to most aboard the Spanish ships, engrossed as they were in celebrating the occasion, the Armada itself had been sighted and was under surveillance. Captain Thomas Fleming was already hastening to Plymouth to broadcast the good news.

Later, everyone in the Armada knew they were observed as they watched intrigued by the beacons of lights twinkling and the columns of smoke rising from the headlands heralding their approach.

Warning beacons

WARNING BEACONS to alert everyone to the approach of the Spanish Armada were provided with watchers who were paid eightpence a day and provided with a plentiful supply of fuel in the form of three trees per beacon. Dogs were not allowed to accompany a watcher lest he be distracted from his duty by the animal. Justices of the peace were required to keep watchers under close scrutiny. During bad weather, watchers were provided with huts — rather like sentry boxes — to protect them, but a seat was not provided because it might tempt a watcher to sleep. Said Lord Macaulay:

From Eddystone to Berwick bounds, from Lynn
    to Milford Bay,
That time of slumber was as bright and busy as
    the day;
For swift to east and swift to west the ghastly
    war-flames spread,
High on St Michael's Mount it shone, it shone
    on Beachy Head.
Far on the deep the Spaniards saw, along each
    southern shore,
Cape beyond cape in endless range, those twink-
    ling spots of fire.

8. England prepares for invasion

A T THE BEGINNING of 1588, when the Marquis of Santa Cruz in Lisbon was still frantically assembling and provisioning the Armada with the constant interference of Philip II, the King's enemies in England were similarly embroiled, plunged by turns into gloom and despondency then uplifted to heights of delight by their own Queen.

It was Elizabeth who played a devious game of politics in the early weeks and months of 1588, politics with men and countries, with the Navy and with their enemies. A man — a king — could not have handled the situations which arose with the skill and deviousness she displayed: it needed the deft touches of a woman, the quick-wittedness capable of dealing with the clashing desires of a handful of men — the ruler of an empire, the Duke of Parma, the Treasurer of the Navy, the queen-maker Burghley, the spy-catcher Walsingham, the clutch of courtiers like Cumberland, Leicester, Essex, not to mention the piratical sea-dog Sir Francis Drake. Who but a woman could have handled these men with the consummate skill of a conjuror: who but a queen, and a Queen of England too?

It cannot have been the Queen's innate skill in handling money matters that enabled her to get away with some of her decisions that autumn, winter and spring before the Armada campaign. The lack of preparedness in England to combat an invasion was not far short of criminal. Parma declared that had he attempted the crossing of the Channel from Flanders to Kent in the October of 1587 he would have done so virtually unopposed — and he would have marched straight to London. That he did not do so was due, in part at least, to Drake's raid on Cadiz earlier in the year.

He may, of course, have been wrong, but his confidence has something to say about the known lack of preparations for England's defence.

When Walsingham warned Elizabeth that Santa Cruz was likely to come out of Lisbon before Christmas 1587 her reaction seemed more one of womanly intuition, sensing a true danger, rather than one arising from a careful consideration of the alarming views of her naval advisers. Yet the decisions were right. The orders went out. The result was that within a fortnight all the Queen's ships and most of the auxiliary merchantmen were armed, provisioned (up to a point) and mobilized for war.

Yet stranger than the mobilization was the dismantling. No sooner did it seem apparent that an invasion was not materializing than she had the courage to reverse the operation and to put the fleet back into the sixteenth-century equivalent of mothballing. Plymouth and the Medway became the anchorages for her half-manned reserve fleet again, the ships' masts stark like a petrified forest. A small squadron of four galleons and a handful of pinnaces were exempted from this petrifaction to carry out patrols off the Flanders coast in support of the Dutch. Captains and statesmen were dismayed at the decision, but the saving in the costs of wages and victuals was compelling. Burghley annotated a list of these naval dispositions with calculations showing that the Queen would save £2,433 18s. 4d. every month. Elizabeth rated that saving most handsome: it made the decision to confine the Navy to its anchorages quite easy.

But there were some things the Queen could not undo. She could not (even had she wished to) arrest the feeling of nationalism and patriotism that swept the country: it was a bad time for aliens and foreigners in England. Ubaldini records that 'it was easier to find a flock of white crows than one Englishman who loved a foreigner'.

Other defensive preparations were allowed to proceed: a bar was laid across the Thames estuary from Gravesend in Kent to Tilbury in Essex, a chain and line of boats with the dual purpose of denying passage to enemy assault ships and acting as a bridge to allow troops to cross from one county to the other. Peter Pett was the engineer in charge, enlisting the help of the Italian Giambelli. Even while the Armada sailed past Torbay they were still putting the finishing touches to this patent bar-cum-bridge.

The Queen appointed Deputy Lieutenants for the West Country, an act which would cost her nothing: five for Devon and two for Cornwall. Raleigh, as Lord Lieutenant for Cornwall, now received support from his cousin Richard Grenville as Deputy Lieutenant.

Across the southern counties, and even farther inland, defensive trenches were dug in the fields, forts were repaired, warning beacons were constructed on high ground till a pattern criss-crossed the land. It would take but a minute with a flaming torch to set

Lord Howard of Effingham reads the proclamation of a call to arms at Plymouth Quay, 1588, in a late Victorian picture by John Seymour Lucas.

the alarm ablaze, spreading the news of the arrival of the Armada. At the first sight of flame and smoke and the following clangour of church bells men were to muster at given rallying points to be led by their Lords Lieutenant to meet the enemy.

As the months dragged on throughout the winter of 1587–8 and the spring of Armada year, the English musters became better trained and armed, while in Flanders the Duke of Parma's men, wintering in cold army cantonments and not campaigning, suffered sickness and poor food. The army's combat potential dwindled from a high in September 1587 until by July 1588 it had reached its nadir, as well as suffering a fall in strength from 30,000 to 17,000. The advantages for the assailants were lessening. The Enterprise of England was not looking quite so promising any more.

Sir Francis Walsingham, head of Queen Elizabeth's secret service. Camden wrote of him: 'He was a person exceeding wise and industrious . . . a diligent searcher out of hidden secrets.' He had an implacable hatred of Spain, and persecuted Roman Catholics remorselessly. Elizabeth called him 'her Moor'.

William Cecil, first Baron Burghley, Secretary of State to Queen Elizabeth I — her 'Eyes', as she called him.

But what of the sea? More and more the English had come to realize the importance of their dependence upon the sea. By 1588 Elizabeth I was mistress of the most powerful navy yet seen in Europe. Thirty-four Queen's ships assembled for the Armada campaign (see *The Opposing Fleets* in Supplement 1). Ten of these thirty-four were modern galleons, all of them built or entirely rebuilt in the 1580s, while another seven were built or rebuilt in the previous decade. These seventeen ships ranged in size from 800 down to 200 tons.

These fine modern galleons of new design and construction bore the stamp of John Hawkins's work and became described as race-built. The word derives from raze, not race, and relates to the razing — i.e. the demolishing of the high upperworks of a ship. They were ships capable of out-sailing any other vessel afloat. They were better armed than any other ships of their size, and the new profile with the lower after-castle gave them an altogether sleeker look. In practical terms, they were more weatherly ships.

The three largest ships in the fleet were of older design and construction. The largest by far was the enormous 1,100-ton *Triumph*, flagship of Martin Frobisher: she was an elderly lady built in 1561. Lord Sheffield's 1,000-ton *White Bear* was only two years younger. The third largest was Sir Robert Southwell's 900-ton *Elizabeth Jonas*, one of the oldest ships in the fleet with thirty years' service to her credit.

Of the smaller ships, those below 200 tons, there were eight which were not more than five years old, with another three a little older. At the lowest end of the scale a fine squadron of pinnaces, like the frigates of Nelson's era — the maids of all work, scouting, carrying despatches, 'repeating' signals — completed the fleet of the Queen's ships.

To John Hawkins must go much of the credit for the concept of the modern galleons. For ten years he had charge of construction and design and he had clear-cut ideas of what was wanted, based principally on his own long experience of commanding ships. Already galleons were longer and leaner than their merchant-ship counterparts. Hawkins designed them longer still, enabling them to sail closer to the wind and to carry more guns along their length. He had the waists decked over, giving greater comfort to the otherwise exposed guns' crews. After-castles were trimmed down drastically: they were used to house small guns, the man-killers, as well as acting as a platform for musketeers and arquebusiers. Reducing the after-castle gave better stability, reduced rolling, enabled different and bigger guns to be mounted. Ship-smashing guns were selected rather than those for man-killing. Sir William Wynter was largely responsible for this. No friend of John Hawkins, he spoke in a blunt Bristolian fashion; nevertheless, he collaborated closely with Hawkins at this time.

Iron guns gradually began to be replaced by those cast in brass or bronze. The 30 lb demi-cannon ship-smashers of unreliable accuracy became largely replaced by culverins and demi-culverins, throwing shots of 18 lb and 9 lb with better accuracy over greater ranges. There is no way now of determining exactly which ships were armed according to Wynter's wishes, but what is quite clear is that the Hawkins–Wynter type of collaboration gave untold advantages to Elizabeth's captains. The fact that these guns failed to sink even one enemy ship will be referred to later.

What England did not encourage was galleys. She only had one and this was cooped up in the Thames — 'wisely kept out of harm's way' as one historian put it. This contrasts interestingly with Spain's experience with galleys. It will be recalled that the Marquis of Santa Cruz was a 'galley man'. In 1571 he had handled a fleet of galleys as no one had ever done before; while the Mediterranean-orientation naval thinking of Spain was biased towards galleys rather than the galleons favoured by other maritime seaboard nations like England, France, Portugal. Forty galleys and six galleasses formed the very foundation of the Spanish effort and were the pride of both Philip and Santa Cruz, even though the Armada was well furnished with other fine ships. It had great ships such as the Portuguese Royal Fleet, confiscated by the conquering Spaniards in 1580; and it had what was called the Indian Guard, those galleons built specially for service in the long Atlantic rollers to escort homeward-bound merchant ships trading in the West Indies. The harsher conditions of the Atlantic, with fierce gales from the south-west and battering seas, highlighted the galleys' shortcomings.

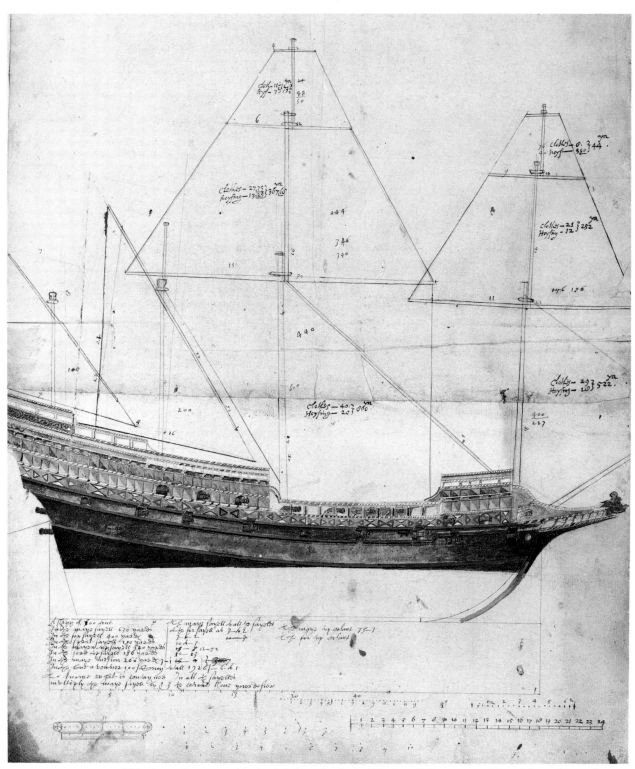

This sixteenth-century drawing is believed to be by Matthew Baker, master shipwright to the royal dockyards. It shows a broadside view of a race-built galleon with its sail plan, typical of many of the modern English ships used in the Armada campaign.

ÆTATIS SVÆ LVIII
Anno Dñi 1591

Sir John Hawkins was Treasurer of the Navy, and largely responsible for the modernization of the Queen's ships enabling them to outperform the ships of the Armada. His achievement merits comparison with that of his modern counterpart R.J. Mitchell (1895–1937), who designed the graceful Spitfire, the most famous of all Second World War fighter aircraft.

However, Cadiz had taught Philip a valuable lesson. There the conditions were overwhelmingly in favour of the galleys. The confined space, the lack of sea room, suited oared vessels rather than sailing vessels, yet they performed abysmally. Six of them were brushed aside by Drake's sailing-ships with almost contemptuous ease. The galleys' limitations were exposed. Their meagre five guns were no match at all for the powerful array of thirty-five guns mounted in the English ships, a single broadside from which could cripple them.

To his credit, Philip reacted with uncharacteristic speed. He reduced the number of galleys in the Armada from forty to only four — and Portuguese ones at that, not Spanish — and not one of the four reached the Chops of the Channel, let alone participated in the Channel Pursuit or the north-about attempt to escape. Wisely, Philip assembled sixty-five galleons and great ships comprising twenty-four true galleons and forty-one lofty merchant ships armed with guns which made their transition to heavy warships quite comfortably.

The fleet train comprised twenty-five urcas or hulks, four Neapolitan galleasses, the four galleys that the storm off Cape Finisterre sent scurrying for harbour and thirty-two lighter-weight vessels — the pataches and zabras which we would call pinnaces.

*   *   *

Elizabeth, as we have seen, kept the Queen's ships on a very tight rein — secured alongside or anchored, half armed, half manned, with half the crews living ashore, enjoying fresh food at their own rather than her expense, ships not deteriorating as they would do battling against an Atlantic winter. Money, as Burghley showed, was the final arbiter. While her ships lay quietly in their harbours she conducted her devious machinations with Philip, with Parma, and even with her allies, the Dutch.

She swept through the corridors of diplomacy, intriguing here, trying to do a deal there; persuading, cajoling, manœuvring, trying to bribe, all the while fending off Drake's and Burghley's protestations and approaches.

She tried to buy off Parma by offering him the independent sovereignty of the Netherlands, without telling her Dutch allies, who might well have had conflicting views on the matter.

To be fair to Elizabeth, she genuinely seemed to want to avoid all-out war and she suspected that Philip wanted to as well. In this assumption she was not altogether right; Philip had long since reached the point of no return. The Armada was committed; it was only a question now of when, not whether. Unless — and this is the crucial point — unless he could get all he wanted without committing the fleet to battle. Heaven knew, he had lost face often enough at the hands of Elizabeth and Drake and he could not possibly face another humiliation in the eyes of the world. Philip made no attempt to disguise his preparations for mounting an assault on England. Perhaps — and we can now never know for certain — perhaps he was playing a clever war of nerves; perhaps he cherished the fervent hope that the magnitude of his preparations might frighten Elizabeth into submission.

Drake had no illusions about the situation. Even after legend has been discounted, Drake is still left on a level metaphorically head and shoulders above any of his contemporaries. Indeed, one could go further and assert that he had a prescience about naval strategy and tactics far and away in advance of anyone else.

His submissions to the Queen involved two strategical concepts which seem never to have been considered before; and yet after the Armada they became established as the accepted norm. Some historians believe that Drake stumbled upon these ideas; others, more generous, see them as the outcome of genius. These concepts merit our attention.

The first relates to the defensive deployment of a fleet against a seaborne invasion of England, and deserves examination in relation to the Armada. The usual plan for the defence of England was at first sight quite logical: naval forces should assemble at the narrowest part of the Channel in the Straits of Dover, preferably over towards the French ports, and thus help thwart an invasion crossing. Drake saw this as fundamentally wrong. He expressed it this way: the prevailing wind in the Channel was westerly: *any defending fleet must keep to windward of the invading force — that is, to the west of it.* Thus the massing of a fleet in the Straits of Dover — far to the east — was patently wrong. Such a deployment would allow an aggressor to mount a landing almost anywhere along the whole length of the south coast from the Lizard to Beachy Head.

Sir Francis Drake

*T*HE DIFFICULTY with Drake is to sift the truth from legend: fact from fiction: honesty from conjecture. What is not in doubt was his almost fanatical Protestantism and his staunch patriotism. His sharp intelligence manifested itself in his quick thinking, his swift grasp of the essentials of a debate or course of action. This made him intolerant of others, slower to comprehend. Here are some contemporary views of the man. The first is virtually a descriptive caption for the illustration; the fourth is a little more embellished . . .

Round-headed, brown hair, full-bearded, his eyes round, large and clear, well-favoured, fair and of a cheerful countenance.

John Stowe, *Annales*, 1580

He is called Francisco Drac, and is a man of about 35 years of age, low of stature, with a fair beard, and is one of the greatest mariners that sail the seas, both as a navigator and as a commander . . .

Don Francisco da Zarante in Richard Hakluyt's *Principall Navigations*, 1589–1600

I remember Drake, in the vaunting style of a soldier, would call the enterprise [of Cadiz 1587] the singeing of this King of Spain's beard.

Francis Bacon (1561–1626)

He is so boastful of himself as a mariner and a man of learning. . . Drake is served on silver dishes with gold borders and gilded garlands in which are his arms. . . He dines and sups to the music of viols . . .

Gaspar de Vargas, Chief Alcalde of Gautulco, Mexico

Drake's second strategical concept is equally commonplace today, and still holds good, having stood the test of four centuries of naval warfare. It is this: the offensive in naval warfare — including the use of the offensive even in defence — is fundamental. Admiral of the Fleet Lord Fisher would have bellowed his approval: one of his delights was 'Hit first, hit hard and keep on hitting'. In fact Drake was not allowed to follow out this strategical concept, but in a sense he had already demonstrated it at Cadiz the previous year. It was expressed as 'The watergates of England are the ports of the enemy.'

The southern frontier of England in its war with Spain was not Hampshire, Dorset, Devon or Cornwall, but the enemy ports of Corunna, Lisbon, Cadiz, where the enemy forces assembled. The attack on Cadiz illustrates the fundamental truth of this principle.

Drake nearly persuaded the Queen in January 1588 to allow another assault upon the ports of Spain or Portugal in order to thwart the build-up of enemy ships, but at the last moment Elizabeth changed her mind and called off the operation. Drake was persistent and wrote to the Council in London at the end of March expressing his second strategical concept in tangled phrases: 'If her Majesty and your Lordships think that the King of Spain meaneth any invasion of England, then doubtless his force is and will be great in Spain . . . If there may be such a stay or stop made by any means of this fleet in Spain, that they may not come through the seas as conquerors — which I assure myself they think to do — then shall the Prince of Parma have such a check thereby as were meet . . . My very good Lords, next under God's mighty protection, the advantage again of time and place will be the only and chief means for our good; wherein I most humbly beseech your good Lordships to persevere as you have begun.' Drake went on to exhort their Lordships 'not to fear any invasion in her own country but to seek her Majesty's enemies wherever they may be found . . . for that with fifty sail of shipping, we shall do more good upon their own coast than a great many more will do here at home.'

A fortnight later on 13 April Drake addressed the Queen: 'If your Majesty will give present order for our proceeding to the sea and send to the strengthening of this fleet here four more of your Majesty's good ships and those 16 sail of ships with their pinnaces which are preparing in London, then shall your Majesty stand assured, with God's assistance, that if the fleet come out of Lisbon, as long as we have victual to live withal upon that coast, they shall be fought with . . . God increase your most excellent Majesty's forces both by sea and land daily; for this I surely think, there was never any force so strong as there is now ready or making ready against your Majesty.'

Drake did not rest there: he exhorted further: 'The advantage of time and place in all martial actions is half the victory, which being lost is irrecoverable . . . Wherefore if your Majesty will command me away with those ships which are here already and the rest to follow with all possible expedition, I hold it, in my poor opinion, the surest and best course.'

Two days after the date of this letter the Duke of Medina Sidonia was having his standard blessed at the altar of Lisbon cathedral by the Pope.

But Elizabeth did not command Drake away. She stayed his hand for another fortnight or so when he was emboldened to press her further. 'Most renowned Prince,' he began in a phrase which presaged greater demands, 'I beseech you to pardon my boldness in the discharge of my conscience, being burdened to signify into your

Highness the imminent dangers that in my simple opinion do hang over us . . . The promise of peace from the Prince of Parma and these mighty preparations in Spain agree not well together . . . these preparations may be speedily prevented by sending your forces to encounter them somewhat far off and more near to their own coasts which will be cheaper for her Majesty and her people and much dearer for the enemy.'

By the beginning of June, when Howard arrived at Plymouth, Drake brought his chief round to his own point of view. Drake could be a compelling debater. Indeed, a command structure with Drake being forced to accept the superiority of Howard in command of the fleet must have been humbling for the Devonian, and seemed bound to lead to disharmony. But it was to the credit of each man that they formed an excellent working relationship, though Howard must at times have been appalled and stupefied by this adventurer — a man who normally yielded to no one save his Queen, who displayed arrogance born of the belief that he was always right. Drake was a difficult man to command. He was religious to the point of devoutness; proud, dynamic, insufferable at times but described too as a 'jolly' companion.

The 52-year-old Howard must have been the soul of tact and discretion: his position cannot have been easy. Nor did he stand to gain much from his command. If the Armada were routed the credit would undoubtedly go to Drake, and in the event of defeat the blame would rest with himself as senior commander. He was an honourable man, conscientious, fervently Protestant and devoted to the Queen.

Drake accepted Howard's supremacy with a rare graciousness. The official ceremony of Drake hoisting his flag — newly brought by Howard — as vice admiral of the combined fleet took place on 2 June 1588. The scene was beautiful. It was a bright early summer's day, with the Devonian countryside of lush green fields a backdrop to the colour of the massed ships and boats in the Sound at Plymouth, the whole scene one of frenzied activity, the rush of provisioning ship. Howard, the Lord High Admiral, wrote of the occasion to Burghley:

Upon Tuesday last . . . the wind serving exceedingly well, I cut sail at the Downs, assigning unto my Lord Henry Seymour those ships appointed to stay with him on the Narrow Seas . . . and with a pleasant gale all the way long came and arrived this day 2 June about eight of the clock in the morning at this port of Plymouth, whence Sir Francis Drake came forth with sixty sail very well appointed to meet with me; and so, casting about, he put with me into the haven again, where I mean to stay there two days to water our fleet, and afterwards, God willing to take the opportunity of the first wind serving for the coast of Spain with intention to lie on and off betwixt England and that coast to watch the coming of the Spanish forces.

The force that Howard left in the charge of Lord Henry Seymour in the Straits of Dover–Thames estuary area numbered about forty ships. They were strung out along Gillingham Reach, past Chatham's dockyard, with the small pinnaces within sight of Rochester and the galleons as far down the estuary as Queensborough. It was still too great a force to be simply watching and waiting for an assault by invasion barges. Several of them should have accompanied Howard to Plymouth: certainly the two flagships — *Rainbow* (Seymour) and *Vanguard*, flag of Sir William Wynter, both of them new 500-ton galleons of Hawkins's latest design. As it was they were kept in reserve off Dover and only took part in the one day's battle of Gravelines.

Howard, however, was shocked at the state of the fleet's provisioning programme. Several days later — on 7 June — he was still in port and complaining bitterly to Burghley: 'I perceive that the ships and also the victuals be nothing in that readiness that I looked they should be in . . . We have here now about eighteen days victuals and there is none to be gotten in all this county . . .'

In a second letter the same day he expressed the fine state of the seamen. 'There is here the gallantest company of captains, soldiers and mariners that I think ever was seen in England. It were a pity they should lack meat when they are so desirous to spend their lives in her Majesty's service.' For some time now messes aboard the English ship had been scanted 'six upon four', meaning that six men were receiving food for four and sharing it between them.

Another fifteen days passed and Howard was still at Plymouth when he wrote again to Burghley on 22 June: 'If they come not [he was referring to the Armada] our extremity will be very great for our victuals ended 15th of this month . . . men have fallen sick . . .'

More badgering was necessary before the victuallers delivered a month's supply. Writing to the Queen on 3 July, Howard expressed his relief: 'On Saturday late at night they came to us. They were no sooner come, although it were night, but we went all to work to get in our victuals which I hope will be done in 24 hours, for no men shall sleep nor eat till it be despatched, so that God willing, we will be under sail tomorrow morning being Monday.'

And to Walsingham, Howard wrote at 12 pm: 'God willing I will set sail within this three hours . . .'

While Howard was exchanging these letters with London on the subject of victuals, there were other matters engaging his attention. He gave full support to Drake's views — now also supported by Hawkins and Frobisher — on attacking King Philip's forces in Spanish ports. Time, it is evident, was beginning to run out. Howard received intelligence of the Armada leaving Lisbon, becoming storm-bound and then taking shelter in Corunna. There was no time to be lost.

Then, almost unbelievably, there came permission from the Queen for the fleet to sail. She had yielded to the persuasion and logic of Drake's strategy, and as if to underline the change to good fortune for the fleet, a fair, fresh wind sprang up from the north-east. Howard, Drake and Frobisher abandoned provisioning and nearly a hundred ships spread their canvas and hastened anxiously to get away before the Queen changed her mind and recalled the fleet.

In his letter to Walsingham on 4 July announcing the fleet's departure, Howard explained his dispositions:

I have divided myself [the fleet] here into three parts, and yet we lie within sight of one another so as, if any of us do discover the Spanish fleet, we give notice thereof presently the one to the other and thereupon repair and assemble together. I myself do lie in the middle of the Channel with the greatest force. Sir Francis Drake [vice admiral] hath twenty ships and four or five pinnaces which lie towards Ushant: and Mr Hawkyns [rear admiral] with as many more lieth towards Scilly.

In making these dispositions Howard made it clear he did not believe that Ireland was one of the Armada's objectives. If Scotland was to be a target area, he intended to follow the Armada through the Narrow Seas (the Channel). If England were the target,

Cost of living

WHILE ships' crews were fed with substantial quantities of food both at sea and in harbour — albeit often stale or rotting food — their families ashore coped with a housekpeeing bill running into shillings a week. A gunner, as we have seen elsewhere, would earn £9 15s. 6d. a year, or about 3s. 9d. a week. It is almost impossible to get a true comparison of money values over so long a period as four centuries, if only because the social patterns of living in the two eras bear little relation to each other. However, if one bases calculations on the level of Consumer Prices (the General Index of Retail Prices) with 1974 = 100, then 1588 = 4.8 and 1988 = 388, a factor of 80 times greater.

A quail = ½d.
200 white herrings = 3s. 0d.
A goose = 4d.
Best mutton = 1½d. lb
2 lb jar marmalade = 5s. 0d.

Oysters = 4d. a bushel
A chicken = 1d.
Best beef = 3d. lb
Raisins = 3d. lb
Tankard of ale = ½d.
Cost of a meal at an Inn of Court = about 3d.
Weekly meals for Cambridge student = 5s. 0d.
Bottle of Gascony wine = 2s. 0d.

Higher up the social ladder these costs have been recorded:

Annual fees for Bedford Grammar School, £13.
Charge by Hilliard for one of his beautiful miniatures, £40.
Pair of ornamental breeches, about £7.
Pair of stockings, about £1.
A fine shirt, about £1 or more.
Cost of building Kenilworth, county seat of the Earl of Leicester, £60,000.
Canvas for making servant's livery, 4d. a yard.

his fleet would attack the Armada, while Lord Henry Seymour with his flag in the *Rainbow*, commanding the detached squadron in the Downs, would watch Flushing, Dunkirk and the Straits of Dover.

Within two days of departure from Plymouth, the fleet was in the middle of the Bay of Biscay, two-thirds of the way between Ushant and Corunna, and all looked well set for a battle royal in Corunna — except the weather. Howard was impelled to write to London: 'I know not what weather you have had there, but there was never any such summer seen here on the sea. God of His mercy keep us from sickness, for we fear that more than any other hurt the Spaniards will do.' Some sickness did strike the ships, but the mood and confidence in the mariners of the fleet was clearly defined by Thomas Fenner of the *Nonpareil*: 'There never happened the like opportunity to beat down the Spanish pride.'

No wonder the mood was one of confidence. In prospect was a battle with plunder and spoil such as would make the Cadiz expedition of the previous year look pretty small. The English had the chance to surprise the Spanish Armada — storm-damaged it was true, but nevertheless a great fighting force — at anchor without sea-room, disadvantaged beyond measure. Even the most cautious minds dwelt longingly on the prospects.

Then, perversely, the wind dropped away, the fleet became becalmed and when a fresh wind arose it had backed to the south and blew steadily. Suddenly the tables were turned. Hopes of the wind carrying the English fleet to Spanish ports to provision before attacking Corunna now went overboard. If it tried to beat south in the face of such a wind this would be time-consuming, provisions would again fall dangerously low, but — far more dangerously, in tactical terms — the southerly wind which blew adversely for Howard blew fair for the Armada should it be capable of leaving port. In such an event Howard might even miss his enemy as he headed north, and the Armada would be sighting Land's End just about the same time as the English Admiral reached Corunna — to find the anchorage deserted. Howard had no option but to turn about and set course for Plymouth.

On Friday 22 July the English fleet dropped anchors in Plymouth Sound. Thankfully, it had beaten the Armada to it. Unknown to Howard, it was that very same day that Medina Sidonia weighed anchor at Corunna and headed north for England. It had been a close-run thing.

9. *The point of no return*

PREPARATIONS BEGAN immediately to re-provision the English ships and to effect maintenance repairs. Sickness among the men had taken its toll, and newly pressed men were needed to replace the men sent ashore. Local justices of the peace in Devon and Cornwall were hard put to locate suitable numbers of men of the quality looked for by the admirals and captains.

They were days of intense activity, with many of the world's greatest seafarers concentrated in Plymouth, striving to get their ships into the finest order. John Hawkins was pleased enough, and wrote to Burghley telling him some of the ships were 'in most royal and perfect state'.

The Lord High Admiral's flagship, the 800-ton *Ark Royal*. She carried a total of 430 mariners, gunners and soldiers apart from officers, gentlemen volunteers and supernumeraries, which would have brought the total to about 500. Her original name was *Ark Ralegh*, and it changed again in 1608 when she was rechristened *Ark Anne* in honour of the queen of James I. She stove in her timbers and was broken up in 1616. It was to be 1914 before a second *Ark Royal* was launched.

Howard himself was also delighted. He commanded the fleet from aboard the *Ark Royal* (originally the *Ark Raleigh*, and popularly referred to as the *Ark*). This 800-ton ship had been built originally for Sir Walter Raleigh, and he had given it to the Queen in exchange for an IOU for £5,000 (which was honoured in 1592, being deducted from his debt to the Crown!) Howard expressed his delight in the ship to Burghley: 'I think her the one ship in the world for all conditions, and truly I think there can be no great ship make me change and go out of her . . .'

The talent accompanying Howard at Plymouth upon whom he relied most heavily included his vice admiral, Sir Francis Drake, with his flagship, the *Revenge*. His rear admiral was John Hawkins in the splendid, modernized *Victory*. Commanding the enormous *Triumph* was Martin Frobisher, stubborn, rough-cast leader of three NW Passage expeditions. There was Thomas Fenner, an experienced seaman who had shipped with Drake to the Indies and Cadiz, and his cousins George and William Edward Fenton, protégé of Frobisher, commanded the *Mary Rose*. There were captains James Lancaster, Luke Ward and young Richard Hawkins, and many more talented seamen. There was also more than a hint of nepotism. Several noblemen present included Lord Thomas Howard, the admiral's cousin; Lord Sheffield, the admiral's nephew; Sir Robert Southwell, his son-in-law.

Contemporary artists employed considerable artistic licence in depicting details of their subjects. The illustration on p.85 is a contemporary woodcut, while the one above is third in a series of ten engravings by C.J. Visscher (1550–1612). Both are of the *Ark Royal*.

Commission to Lord Howard

ELIZABETH, by the Grace of God, &c, to all to whom &c greeting: Know ye that we, reposing special trust and confidence in the fidelity, prudence, zeal, experience, circumspection, industry and diligence of our beloved Councillor, Charles, Lord Howard, Baron of Effingham, Knight of our illustrious order of the Garter, High Admiral of England, Ireland, Wales and of the dominions and islands thereof, of the town of Calais, and the marches of the same, of Normandy, Gascony and Acquitaine, and Captain General of the Navy and mariners of our said kingdoms of England and Ireland — do by these presents, design, make, constitute, ordain and depute the said Charles to be our lieutenant-general, commander-in-chief, and governor of our whole fleet and army at sea . . .

The Commission is dated 21 December 1587.

A Knight of the Garter.

Pine's engraved chart of the Channel from Land's End to Plymouth, with a most elaborately embellished cartouche.

In the Medway Lord Henry Seymour commanded the eastern squadron, comprising the Queen's ships *Rainbow, Antelope, Swallow, Bull, Tiger, Tramontana, Scout, Achates, Bonavolia Galley, Merlin, Spy, George, Sun* and *Cygnet*. He hoisted his flag in the *Rainbow*, a modern 500-ton galleon. His vice admiral was the vastly experienced Sir William Wynter aboard the 500-ton *Vanguard*. Lord Howard had inspected these ships when he was in the Medway, crawling into fore peaks and bilges — and other places not meant for admirals to check into. 'I have been aboard every ship', Howard was to report, 'that goeth out with me, and in every place where any may creep, and I do thank God that they be in the state they be in: there is never a one of them that knows what a leak means.'

Even Wynter agreed: 'Our ships doth show themselves like gallants here. I assure you it will do a man's heart good to behold them and would to God the Prince of Parma were upon the seas with all his forces, and we in view of them!'

*　　*　　*

In discussing the composition of the English fleet it is impossible to reconcile figures one with another. The most authoritative sources do not agree, but this should not deter us from examining what figures are available. The number of ships listed totalled 197 (see Supplement 1) and they carried a total of 15,541 men. This is the figure quoted by W. Laird Clowes,* but the equally authoritative Professor Laughton† gives

* *The Royal Navy*, 7 vols. 1897–1903: see Vol I pp. 539–604.
† *State Papers Relating to the Defeat of the Spanish Armada*, 2 vols, 1894, reprinted 1981.

The state of the fleet

'THE SHIPS sit aground so strongly and are so staunch as if they were made of a whole tree.'

Thus wrote William Hawkins from Plymouth in February 1588 to his famous brother John, Treasurer of the Navy, who had worked so unceasingly to equip the nation with first-class fighting ships. Later, in July, on the eve of the Armada campaign John Hawkins himself saw the ships and described them to Lord Burghley: 'The four great ships, the *Triumph, Elizabeth Jonas*, the *Bear*, and the *Victory* are in most royal and perfect state: you could not tell that they had been at sea more than if they had ridden at Chatham.'

Yet these ships had been in all the gales and storms of the summer, sweeping the Channel and off the coast of Spain.

15,925. Furthermore, Laughton reckons one should add to these figures the many recruits sent from Plymouth and other volunteers who joined the fleet during its voyage up the Channel whose accession went unrecorded. It is thought probable, therefore, that the total number of men fell between 17,000 and 18,000.

Of the 197 ships summoned to oppose the Armada, the most important were the Queen's ships, of which there were thirty-four. These were deployed fourteen-to-twenty between the eastern and western squadrons, with the Plymouth-based squadron having the pick of the heavier ships. These were the nucleus of the English fleet, the front-line ships, the warships that would engage the enemy galleons, and these were the ships of which Howard, Hawkins and Wynter spoke so highly.

Another thirty-four vessels were merchant ships serving under Francis Drake, then there were eighteen more under the Lord Admiral, thirty were paid for by the City of London and fifteen were acting as victuallers. The coasters and voluntary ships serving both Lord Seymour and the Lord High Admiral numbered another sixty-six ships.

Not all of these ships saw action against the Armada — indeed, most of them did not. Even Lord Seymour's squadron did not join the Lord High Admiral until 6 August, in time for the final battle at Gravelines. There was much movement among his ships: he sent four ships to escort a convoy, and he discharged another six for lack of victuals. He judged the galley *Bonavolia* unseaworthy, and at the last moment sent her back to the Medway. The eight London ships led by Nicholas Gorges in the *Susan Parnell* of the Levant Company did not leave the river Thames till after 8 August, as did the ten London ships under Henry Bellingham in the *George Noble*, both squadrons joining Seymour after the battle of Gravelines on the admiral's return from the North Sea.

Furthermore, there was much coming and going of personnel. The fifteen small victualling ships under the command of Francis Burnell sailed west down the Channel in July, and all of them were probably discharged quite early on in the pursuit of the Armada. Their men would have been pressed for service immediately into the Queen's ships.

It is interesting to compare the relative strengths of the royal ships in the opposing fleets and to expose a myth which has persisted for four centuries. Ever since the broadsheets of the sixteenth century, the idea has been perpetuated of small English ships contending with huge Spanish galleons for control of the Channel. Even Lord Howard pointed up the difference in a letter to Walsingham when the bulk of the

This engraving appears in *Fragments of Ancient Shipwrightry* by Matthew Baker, published in the sixteenth century, and now preserved in the Pepysian Library.

fighting was over and he pursued the remnants of the Armada in the North Sea: '. . . their fleet consisteth of mighty ships and great strength'.

True, the Spanish ships *looked* big. They carried huge after-castles in the fashion of warships of the early-to-mid sixteenth century, and huge fore-castles, too. Even Raleigh was bound to say they had 'majesty'.

Furthermore, the Spanish method of assessing tonnages of ships differed considerably from the English, with the result that they gave significantly higher tonnages to their ships, averaging perhaps 20–25 per cent above the English calculations. For example — and this is a fairly extreme example, but an accurate one tested by actual measurement — the *San Salvador*, which was captured in the Channel, was registered as 958 tons by the Spanish, but when measured by the English it was rated no higher than 600 tons. The Spanish figure was more than half as much again as the English measurement.

It is interesting to compare the tonnages of the major royal ships of each fleet. If, as we have seen already, the Spanish Armada consisted of twenty-four galleons (i.e., the ten of the Portuguese Squadron, the ten of the Indian Guard and the four great ships of Spain), then we put outside our consideration all the armed merchant ships, many of them registered as over 1,000 tons, but none of them constructed as King's ships. If we consider alongside these major Spanish galleons the biggest of the Queen's ships, we have the following comparatives:

Queen's Ships	Tons	King's Ships	Tons
Triumph	1,100	San Juan (Port.Sqdn)	1,050
White Bear	1,000	San Martin	1,000
Elizabeth Jonas	900	Florencia	961
Ark Royal	800	Santa Catalina	882
Victory	800	La Trinidad	872
Elizabeth Bonaventure	600	San Luis	830
Mary Rose	600	San Felipe	800
Hope	600	San Marcos	790

It can be seen that the greatest ship on either side was Frobisher's *Triumph*, followed closely by the vice admiral of the Portuguese Squadron, the *San Juan*. Sidonia's flagship, the *San Martin*, and Lord Sheffield's *White Bear* each registered 1,000 tons. If we extend the table further, we get:

Nonpareil	500	San Mateo	750
Revenge	500	San Juan Bautista	750
Vanguard	500	N.S. de Begoña	750
Rainbow	500	San Cristobal	700
Golden Lion	500	San Juan Bautista	650
Dreadnought	400	Santiago el Mayor	530

However, we have already established that the Spanish method of calculating tonnages resulted in much higher figures than the English. If an allowance of about 20 per cent is made in the Spanish figures it can be seen quite readily that the actual differences between the tonnages of the opposing warships are remarkably small: indeed, the shift in advantage is to the English.

The rule of tonnage

JAMES BAKER was employed by the Crown as a craftsman 'pensioner' at the rate of about fourpence a day in 1537. Henry VIII retained such craftsmen so he could call upon them in time of need. Baker's son, Matthew, earned renown greater than his father's — as a shipbuilder and surveyor of men-o'-war, with a specialist knowledge of mounting heavy cannon inboard. He was the first man to be called a Master Shipwright and he continued to give good service to Queen Elizabeth I. He undoubtedly knew John Hawkins, and it was probably through this connection that he was selected to devise a satisfactory means of measuring ships and calculating tonnages.

He selected a vessel named the *Ascension* of London. Baker found she carried 320 butts of wine in her hold. Two butts went to the ton, so he described her as of 160 tons burden — that is, she could carry a burden or load of 160 tons. Baker measured the ship as follows: she was 54ft on the keel, 24ft broad inside the plank and 12ft depth of hold. If one multiplies these figures the product is 15,552. Baker then sought a divisor which would give the 160 tons answer he wanted. This proved to be 97·2, which he then seemed to round up to 100.

In order to calculate the ship's deadweight for purposes of registering, he thought it proper to add one-third to the burden. He published all these findings in his *Rule of Tonnage*.

A century after Baker's calculations in 1552, shipwrights on the Thames claimed that Baker divided by 94, and measured *outside* the plank for breadth and to the keel bottom for depth. This could have the effect of increasing the tonnage by as much as 20 per cent. As shipwrights were paid by the ton when they sold a ship to the King, this was to their considerable advantage. But King Charles II's good advisers enabled him to refer to Matthew Baker's calculations established in Queen Elizabeth's time.

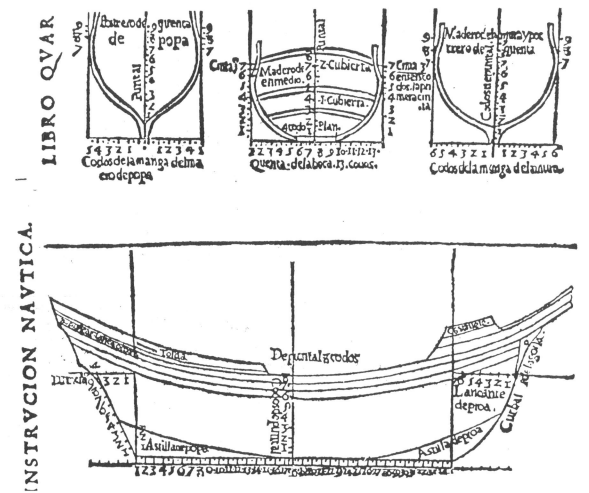

The oldest Spanish work on shipbuilding was published in the year before the Armada campaign, 1587, and it contained these plans by Dr Diego Garcia de Palacio.

There is, however, another aspect of this matter: we have excluded from our lists the names and tonnages of the armed merchant ships, and here the Spanish greatness is manifest. The ten ships of the Levant Squadron commanded by Martin de Bertendona were huge vessels, the largest being the 1,249-ton *La Regazona* and the smallest still a sizeable 666 tons. Howard had nothing like these in his fleet. His two largest supply ships were 400-tonners, the Earl of Leicester's *Galleon Leicester* and the Levant Company's *Merchant Royal*. There were four 300-tonners, Raleigh's *Roebuck*, the London ship *Hercules*, a West Country *Sampson*, and the Levanter *Edward Bonaventure*.* Then came five 250-tonners and another twenty-three of 200 tons or thereabouts.

What is now evident is the fact that there was not the great disparity in the sizes of ships that could support the David and Goliath scenario painted by some historians throughout the years. Nor was there a great disparity in the numbers of ships opposing each other. Tonnages and numbers of ships gave neither side a significant edge on the other. What *was* of great advantage to the English was the modern construction and design of many of the Queen's ships, which made them weatherly and nimble in handling by skilled crews, plus the quality of their ordnance.

* It was her voyage of 1591–3 which helped found the East India Company.

*   *   *

We left the Armada marshalling its forces within sight of the Lizard, poised on the threshold of its greatest enterprise. The point of no return had been reached. The fleet rolled in the Atlantic swell, waiting for the stragglers to come up. It must have been a magnificent sight with the masts emblazoned with flags and ensigns stiffening in the wind and banners streaming aloft from the bare masts.

Such was the unforgettable sight presented to Captain Thomas Fleming aboard his tiny 50-ton pinnace or bark, the *Golden Hind*, as he patrolled the Chops of the Channel eager to gain early intelligence of any approaching Spanish forces.

One of history's greatest battle-fleets lay within his vision. He headed the *Golden Hind* round and ran for the Sound. When he arrived there he was told that Howard and Drake were up on the Hoe . . .

*   *   *

Speed of ships 1570–1988

Year & ship	Knots	8	10	12	14	16	18	20	22	24	26	28	30
16th c. Oared galleasse	~~~~~~~~	~~											
1588 *Revenge*	~~~												
1665 *Royal Charles*	~~~												
1700 *Royal Sovereign*	~~~~~	~~											
1755 *Royal George*	~~~												
1800 *Victory*	~~~~												
1860 *Warrior*	~~~~~~	~~~~	~~	steam / sail									
1870 *Devastation*	~~~~~~	~~~											
1906 *Dreadnought*	~~~~~~	~~~~~	~~~~~										
1916 *Iron Duke*	~~~~~~	~~~~~	~~~~~~	~									
1941 *King George V*	~~~~~~	~~~~~	~~~~~~	~~~~~~	~~~~~								
1988 *Resolution*	~~~~~~	~~~~~	~~~~~~	~~~~~~	~~~~~~	~~~							

Range of weapons 1588–1988

Period & weapon	1	3	5	7	9	11	13	15	17	19	21	23 miles
1588 cannon	🔥 *Revenge*											
17th c. cannon	🔥 *Royal Charles*											
18th c. cannon	🔥 *Royal Sovereign*											
19th c. cannon	🔥 *Victory*											
1906 12″ gun				🔥 *Dreadnought*								
1916 15″ gun										🔥 *Iron Duke*		
1941 15″ gun										🔥 *King George V*		
1988 missile									Polaris sub *Resolution* *🔥			

*4630 Kms (2893 miles)

When Howard and Drake had finished their leisurely game of bowls they returned to their ships in the Sound where preparations for leaving harbour were well advanced, as Drake knew very well they would be. Part of his easy nonchalance was born of the knowledge that his crews knew precisely what needed doing without so much as a nod from him. Looked at critically, many would think the Spaniards had scored an initial tactical advantage in seafaring terms, in both time and place: catching the Queen's fleet in Plymouth harbour, their vast Armada had surprised their enemy, harbour-bound, to leeward while they held the weather gage. One historian declared that the fleet and fortune of England had been placed in peril: 'To such a pass had Elizabeth, her vacillations and economies brought them. The campaign could hardly have opened under auspices more discouraging for England.'

But all was not as it seemed. The earliest time the Armada could enter the Sound — if indeed that was the intention — would be on the flood tide the following afternoon. By then the English had every intention of being at sea.

That evening with an ebb tide and a wind which 'was very scant' the royal galleons and the heaviest of the armed merchantmen warped their ships out of the inner

The legend of Drake on Plymouth Hoe

PERHAPS THE MOST romantic of all the legends attaching to Sir Francis Drake's life is the portrayal of his playing bowls on Plymouth Hoe on the afternoon of Friday 29 July 1588. After a midday meal with the Lord High Admiral, Drake strode up to the Hoe with Howard, where they gazed out over the Sound with its splendid views to seaward.

It was probably about three o'clock (this is conjecture, for no contemporary report carries the time of day: but it is likely to have been between three and four in the afternoon). Captain Thomas Fleming of the 50-ton pinnace *Golden Hind* (not Drake's ship which circumnavigated the world) came bustling up to the Hoe with long-awaited intelligence. Earlier that day — probably at dawn when most sightings are made — Fleming had sighted the Armada. Well, it was not all the Armada, probably just the squadron commanded by Don Pedro de Valdes which had run ahead of the storm and the rest of the fleet, and now had been waiting days for the rest to come up. Fleming beat back to Plymouth in the face of a south-westerly breeze.

If it was Howard bowling with Drake, Fleming would have reported to him as Lord High Admiral, not to Drake, the vice admiral, but having done so it is not inconceivable that Drake would have replied, 'We have time enough to finish the game — and the Spaniards, too!' And in doing so he would give his non-seaman admiral thinking time.

It also dovetails nicely with the nature of this quick-thinking seaman: although he was casually playing bowls, his seafaring professionalism would tell him the state of the tides and all that that entailed. It was dead low water that afternoon, and the fleet could not move against the floodtide, possibly now beginning to run strongly at about one knot: the tide would have to slacken again that evening before the ships could get out. No one could clear Plymouth with a tide running against a south-west wind.

Drake knew all this instinctively: he realized there were hours to wait before the ships could even be warped out of harbour: 'Time enough to finish . . .' The quick reply, the response of a cool-headed leader, the gesture of nonchalance was completely in character with the man. Howard, one senses, would nod wisely in agreement.

One may be certain that Drake would have said something else to Fleming, something out of ear-shot, but something downright seamanlike and earthy, leaving Fleming in no doubt whatsoever that all captains, boatswains and mariners were to get cracking then and there to take advantage of every minute. This message, never explained, must also have been in character with the vice admiral.

The story of the game first appeared in print in a pamphlet in 1624, within living memory of the event, and is therefore unlikely to have been fabricated. Drake's response did not appear in print until 1736, nearly 150 years after the game. It could harbour, laboriously towing them through the narrows with their rowing-boats or hauled along by cables run out from the shore, then coming to anchor in the lee of Rame Head where they waited for daylight and the morning ebb due at about eleven o'clock. Some ships found enough wind to begin to beat down the Sound. The next morning, Saturday, the wind got up from the south-west and the fleet managed by tedious hard work and great skill — and with just a hint of wind to assist — to beat clear of the Sound. The race-built ships and pinnaces probably found it easier than the other ships, using just enough canvas to give steerage way and allowing the tide to help. It was a good display of seamanship, barely commented upon. Drake made no mention of it in his letter the following day to Lord Henry Seymour. Howard wrote to Walsingham the same day:

> We first warped out of harbour that night and upon Saturday turned out very hardly, the wind being at south-west and about 3 of the clock in the afternoon descried the Spanish fleet through squalls of rain, upwind of them to westwards as far as Fowey.

well have become elaborated — even invented. The painting by Seymour Lucas captured the serene self-assurance of the noblemen and clearly depicts the signal beacon behind them blazing into flame to announce the arrival of the Armada. The legend has survived four hundred years. It deserves to endure another four hundred.

The facsimile signatures identify the personalities: Richard Grenville, Humphrey Frobisher, Martin Frobisher, Francis Drake, Howard of Effingham, Edward Fenton, John St Leger, Ambrose Manington, John Hawkins, Walter Raleigh, Robert Southwell, Thomas Fenner, Thomas Fleming and Richard Hawkins.

Howard and Drake had fifty-four ships with them at 3 p.m. close to the Eddystone Rock, a cluster of dangerous rocks nine miles south of Plymouth: four hours to cover so few miles shows the tedium of beating to windward.

Frobisher in his huge *Triumph* had had a struggle to clear the Sound and he left it with ten other ships last of all. All day Saturday and Saturday night he was working up to windward making short tacks inshore of the Armada.

*   *   *

At about midnight a pinnace commanded by Ensign Juan Gil returned to the *San Martin* with four Falmouth fishermen he had captured near Plymouth. These poor bewildered men were persuaded to reveal that they had watched English ships being towed out of harbour — not just Drake's squadron, but the whole fleet commanded by the Lord High Admiral. This information added to Sidonia's worries. He had thought that Howard with the main element of the fleet was 250 miles farther away up-Channel. But there was nothing he could do about it and the Armada continued to sail eastward under shortened sail with a wind astern which soon began to veer WNW.

Flores de Valdes warned Sidonia that they were in danger of getting ahead of the emerging English ships and of forfeiting the weather gage. So the Armada anchored.

Howard and Drake took advantage of a south-wester which sprang up in the night. In the light of the moon the Spaniards could see ships some miles away to the east, safely to leeward. But Howard and Drake stood out to sea across the bows of the anchored Armada.

At first light on Sunday 31 July Howard and Drake were to windward of the Spaniards with plenty of sea room, while stragglers who had been beating upwind inshore on short tacks were fast catching up. Howard put about and bore down onto the enemy's weathermost tip — Bertendona's Levant Squadron.

The Duke of Medina Sidonia awoke to see Howard's and Drake's ships five miles west of the Eddystone Rocks — no less than eighty of them, away to the south-west, *to windward of his Armada, and with Frobisher needing just one more tack to join them*. He must have been astonished at the display of seamanship of the English — so cleverly had they beaten to windward to gain the weather gage. They had been land-locked on a lee shore yesterday, and now it was they who could decide when and where to attack. The Duke had been beaten at every turn, and had lost the chance of a lifetime, of catching the English fleet embayed.

Without having fired a shot in anger, the English had gained the upper hand. Sidonia was now compelled to give battle at the enemy's convenience: he was committed to an uncomfortable rearguard action. It was going to be a tedious voyage up-Channel.

The Duke reflected gravely about Parma on that Saturday as his fleet lay hove-to ten miles off Plymouth, within sight of the smoking beacons, allowing his stragglers to catch up with the main fleet. He wrote to the King:

> I am astonished to have received no news of him for so long. I can only proceed slowly to the Isle of Wight and go no farther until he informs me of the state of his forces. All along the coast of Flanders there is no harbour to shelter our ships . . . I have decided to stay off the Isle of Wight until I know what the Duke is doing, as the plan is that the moment I arrive he should come out with his fleet, without making me wait a minute. The whole success of the enterprise depends upon this. . . .

The English Mercurie

THE FIRST sighting of the Spanish Armada in the Channel was presented by the *English Mercurie* on its front page in this fashion. The dates, of course, refer to the Old Style calendar, not to the new one used throughout this book. This sober, unflurried account published at a time when England expected invasion within days bears the stamp (if it reflects public opinion at the time) of imperturbable, almost clinically efficient reportage without a hint of panic or nervous agitation. Compare it with its modern equivalent, Winston Churchill's broadcast in June 1940 at the fall of France: 'The news from France is very bad . . .'

[1]

THE

English Mercurie.

Publiſhed by AUTHORITIE.

For the Prevention of falſe Reportes.

Whitehall, July 23d, 1588.

EARLIE this Morninge arrived a Meſſenger at Sir *Francis Walſingham's* Office, with Letters of the 22d from the Lorde High Admirall on board the *Ark-Royal*, containinge the followinge materiall Advices. On the 20th of this Inſtant Capt. *Fleming*, who had beene ordered to cruize in the Chops of the Channell, for Diſcoverie, brought Advice into *Plymouth*, that he had deſcried the *Spaniſh Armado* neare the *Lizard*, making for the Entrance of the Channell with a favourable Gale. Though this Intelligence was not received till near foure in the Afternoone, and the Winde at that time blew hard into the *Sound*, yet by the indefatigable Care and Diligence of the Lorde High Admiral, the *Ark-Royal*, with five of the largeſt Frigates, anchored out of the Harbour that very Eveninge. The next Morninge, the greateſt Part of her Majeſtie's Fleet gott out to them. They made in all about eighty Sail, divided into four Squadrons, commanded by his Lordſhip in Perſon, Sir *Francis Drake* Vice-Admiral, and the Rear-Admirals *Hawkins* and *Forbiſher*. But about one in the Afternoone, they came in Sighte of the Spaniſh Armado two Leagues to the Weſtward of the Eddiſtone, ſailing in the Form of a half-Moon, the Points whereof were ſeven Leagues aſunder.

B

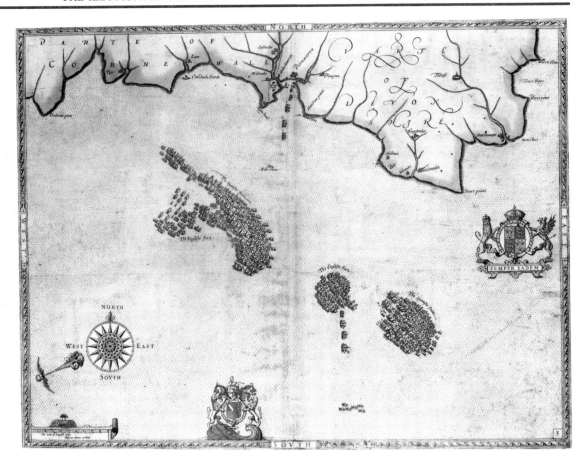

Robert Adams produced a series of eleven Armada prints between 1588 and 1590 which were published in his *Expeditionis Hispanorum*. This is No. 2 in the series, showing the opposing fleets between Dodman Point and Start Point early during the Channel pursuit.

Just how worried Sidonia was by the situation is shown by the fact that he was prepared to disobey the most precise orders from the King *not* to stop at the Isle of Wight.

Sidonia's war council on this Saturday decided not to attack Plymouth in a replication of Drake's attack on Cadiz. However tempting were the prospects to even the most cautious minds, the circumstances were quite dissimilar from those at the Spanish port. The Armada was not a mobile, tactical strike force; it was a huge convoy hampered by numerous ponderous ships carrying troops and provision. Furthermore, Plymouth's tidal stream, powerful shore batteries and miles of inland waters lent itself to sound defence, unlike Cadiz: Plymouth, in short, was seen to be impregnable, although de Leiva (a cavalry officer of some distinction) viewed the prospects of a land assault with some relish. More sensible counsels prevailed. The Duke, worried though he was, ordered his fleet to begin its voyage up-Channel at least as far as the Isle of Wight with the daily expectation of a pinnace bearing despatches from Parma.

The Armada adopted its new, curious, massive crescent formation, the very sight of which intrigued Howard and Drake and filled many Englishmen with some feelings of apprehension. The Armada began its laborious 'caping' up-Channel.

The crescent formation was the result of months of debate and argument in Lisbon: it had been worked out with military-like precision.

The principal fighting ships were carefully deployed in three major divisions: vanguard, main-battle and rear-guard — standard military (as opposed to naval)

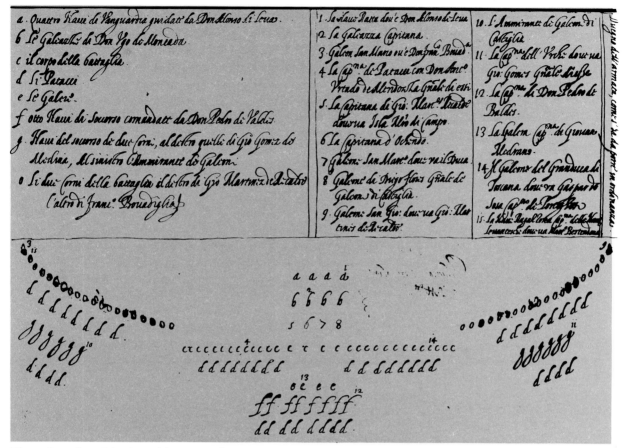

This sailing plan of the Armada's crescent formation was sketched by the Grand Duke of Tuscany's ambassador to Lisbon on 18 May 1588. It reveals the Spanish captains' names and their ships' position in the formation. When adopted at sea it proved incredibly effective against the English attacks.

practice. This marching formation changed on the battlefield in traditional ways: the vanguard fell back and to the right of the main battle force, while the rear-guard took position on the main-battle's left.

The main battle force was formed by Sidonia's most powerful war galleons, led by the *San Martin* and the Portuguese Squadron, and the Indian Guard and galleons of Castile under Don Flores de Valdes. The vanguard comprised the twenty ships of the Levant and Guipuzcoan Squadrons commanded by Don Alonso de Leiva with Martin de Bertendona and Oquendo as divisional commanders.

The rearguard under Juan de Martinez Recalde comprised twenty ships of the Biscayan and Andalusian Squadrons.

The urcas and transports were placed for main protection in the centre of the formation, the whole forming a crescent or moon shape with a thickened centre, and 'wings' of ships in echelon providing long, trailing horns. Nothing like it had been seen by English seamen. It appeared more puzzling than daunting, but one thing was certain: it was a formation of powerful defensive strength. One chronicler described it with awe:

> The Spanish fleet with lofty Turrets like Castles, in front like a half moon, the Wings thereof Spreading out about the length of seven miles, sailing very slowly through with full Sails, the Winds being as it were tired of carrying them, and the Ocean groaning under the weight of them.

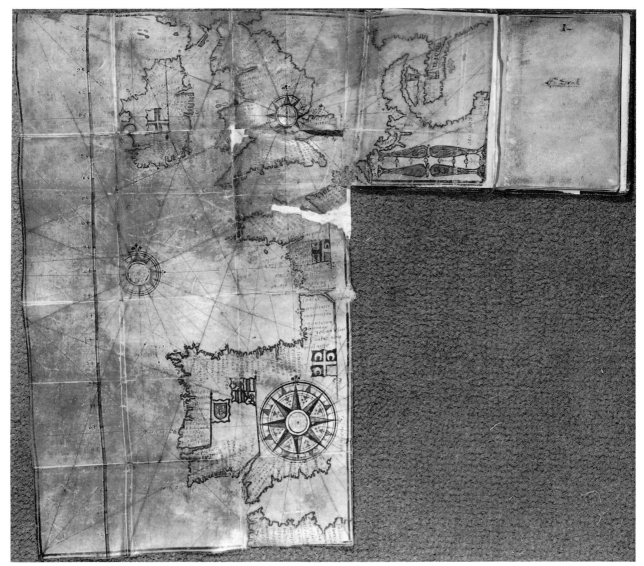

Drake used this chart so frequently it became worn and torn at the creases where it folded into his notebook. It is now preserved in the Pepysian Library, Cambridge.

Any ships with wind advantage attacking the formation could only attack the craft forming the protective wings or horns — where, of course, the enemy placed his strongest ships. Furthermore, any ship which might become damaged could be recovered easily into the bosom of the fleet. And again, any attacking ships daring to venture too far into the horns could soon find themselves lacking sea room, enveloped by the enemy as the horns began to close about them like a crab's claws.

Surprisingly, the Armada's lines of ships were abreast. The Spanish ships' guns were already on the broadside, so line ahead was the logical formation to give clear arcs of fire, but this was a transitional era, and line abreast still held firm. Again, the ships were so close together — supposedly fifty paces apart — that any enemy penetrating the ranks would immediately be boarded on both sides. This was the mode of fighting that the Armada understood.

The formation was conducive to creating a mêlée type of battle, most unsuited to the English and their new gunnery tactics but suited to the grappling techniques of the high-castled galleons of Spain. The English found these Spanish tactics frustrating and disconcerting.

The first encounter of the Armada and the English fleet was about to take place, the outcome of which was totally unpredictable because each of the two combatants employed a fighting style completely alien to that of the other. The English would be intent on cannonading from a distance, able to attack the nearest edges of the Spanish formation but not the centre. The Spaniards for their part wanted close combat, but had simply no chance at all of accomplishing it so long as they maintained their tight, defensive crescent formation. However, contact there was, but the encounters were often indecisive, almost painless, seemingly meaningless — yet significant none the less.

10. *Battle off Plymouth*

*T*HE ARMADA HAD hardly weighed anchor and got under way before the Duke was up top trying to make out the ships he saw bearing down on his southernmost squadron; he believed they came from another English fleet or squadron, so unexpected had been their appearance from windward. But he was wrong. Howard, Drake and Frobisher with all their ships were about to give battle, having already demonstrated some of the skills of naval tactics. Sidonia hoisted the royal standard from his foretop, the signal for his ships to engage.

It is to Captain Jonas Bradbury, commanding the 80-ton pinnace *Disdain*, that there goes the honour of firing the first shot of battle with the Armada, and he did it with a theatricality reminiscent of old-time chivalry in war. At nine o'clock on Sunday, 31 July the Lord High Admiral dispatched the bark or pinnace 'to give the Duke of Medina defiance' — the equivalent of a medieval knight hurling down his gauntlet. Bradbury sailed his pinnace at speed towards what he thought was Sidonia's *San Martin*, and when almost upon her she hauled up and fired a culverin shot at the hull of her giant adversary. She then scurried back up-wind to rejoin the admiral. The shot that rang out signalled the beginning of the end of the Armada.*

The Spanish sources are probably more reliable in relating the events of this first encounter of fleets in the Channel, though it is only fair to say that all reports, Spanish and English, differ quite considerably in all aspects — to such an extent that one wonders sometimes if the same events are being described. Perhaps this is understandable, because never before had 250 ships fought over such huge areas: anyone aboard a vessel taking part could only describe with any accuracy what he saw actually happen aboard his own craft. The only semi-official English version of the battle comes in a document entitled *Relation of Proceedings*. It had two versions, one based on talks with Howard and the second with Drake's views written down by Petruccio Ubaldini, a non-seafaring Italian of undoubted anglophile feelings but questionable reliability: he occasionally confused east with west and windward with leeward.

Howard's description of the day's encounter was remarkably brief: 'At nine of the clock we gave them fight which continued till one . . .' he wrote to Walsingham 'From aboard the *Ark*, athwart Plymouth.' He added: 'We durst not adventure to put in amongst them, their fleet being so strong.'

What is believed to have occurred is this: Howard led his *Ark Royal* to attack the outermost ship on the starboard horn, which he had assumed to be the Duke's flagship, but which was in fact Don Alonso de Leiva's 820-ton Levant ship, *La Rata Coronada*. As *Ark Royal* began to cross Leiva's stern, down went the Spaniard's helm and both

---

* No *State Papers* mention this incident as described, but the pinnace *Disdain* does receive mention.

flagships swung north, broadside to broadside, steering towards the far, landward horn of the crescent. Howard maintained a distance from the enemy of about 400 yards, close enough for his master gunners to strike the enemy and just too far for the less expert Spanish gunners to score hits.

The rest of the Levant Squadron turned north to conform with and support de Leiva, and they tried hard to grapple with the English ships in the fashion they knew, but Howard's close-winded galleons kept their distance, throwing shots at the enemy and never giving the high-castled Spanish ships the chance to get to grips. This inconclusive skirmish ended with little damage and few casualties.

Meanwhile, on the landward wing of the crescent formation English ships fetched up on the windward side of Recalde's squadron of Biscayan ships and met with a totally different reception. A line of English ships led by Drake in the *Revenge* included Hawkins in the *Victory* and Frobisher in his enormous *Triumph*: this line headed for the flagship, Recalde's *San Juan de Portugal* of 1,050 tons and 50 guns. Then a remarkable development occurred.

The *San Juan* turned about as if in an act of pugnacious defiance to face Drake's ships. It was not out of character for the veteran Recalde, but whether due to confusion or interpretation of signals, another error of some sort, or some inexplicable reason (Recalde may simply have wanted to fight face to face with the mighty Drake) the rest of Recalde's squadron carried on sailing down-wind as if leaving him to the mercy of the English ships.

Very soon the *Revenge, Victory* and *Triumph* were pouring broadsides of culverin and cannon shot into the enemy flagship and, like Howard on the far wing of the crescent, maintained a range of about 300–400 yards, giving Recalde no chance whatsoever of grappling.

This went on for perhaps an hour, Recalde accepting the punishment possibly in the hope he could tempt one English ship to come close enough to enable him to get his grappling hooks into her. What was confusing for him was the English tactics. In the whole centuries-long story of war at sea, boarding was the only way a superior force could ensure capturing a prize — yet here were the English ships standing off and declining to board. He was sure that if he grappled with one — or better still two — English ships he could hang on till support arrived. But no such chance was presented. Drake was too canny. He stood off until Spanish reinforcements arrived to support Recalde. The 1,160-ton *El Gran Grin*, carrying aboard Colonel Pimentel, the officer commanding the *tercio* or brigade (but in other reports he is placed aboard the *San Mateo*) arrived with other ships of the squadron, and fighting raged for about two hours. During this time the Duke's flagship *San Martin* and the galleon *San Mateo* also came to Recalde's assistance.

It was now about midday, and ammunition on both sides was being expended at a great rate. Howard was now in a position to gauge how the fighting was going on the landward horn of the crescent, and when he saw an increasing number of Spanish ships joining Recalde he signalled to break off the action. The Spanish ships returned to their stations in the Armada and the English ships withdrew.

Howard was much criticized for his apparent half-heartedness in not pressing more strongly, giving the enemy the impression he was irresolute, unsure, even afraid. But on balance he was probably right. There was a feeling of the unknown about the encounter of these two great fleets: new tactics, newly designed ships, these and many

Lord Sheffield hoisted his flag in the *White Bear*, one of the oldest and largest of the Queen's ships. At the time of the Armada she was twenty-five years old, and she carried 490 men aboard. This engraving shows the heavy after-castle of an old ship, and this is possibly Sheffield's flagship.

other factors fresh to sea warfare were being tested, and at stake was the throne and the very land of England.

Pedro Coco Calderon was the Armada's Paymaster General aboard the urca *San Salvador* and his records of the campaign have survived the centuries. He gave his views of this skirmish, naming seven Spanish ships which engaged the English. He referred to Recalde's early single-handed attack: 'During the morning certain ships basely took to flight until they were peremptorily ordered by the flagship to luff and face the enemy.'

Sidonia noted in his diary, 'The enemy attacked him [Recalde] so fiercely with gunfire (but without coming to close quarters) that they crippled his rigging and hit his foremast twice.' They also, incidentally, shot off an officer's leg.

That night the Duke wrote yet another letter to Parma. It was superscribed: 'Two leagues off Plymouth 31st July 1588.' It was to be sent by the trustworthy Ensign Juan Gil who had captured the fishermen some days earlier. The Duke described the morning's engagement, then went on:

I intend with God's help to continue my voyage without letting anything divert me, until I receive instructions from Your Excellency of what I am to do and where I am to wait for you to join me. I implore Your Excellency to send someone with the utmost speed, bringing replies to the points on which I have written to you: also to send me pilots for the coast of Flanders, for without them I am ignorant of the places where I can find shelter for ships as large as these in case I should be overtaken by the slightest storm.

In the postscript Sidonia added:

the enemy continues to harass our rear and . . . their ships now seem to have increased to over one hundred sail. Some are excellent vessels, and all of them very fast sailers.

Poor Sidonia! Even this begging letter went unanswered. Wrapped around by indecision and the unknown, he must have pondered hard and long on what exactly to do — stop at the Isle of Wight? Head on to Calais? Dover? Flanders? Margate?

He was bemused too by the tactics adopted by the English ships. He could not fathom why they did not come to close quarters: 'their ships [the English] are so fast and so nimble, they can do anything they like with them.'

Howard was equally baffled by the defensive formation of the Armada and he wrote confirming his worries to Walsingham, but he had other worries too: 'Sir, for the love of God and our country, let us have with some speed some great shot sent to us of all bigness, for this service will continue long; and some powder with it.' Like many commanders before and after him, Howard was learning that high command was a constant headache, facing the dark unknown hedged about with untold risks.

Before we leave this day of battle we must record two other incidents on the Spanish side which were to have repercussions later. The first was an accident, a collision of two ships — a common enough experience, and more or less to be expected in a fleet of such close formation. Don Pedro de Valdes's 1,150-ton flagship *Nuestra Señora del Rosario* was regrouping with the other ships of the fleet in a rising sea when human error led to the *Rosario* colliding with a Biscayan ship. (Some sources place this collision later in the day, after the explosion in the *San Salvador*.) Then as the *Rosario* swung round after the collision she fouled another ship of her own squadron, the *Santa Catalina* of 730 tons, losing her own bowsprit and carrying away the mainstay of her foremast.

While all seemed confusion with the *Rosario* an enormous explosion blasted the fleet. The 958-ton *San Salvador* of Oquendro's Guipuzcoan Squadron had blown up and was blazing fiercely.

All at once Sidonia had three casualties in his fleet: Recalde's ship was shot through and through, the *Rosario* had collision damage and the *San Salvador* was seriously mauled in the explosion.

The catastrophe had occurred at about 4 p.m. No one knows how the accident came about, though the simplest and possibly the most plausible explanation was to attribute it to a gunner's carelessness. But rumours abounded and as always became embroidered in their telling. A popular story is one related by Calderon. He tells how a pressganged Fleming had managed to smuggle his wife aboard and conceal her (some reports say his daughter, too) till she was discovered by a Spanish infantry captain who claimed *droit de seigneur*. The anguished and infuriated Fleming laid a trail of powder to the magazine, ignited it and leaped overboard.

Whatever the reason — and simple carelessness is the likeliest cause — the resultant explosion killed no less than 200 men and created tremendous damage to the ship; her poop and her two highest after-castle decks were wrecked, and her stern was blown out.

Sidonia fired a cannon to halt the Armada and allow him to investigate. Boats were rowed across to take off soldiers, mariners, the Paymaster General and the heavy chests of imperial gold intended to help finance the invasion of England. The fires were doused but the stench of burning timbers and bodies was overpowering. Lines were secured aboard and the smouldering hulk was taken in tow.

Gusting winds brought about a chop in the Channel and this led directly to the second disaster. The *Rosario* was almost impossible to steer properly. As the ship pitched and tossed in the rising sea the weakened foremast began to whip and crack. With a frightening noise, it sheared at deck level and fell aft with awful tangling of rigging, cordage and canvas, on to the mainmast yard. Pedro de Valdes let off a distress signal to bring attention to his plight.

Alexander Farnese, Duke of Parma, largely responsible for the failure to mount the invasion of England from Dunkirk, 1588.

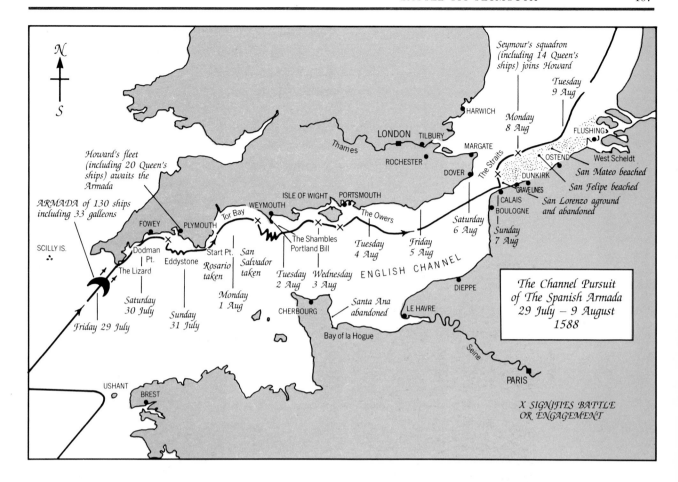

The Duke again fired a cannon to bring the Armada to a halt and the *San Martin* hauled round to the rear to assist Don Pedro. A number of pataches, the *almirante* of the Squadron, the *San Francisco*, and a galleasse were now busily clustered around the stricken ship, giving what assistance they could.

The Duke took command of the rescue and the *San Martin* herself was the first to pass a cable across. It was a most curious situation: the Armada's flagship had no good reason to become embroiled to such an extent in a rescue, unless in the direst of emergencies. There were plenty of other ships to undertake a tow. However, the flagship's sailing master, Captain Marolin de Juan, handled the seamanship aspect of the operation professionally, and the tow was secured. In the rough seas the ship's movements parted the tow, and in the increasing seas and weather conditions it became impossible to pass another.

Aboard the *San Martin* Sidonia was having to listen to some unpalatable advice from his chief of staff, the experienced commander of the galleons of Castile, Diego Flores de Valdes. The situation bore heavy overtones of irony. Diego Flores was the cousin of Pedro de Valdes, and there was no loving kindess in their family relationships. Indeed, it would be accurate to say they were always at loggerheads, and it would not be too much to assert they were implacable enemies. Diego must have watched the predicament of his cousin with considerable satisfaction.

But from a professional standpoint, he quite rightly protested at the *San Martin*'s involvement in the rescue. The Duke's station lay at the head of the fleet. The fleet itself should be under way, on its easterly course, not bucking at the whim of the sea and wind under shortened sail, with the prospect of scattering in the approaching darkness. The Duke was imperilling the whole enterprise for the sake of one ship.

He was finally persuaded, though he remained on deck, where he had stayed all through the tiring day in order to watch and satisfy himself that the small galleon flagship of the screen, commanded by Ojeda, with four pinnaces were stationed around the crippled *capitana* of the Andalusian squadron.

Sidonia sent a message to Pedro de Valdes inviting him to leave the *Rosario* and join the Duke aboard the *San Martin*, but on a point of honour Don Pedro declined firmly. As it turned out this proved to be one of the most momentous decisions of his life.

The *San Martin* hauled around and made to take up her station leading the Armada, which now increased sail and resumed its progress. The *Rosario* and her escorts gradually fell astern. As the Duke watched a boy brought him cheese and hard tack, his first food of the day. He knew there would be much talk aboard the ships that night. To many officers, gentlemen and noblemen in the fleet — indoctrinated since childhood with codes of conduct, and taught to respect honour — the apparent desertion of the *Rosario* by the Duke seemed unforgivable. It is reported that by his decision to leave Don Pedro the Duke not only infuriated the unfortunate captain but also lost all respect from the younger officers of the Armada.

Flores de Valdes took most of the blame for his share in what was regarded as the dishonourable desertion of Don Pedro. He became the most despised man in the Armada, and it was this episode more than anything else which subsequently helped commit him to gaol.

Later that night the ships of the Armada clearly heard the rumble of cannon fire coming from the direction of the *Rosario*'s estimated position.

11. Capture of the Rosario

A S DUSK FELL on Sunday night, 31 July, Howard broke out the flag to signify a council of war aboard the *Ark*. That council decided that the balance of honours for the day lay with themselves. After all, as a basic fact, an invasion of Plymouth or Devon had been thwarted, prevented, averted — call it what you like: an invasion had not taken place, and this was the prime objective of the English fleet.

However, the English commanders could not have expressed much gratification with their own gunnery; despite its accuracy, it failed to smash the enemy ships as had been hoped. True, they had witnessed the shattering of the *San Salvador* and the ordeal of Recalde's flagship *San Juan*, but neither of these events reflected greatly to the credit of the English gunners. The *San Salvador*'s explosion was at best an accident, at worst an act of sabotage — it was nothing to do with the English.

The *San Juan* engagement, on the other hand, was a disturbing experience for a number of reasons. We have seen, for example, that Recalde's ship had been subjected to a murderous rate of fire at a range of 300–400 yards from the *Revenge, Victory* and *Triumph*, three of England's hardest-hitting ships, armed with the most advanced ship-smashing cannons, and 'several other ships' — Sidonia actually quotes eight other ships. After that morning's baptism of fire at the hands of the English the *San Juan* was believed to have been disabled beyond repair, yet a few hours later she was perfectly able to hold her own in the thick of the fighting, and to take a further battering. What, then, was wrong with the English gunnery?

The fact of the matter is that the shots from the English cannons and culverins, even at the close range of less than a quarter of a mile, were simply not performing as had been expected. The shots were not penetrating the enemy hulls. They were striking, they were damaging, especially the masts and the rigging, but the hulls remained basically intact.

The range, it was resolved, must be reduced, or the size of the guns enlarged; or both. These were the unpalatable facts brought home to the war councillors aboard the *Ark* after the first day of battle with the Armada.

One further point caused the assembled officers apprehension more than fear: the seeming defensive impregnability of the curious crescent formation of the Armada.

The officers dispersed from the *Ark* to their ships in pensive mood, a mood which would be changed that night to anger and bewilderment by the mysterious events during the hours of darkness.

It all arose from the discussion around the Lord High Admiral's table. It was generally believed by these practical seafaring commanders that the Duke of Sidonia would feel compelled to seize the Isle of Wight. No other sheltered anchorage for the Armada lay ahead. If Sidonia was to meet Parma he would *need* such an anchorage to finalize plans and mount the assault on England.

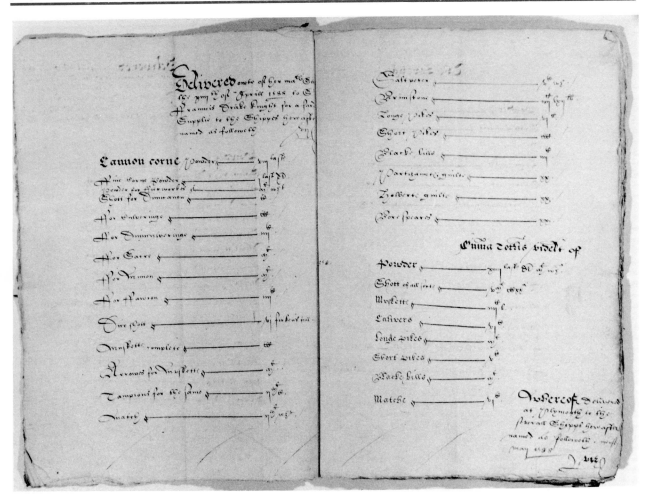

Manuscript list of ammunition and weapons supplied to Sir Francis Drake immediately before the Armada campaign in 1588.

To protect the Isle of Wight the English could forge ahead of the Armada and form a protective screen across the Solent. However, in doing so they would forfeit the wind advantage, and at the same time they would be abandoning the tactics adopted that very day, which had prevented a landing at Plymouth or in Devon. Torbay, the next likeliest landing ground, lay round the next cape: the council decided as a matter of policy that the fleet should continue its tactic of maintaining the windward position and harassing the rearmost ships with attacks at every opportunity.

Drake, it was decided, should have the honour of leading the fleet in its close marking of the Armada, with the rest following the light of the great lantern in the stern of his *Revenge*. The ships took up station and followed the great stern light.

Some hours later the light disappeared quite suddenly. Confusion reigned. No night signals had been concerted. Some ships stopped; others shortened sail. Howard, with the *Mary Rose* and *White Bear* in company, pressed on relentlessly and in time detected a faint light far to leeward. Howard assumed that Drake had outdistanced him, and he set off in pursuit, but when dawn came early on Monday 1 August the Lord High Admiral was disconcerted to discover that he had picked up the stern light of the weathermost Spanish galleon and had blundered almost within shot of the enemy fleet, while the main body of his own fleet was miles away hull down over the

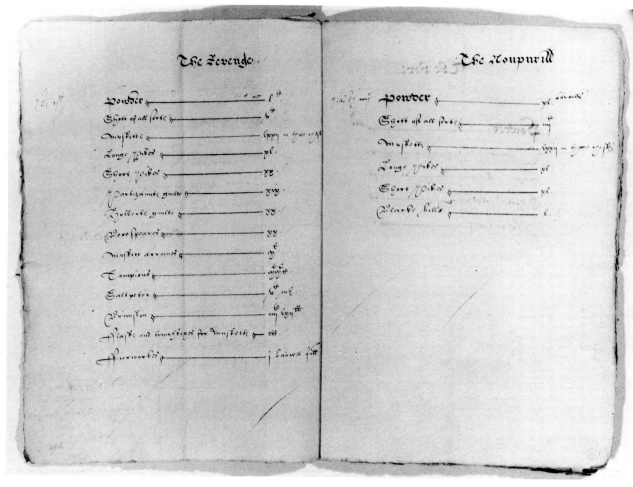

Manuscript pages showing items allocated to Drake's *Revenge* and Thomas Fenner's *Nonpareil*.

horizon. All he could do was haul round with the *Mary Rose* and *White Bear* and beat back to his fleet, now dispersed over a wide expanse of the Channel.

Throughout the day the English ships gradually reassembled. Captain John Fisher of the *Margaret and John* was one of the first to scramble aboard the Lord High Admiral's flagship with an extraordinary tale of adventure concerning the *Rosario* off Start Point. Fisher asked for permission to sail back and claim his valuable prize. It was then that a pinnace secured alongside the *Ark* with a message for the Lord High Admiral from Drake. The message told the story of his night's adventures.

Drake claimed that soon after midnight he saw strange sails passing to starboard on a reciprocal course. He reasoned that they were Spanish ships of the Armada doubling back down-Channel intent on catching the wind. Since this should be prevented, he led round to starboard to follow them, dousing his stern lantern light for fear the fleet would follow him. He had with him only the 300-ton Dartmouth privateer *Roebuck*, owned by Sir Walter Raleigh and commanded by Captain Jacob Whiddon, and two pinnaces.

After a while Drake learned that the ships he was chasing were German merchant ships on their lawful occasions and he called off the pursuit and came about. As he was doing so he sighted a large enemy ship. She was soon identified as none other than

Don Pedro de Valdes's *Rosario*. Unknown, to Drake, the *Rosario* had already experienced a curious set of adventures during the night through the agency of a small English ship called the *Margaret and John*.

This little craft, a 200-ton vessel commanded by Captain John Fisher, was a London merchant ship owned by John Watts, later Lord Mayor of London. Also aboard were John Nash, the master, and Richard Tomson, lieutenant, with a crew of 90 men. The story they told was remarkable by any standards, and it is recorded clearly in a literate deposition to the Queen's council.

Soon after dark they came upon the *Rosario* which had in company the galleon commanded by Ojeda, a galleasse and one pinnace. All these three sheared off unexpectedly as soon as they sighted the approaching *Margaret and John*, leaving the *Rosario* apparently abandoned — no lights, no sails set, not answering her helm and no evident sign of life aboard. Fisher sent a boat alongside but the *Rosario* was too big and the rough seas too high to allow the Englishmen to board her. A volley of muskets was fired to elicit some response, but to no avail. Then 'presently they gave us two great shot, whereupon we let fire with our broadside through her, doing her some hurt . . . After this we cast about our ship and kept close by the Spaniard until midnight, sometimes hearing a voice in Spanish calling us.'

Yet the curious, inexplicable thing is that 420 men lurked aboard the *Rosario*, making no attempt to repel boarders, or to beat off their small adversary (save for two shots), or to set sail, or to repair damage. It seems unbelievable, but on balance, if Fisher's report is to be accepted in part, it needs acceptance in full.

This extraordinary situation, when a small armed merchantman proved incapable of taking as prize a huge 1,150-ton Andalusian vessel, and with Captain Fisher handling a difficult situation with sense and great presence of mind, now took another strange turn.

At midnight Fisher saw the Lord High Admiral's flagship in the moonlight about two miles away, and 'fearing his Lordship's displeasure if we should stay behind the fleet, we made all the sail we could and followed my Lord to overtake him, leaving the *Rosario* to her own devices.'

Don Pedro de Valdes, vice admiral, Knight of the Order of Santiago, Captain-General of the Kingdom of Andalusia and Governor of Havana.

At dawn Drake was astern of the English fleet, trying hard to catch up, when he came upon the *Rosario*. Of course, he should not have been there at all. His station was in the van of the fleet, as agreed at the previous night's council. Not only was he far out of station, he had disregarded orders, for which many captains had been hanged. Not so Drake, who with an uncanny luck which accompanied him all his life, sighted the apparently deserted and abandoned *Rosario*. He hailed the enemy ship and called on Don Pedro to fight or surrender.

The Spanish commander wanted to know what the terms of surrender would entail and Drake replied peremptorily that the terms would be his own: he was not, he added, 'at leisure to make any long parley'. Nevertheless, there were some flowery exchanges. When Don Pedro realized that his adversary was none other than the notorious Francis Drake he decided that instead of fighting he might gracefully surrender to a man 'whose valour and felicity was so great that Mars and Neptune seemed to attend him'. It was a chivalrous and courteous — if dishonourable — yielding to superior forces.

Whatever the expected outcome of a fight between the two ships, Don Pedro de Valdes seems to have been treated with an unexampled degree of charity. Despite the ignominy of his surrender, Drake accorded him all the honours of war, took forty of his officers and gentlemen aboard the *Revenge* and later accompanied him on a visit to the Lord High Admiral aboard the *Ark*. Don Pedro had the rare experience of watching the battles of the Armada campaign from the decks of the *Ark* or the *Revenge*. He then experienced an honourable internment in England.

Drake, one would have thought, might have treated the prisoner with some contempt, yet Valdes became a minor celebrity in both England and Spain.*

Drake dispatched Jacob Whiddon to command the prize into Dartmouth with orders to strip her of guns, powder and shot, all of which were in short supply in England.

Drake's story, although disbelieved in many quarters, and certainly not accepted in its entirety, enabled him to get away with the whole incident. He must have come very near to being tried before the Lord High Admiral for several breaches of naval disciplines — for desertion, for leaving his admiral uninformed of his movements, for hazarding the rest of the fleet . . . while he sailed off in search of prizes for personal profit. He had exposed an unacceptable face of privateering enterprise.

Frobisher was not so generous in his attitude. Ten days later the injustice of it all was still smouldering inside him and he accused Drake of being a cozening cheat: 'Like a coward he kept by her all night, because he would have the spoil. He thinketh to cozen us of our share of fifteen thousand ducats. But we will have our shares or I will make him spend the best blood in his belly.'

History, though, seems to have acquitted lucky Drake. It seems inconceivable that he would have consciously jeopardized his life, his ship, his nation when on the threshold of invasion in a personal search for prizes during a battle. He was a risk-taker par excellence — but he did not take that kind of gamble.

*   *   *

* On the other hand, Drake masked his feelings well. During his circumnavigation his friend Thomas Doughty rebelled against him and Drake condemned him to death for mutiny. Drake took communion with him, entertained him to dinner, then led him to the block to be executed.

The surrender of a Spanish galleon

DON PEDRO de Valdes, Spanish nobleman of high birth, was treated by friend and foe alike as some sort of minor hero, yet his most heroic action in the Armada campaign was his abject surrender — however graciously it was done — to Francis Drake without firing a shot.

One of the Armada's finest galleons, the *Nuestra Señora del Rosario*, captained by de Valdes, surrendered in the Channel on Monday 1 August 1588. This was not the only mystery surrounding this enormous ship, at 1,150 tons one of the biggest in the Armada.

Earlier in the day the *Rosario* had collided with another Spanish ship and suffered damage to her bowsprit and foremast, which subsequently carried away. Now, this was serious damage, but no more than ships of that period would have been prepared for. *Rosario* is registered as having aboard 304 soldiers and 118 mariners, totalling 422 men, every one of whom in an emergency would have been available to clear away with axes, knives and saws all the dreadful tangle of masts, yards, spars, canvas, rigging and cordage engulfing the ship. A matter of several hours' work would have transformed the *Rosario*: a jury-rig forward would have helped balance the rudder, and competent seamen could have controlled the ship adequately. She would have been sluggish, of course, but certainly capable of giving a good account of herself in a fight. Yet nothing seems to have been done to make her seaworthy.

What is more — and this is a mystery too — when the *Margaret and John* came upon her that night she was wallowing out of control, apparently without watches set, certainly with guns unmanned and mast and yards still fouling her decks.

This was still so when Drake in his *Revenge*, with the *Roebuck* in company, came upon her. In prospect was a great fight: the *Rosario* looked huge to the two English ships. Her sides loomed high, her after-castle was like a mountain impossible to scale — and she was one of the most heavily armed ships in the Armada.

Yet Don Pedro de Valdes surrendered his ship to Drake with a courtly bow and expressions of mutual respect. Without so much as the firing of a musket shot, Drake took charge of this magnificent gift of a galleon, of its 46 guns, its store of powder and shot, and — this was a gambler's lucky streak! — of the huge hoard of golden ducats from de Valdes's cabin.

The final puzzle of the great surrender was the fact that de Valdes became something of a minor hero both in Spain and in England. Surrendering to Drake, it appeared, was an honour! In similar circumstances in the English navy he would have been court-martialled for cowardice; better still, he should have hanged himself for the sake of honour.

The picture was painted by Seymour Lucas in late Victorian days. It is entitled *The Surrender*, and depicts the scene aboard the *Revenge*.

Later on during that same Monday morning of 1 August Sidonia suffered another loss. The damaged *San Salvador* began to fall astern of the fleet. The explosion had started some of her seams and the pumps could no longer cope with the water she was shipping. The remainder of her crew and soldiery were taken off: originally she had a crew of 64 with another 319 soldiers aboard, less the 200 or so who had been killed in the explosion or had jumped overboard. The Paymaster General, with much of his money and documents, had been saved.

As many of the ship's stores as possible were salvaged except, curiously, the powder and great shot in her forward hold, comprising 132 barrels of powder and 2,246 rounds of shot. She was allowed to drift slowly astern. The intention must have been to scuttle her, but something obviously went wrong; perhaps the English came up too fast. Whatever the reason, it was late evening when Howard came up with her. The Lord High Admiral sent his kinsman Lord Thomas Howard and John Hawkins to board the hulk and report on the possibility of salvage.

They found a very pitiful sight [the *Relation* revealed], the deck of the ship fallen down, the steerage broken, the stern blown out, and about fifty poor creatures burnt with powder in most miserable sort. The stink in the ship was so unsavoury and the sight within board so ugly that the Lord Thomas Howard and Sir John Hawkins shortly departed.

Howard instructed the intrepid Captain Thomas Fleming in the *Golden Hind* to tow the virtual hulk into whatever port he could, and the next day the sombre procession arrived in Weymouth like a Turner painting — slowly, with the speed and solemnity of a cortège.

The two prizes, the *Rosario* and the *San Salvador*, brought into the south-coast harbours created ripples of excitement along the whole shore — and inland, too, to the Queen's own Court. Volunteers, adventurers, young squires, noblemen, clamoured to follow 'the King of Spain's Armada' as it 'came upon our coast, thinking to devour us all'. So wrote the 28-year-old Robert Carey (later Earl of Monmouth). The Earls of Oxford, Cumberland, Northumberland, Lord Burghley's sons Robert and Thomas Cecil and other young bucks sought a ship or patron. Sir Horatio Palavicino, a Genoese banker settled in England, joined the Lord High Admiral.

For every one privileged person who managed to get aboard a ship there were hundreds who watched the progress of that summer's battle and the movements of fleets from vantage-points — the high bluffs and headlands along the south coast — right from the first sighting of the Armada off the Lizard on 29 July. The sight of two enemy ships towed into English anchorages showed that the Navy was notching up some victories despite the Armada's stubborn crescent formation.

The good station-keeping of the Spanish captains can be attributed in part at least to downright fear. The Duke called to his flagship all the sergeant-majors and provost majors and sent them in pinnaces to visit each ship in the fleet with plans of the Armada's new formation, giving each captain 'in writing that they should put every ship in her appointed place . . . any ship which did not keep that order or left her appointed place that without further stay they should hang the captain of the said ship'.

This unbending attitude arose from the previous day's apparent desertion of Recalde by several captains who at their first experience of action seemed to panic at the violence and rapidity of the English attack.

Tudor rates of pay

*A*T THE TIME of the Armada campaign the rates of pay for English seamen had been raised — in 1585 — on the representation of John Hawkins, who thought that 'by this means Her Majesty's ships would be furnished with able men, such as can shift for themselves, keep themselves clean from vermin or noisomeness which bredeth sickness and mortality'. The following table shows the annual harbour pay, which was slightly lower than pay for seatime:

Master with meat and drink by the year	£26 1s. 8d.
Boatswain	10 17 3
Carpenter	10 8 7
Gunner	9 15 6
Purser	8 13 9
Cook	7 12 1
Mariner	6 10 0

Another contemporary document gives the following landsmen's rates:

Brewers with meat and drink by the year	10 10 0
Dyers	6 13 4
The Miller, the foredrayman, the under-brewer, blacksmith, butcher, cook	6 0 0
Fullers, clothworkers, shearmen	5 0 0
Whitebakers, cappers, hatmakers, feltmakers	4 13 4
Cutlers and Turners	4 6 8
Sadlers, farriers, fletchers, bowyers, shoemakers, drapers, tailors hosier	4 0 0
Pewterers, the tunman, the other drayman and glovers	3 6 8

Yet another source gives these figures:

Hertfordshire stonemason	10d. a day
Carpenter	5s. 0d. weekly
Housemaid	£4 a year

Financial rewards

*I*N 1588 the superior officers who served against the Spanish Armada received daily pay as follows:

Lord High Admiral	£3 6s. 8d.
Lord Henry Seymour as vice admiral	2 0 0
Sir John Hawkins as rear admiral	1 5 0
Sir Henry Palmer	1 0 0
Sir William Wynter	1 0 0
Sir Martin Frobisher	1 0 0
Thomas Gray, Admiral under Lord Seymour (while in command of a detached force)	6 8
Sir Francis Drake, captain and admiral	1 10 0
Thomas Fenner, his vice admiral	1 5 0
Nicholas Gorges, admiral of the merchant coasters and his lieutenant	13 0

In fixing these payments, social rank and title were given due prominence as well as position in the fleet. In all cases there were allowances and perquisites of unknown amount in addition. Vice admiral Gray is curiously promoted here: he was in fact the Master or senior navigator aboard the *Ark*, the Lord High Admiral's flagship.

It is interesting to compare these financial rewards (Howard's pay was just over £1,200 per annum, his officers commensurate with that figure) with other representative incomes during this Armada year. Various sources have provided these:

A substantial merchant	£100+ per annum
Country gentry	£50-100; some £1000
Contry parson's stipend	£20 per annum
An Elizabethan peer	£1,000 per annum
Archbishop of Canterbury, Matthew Parker	£3,428 per annum
Lord Burghley, Elizabeth's chief minister	£4,000 per annum
Raleigh's wine monopoly	between £800 and £2000 per annum
Financier Sir Horatio Palavicino on his death in 1600, one of the richest men in England, left estate worth	£100,000
Countess of Shrewsbury, 'Bess of Hardwicke', second only to the Queen in personal wealth, had an estimated income of	£60,000 per annum

The reorganization of the Armada referred to had been agreed at a council of war on Monday afternoon. Command of the Andalusian Squadron was given to Don Diego Enriquez, son of the Viceroy of Peru, in place of Don Pedro de Valdes. The rest of the reorganization took this form: Sidonia realized that the defensive formation of the Armada had been justified by events, hence his determination to maintain it on pain of death. But he realized too the need to strengthen the rearguard of his force, where the English attacks had been concentrated. Accordingly he strengthened the rear by adding Don Alonso de Leiva and his vanguard to the rearguard. Leiva was to take command of the combined forces until Recalde, sheltering in the midst of the Armada, had repaired Sunday's damage to his *San Juan de Portugal*. Also transferred to the rear were four of the Portuguese galleons and two more galleasses, so that the Armada now had forty-three of Spain's best fighting ships concentrated in the rear. Medina Sidonia in the *San Martin* remained in the van with about twenty galleons and armed merchantmen ready to engage Lord Henry Seymour's expected frontal attack, though in fact the latter was far away off Margate at this stage in the campaign.

By sunset on Monday 1 August the wind had dropped away, to leave both giant fleets becalmed almost within gunshot distance of each other, drifting to the tidal currents, east, then west, then east again.

Away over to port the bulky lump of Portland Bill could be discerned: it could still be seen in the bright moonlight, and at about five o'clock on the Tuesday morning as a breeze freshening from the north-east began to fill the sails, it still loomed large. Watchers from the shore had a fine vantage-point from which to witness the coming day's battle.

12. Battle of Portland Bill

*T*UESDAY 2 AUGUST dawned bright and fine, and what breeze there was gave the weather gage to Sidonia. He was still simmering over the previous day's incident with Don Hugo de Moncada. Monday evening and night was perfect galleasse weather, when oars could provide the motive power denied to other becalmed sailing vessels. Moncada, an arrogant nobleman of Santiago, sought permission from Sidonia to launch his four galleasses against Howard's flagship. Sidonia denied the request, for honour decreed that only Sidonia himself could attack his opposite number's flagship. Moncada departed in a fit of petulance.

Other commanders saw the good sense of such an attack and prevailed upon Sidonia, who relented and dispatched Oquendo to Moncada with orders, and as a sweetener promised a small estate in Spain with 3,000 ducats. Moncada's hurt pride lingered. He simply ignored the orders, and a fine opportunity for the galleasses was lost. His death a few days later at Calais was probably more honourable than hanging from the yard-arm for flagrant disobedience.

Although Sidonia had the weather gage, he was slow to take advantage of it. The English ships moved first, alert to the fact they were handicapped, and they moved close-hauled to the north-west, led by Howard — towards land, in an effort to out-flank the Spanish left wing and recover the wind. Sidonia moved just in time. He led his own squadron to bear down on Howard's line and head it off. The tactic worked and Howard was forced to come about on the opposite tack, steering south-east, and tried instead to attack the opposite wing. The powerful Spanish rearguard now came into its own. Two of the enemy squadrons led by de Leiva in the *Rata Coronada* and Bertendona in the massive *La Regazona* cut across the English path and managed to bring them to action. The first shots in the battle of Portland Bill rang out.

The fighting was fierce and the Spaniards managed to close the range with the unaccustomed advantage of the wind. At one stage it looked as if Howard intended to close and grapple as he steered in rough line ahead towards the *San Martin*.

Sidonia's galleons stood fast, enjoying the wind, and the rival flagships looked like clashing, but at the last moment Howard avoided the Spanish ship and the rest of his line managed to pass the enemy at increasing ranges. It was a clever example of ship-handling.

The Spanish account of the battle reports:

Captain Bertendona [in *La Regazona* of the Levant Squadron] very gallantly assaulted their admiral, offering to board her, but as he came near her she . . . stood out to sea. In this fight there was also the *San Marcos*, *San Luis*, *San Mateo*, the *Rata [Coronada]*, *San Felipe*, *San Juan de Sicilia*, in which was Don Diego Tellez Enriquez . . . the galleon *Florencia*, *Santiago*, *San Juan de Diego Flores* in which was Don Diego

Enriquez, and the *Valencera* of the Levant Squadron in which was the *maestro de campo* Don Alonso Luzon.

When Howard first moved north-west towards the land a small force led by Frobisher in the *Triumph* with five armed merchantmen had misjudged the situation or disobeyed orders by working inshore, attempting to weather the enemy in a tempting but dangerous move which nearly succeeded. The ships with him were the *Merchant Royal, Margaret and John, Centurion* and *Golden Lion*, all of them London merchantmen, plus the *Mary Rose*.

Frobisher ran out of sea-room and nearly came up against Portland Bill, and to prevent grounding he had to anchor. Howard had avoided this danger, possibly by better judgment. Frobisher was now at great risk and the Spaniards soon saw this. Sidonia realized that Moncada's galleasses could be well employed against the anchored ships: he sent an officer to within hailing distance of Moncada and urged him with implied charges of dishonour to attack Frobisher.

Somewhat reluctantly, Moncada did so. The resulting engagement, fiercely and bravely fought though it was, did nothing for Moncada's credit, and indeed it was Frobisher, valorous and skilled seaman that he was, who scooped whatever honours were to be had. He had started, after all, with the formidable handicaps of a lee shore, at anchor, and with a lack of sea-room. He was also confronted by four well-armed galleasses with over forty brass cannon each, enjoying oared motive power, and with galleons approaching in support.

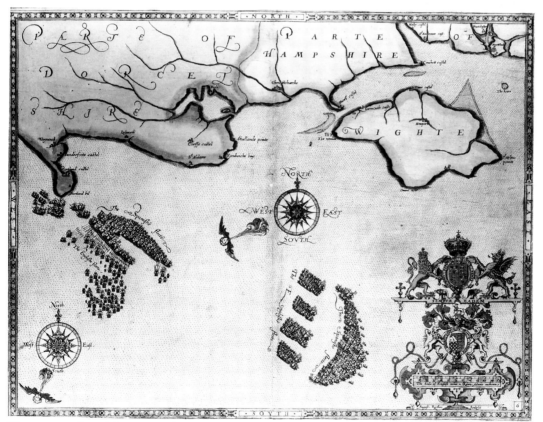

The crescent-shaped formation of the Armada is more clearly defined in Robert Adams's chart No. 6 in his series of eleven depicting the Armada campaign. This print paints the scene from Dorset to the Isle of Wight.

Frobisher's *Triumph* was the biggest ship in the fleet but she was elderly and relatively unhandy — nothing like as nimble as Drake's *Revenge*. In this rather hampered ship Frobisher managed to keep the galleasses at a distance of his own choosing, while at the same time he inflicted cruel damage upon them; their rowers were cut down in swathes, and the long oars snapped, fouling each other and losing rhythm. As his ships lost oared propulsion Moncada had to set sails: he had squandered all his advantages, and Frobisher got away.

While Frobisher was fighting to extricate himself from his precarious position the main battle — a clash of two of the world's biggest fleets off Portland Bill — drifted slowly back towards Lyme Bay. The fortunes swayed first one way then the other. Many times the Spaniards appeared to be getting the upper hand with a mêlée in prospect, but then the superior sailing qualities of the English ships seemed to let them off the hook.

At around midday the wind began to falter, then to veer as it so often does in the Channel with an easterly breeze. Drake, who so far had been frustrated by lack of engagement in the battle, had positioned his squadron so as to take advantage of the wind change. In the afternoon it veered quite quickly, right round to east, south-east, south and finally south-west. Drake took advantage of this and bore down on the Armada, emerging from the gun-smoke to the surprise and consternation of the Spanish, who thought his ships were probably a new fleet coming upon the scene. It numbered, so the Spanish reported, about fifty sail and it charged at the starboard or seaward wing of the enemy formation, broke it up and turned the whole battle front.

Sidonia was concerned at this development. He had attempted two things: firstly to isolate Frobisher's small squadron, and secondly to bring Howard's main force to battle. In both aims he had enjoyed a measure of success, but now he had to meet this third threat, and it promised to be the fiercest of all. Even Recalde's *San Juan*, still sheltering for her own protection in the bosom of the fleet, found herself almost surrounded by English ships, and she put up a formidable defence yet again, despite her damage sustained in the earlier battles.

While Drake's squadron was creating a diversion, Howard took the opportunity to head for Frobisher to render whatever assistance was wanted, but Sidonia detected what he was up to, and led his *San Martin* round with the Portuguese galleons and five others to head off Howard's squadron.

Even as Sidonia did this he saw Recalde's plight and ordered all his squadron to the vice admiral's assistance, leaving himself alone in the *San Martin* to intercept Howard's *Ark*, the *Elizabeth Jonas*, *Leicester*, *Golden Lion*, *Victory*, *Mary Rose*, *Dreadnought* and *Swallow*. In a display of honour the *San Martin* made no attempt to escape from this imposing squadron wearing the Lord High Admiral's flag, and Sidonia even backed her fore topsail, the chivalrous invitation for the enemy flagship to come alongside, grapple and fight. It was a gallant act by the Spanish admiral.

To Sidonia's astonishment Howard made no attempt to come alongside, but kept his distance, sailed by and unleashed a broadside, leading his ships in a rough line-ahead formation, discharging in succession their own broadsides at the *San Martin*. Perhaps unwittingly and even instinctively, Howard was introducing new battle tactics that were to endure for centuries to come. When the line had passed it returned and delivered another series of shots. All told, the Duke reckoned that 500 shots were fired at his ship during this phase of the battle. She must have been peppered with

Martin Frobisher, the brave, tough Yorkshireman who commanded a squadron against the Armada in his flagship *Triumph*.

shot-holes and damage. She replied bravely — all told she got away 80 shots according to Calderon — but inevitably she suffered serious damage to her rigging and sails, her masts were damaged and the holy banner ripped in two.

Before the flagship's plight became desperate assistance came and she was saved from further battering. But the question marks remain: 500 shots from close quarters, and the damage inflicted was not fatal. No reports of holing or penetration, of severe structural damage — just harm to rigging, sails and flagstaff.

By three o'clock in the afternoon Howard signalled to break off the action. Ammunition was now running low and the battle of Portland Bill had spent itself. The *Relation of Proceedings* reported:

> This fight was very nobly continued from morning till evening, the Lord Admiral being always in the hottest of the encounter, and it may well be said that for the time there never was seen a more terrible value of great shot, nor more hot fight than this was.

No doubt Howard and Sidonia breathed sighs of relief. Howard could look back on the day with greater satisfaction than could the Duke, although even he must have been confounded by the inability of the English guns to sink any enemy ships, for some of the Spaniards had taken a heavy battering and many others were severely mauled. He could reflect happily enough on the bloody nose given to the galleasses, and on the fact that the Armada had now voyaged half-way up the Channel without having made a landing.

Sidonia will have gained much satisfaction from not having lost any ships, though he must have reflected gravely on his inability to gain considerably from the morning's advantage of the weather gage, and on missing the golden opportunity of capitalizing on Frobisher's precarious inshore predicament: it was a moment of advantage never again to recur during the rest of the campaign.

Perhaps Sidonia was simply putting a brave face on it when he hailed Moncada later in the day: 'A fine day this has been!' But he found the English tactics distressing. 'These people do not mean to fight, but only to delay our progress.'

But another doubt, nagging like an aching tooth, pestered the Duke. What of Parma? Where? When? Why? The questions loomed unanswered. No lover awaited a message more impatiently than Sidonia . . . although there was little love in his heart for the young, soldierly Duke. Another day had passed, but still there was only silence. . . .

13. Battle of the Isle of Wight

WEDNESDAY MORNING, 3 August, dawned brightly with the Channel barely ruffled by the light westerly breeze. Variable light winds throughout the day drove the opposing fleets forward at a lumbering pace of two knots, offering no advantage to the English, while the Spaniards were perfectly content to be able to maintain their tight defensive formation. All the Spanish ships seemed capable of maintaining their stations except that awkward sailer the 650-ton *Gran Grifon*, flagship of the urcas. Even the clumsy ships in her charge were able to outdistance her. During the very early hours of Wednesday morning she struggled to keep up, but gradually she fell astern and her commanding officer, Juan Gomez de Medina, was frightened to the marrow to find none other than Drake's *Revenge* bearing down on him. There it was again, that uncanny knack of Drake's — his being at the right spot at the right time. He came almost alongside the *Gran Grifon*, now with all canvas piled on desperately trying to recover her station.

The *Revenge* blasted a broadside into the Spaniard as she came abreast of her, sailed past, came about and gave her another, then came under her stern and raked her decks with musket-shot. Other English ships came up and joined in what amounted to good target practice, although to be fair the now damaged *Gran Grifon*, shrouded in smoke, fought back valiantly.

Recalde brought up reinforcements in the form of Oquendo, de Leiva and Bertendona who tried to recover the stricken ship into the relative safety of the crescent formation, while Drake continued to pound the *Gran Grifon* mercilessly until she was no longer under control, seriously damaged and in distress.

(Recalde, incidentally, probably now wore his flag in the *Santa Ana*, transferring his flag from his *San Juan* which had taken such a battering on 31 July and 2 August.)

Other English ships now became engaged in a hot skirmish with the Spanish right wing. During the general engagement that had ensured a Spanish galleasse stroked up to the disabled *Gran Grifon*, secured a line aboard her and towed her to safety. Other galleasses engaged the *Revenge* and claimed they brought down the English ship's main yard — 'having spoiled their admiral's rigging and shot away his main yard'.

When the Duke came up in the *San Martin* with other support and they struck their topsails as a signal for a general engagement the English ships drew off to long culverin shot — a tactic which annoyed the Duke, who interpreted it as a sign that the English did not intend to accept battle, only to delay progress. The fight dwindled to nothing. Indeed, from the *Relations* it would seem the whole incident was less than worth while for it goes unrecorded, perhaps because Howard, whose personal report it is, may have been on the landward side of the Armada, several miles away from the action, and saw nothing of it.

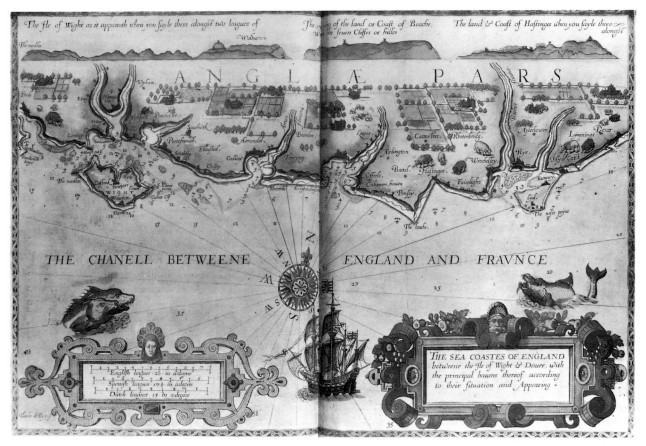

Wagenaer's splendid atlas gave these instructions for entering Spithead on the way to Portsmouth: 'If you will enter at the east end of Wight, keep the Castle right against the Lime-kill that lies above Portsmouth until the Culver Cliff come within a point of the Ile, for then you shall have brought the Lyme-kill to the eastward of Portsmouth: which you must hold until the Castle which standeth to the westward of Portsmouth do appear on the eastside of the wood: and then ply sometimes towards St Helen's Abbey keeping your marks in this sort, you shall then take no hurt on the Shoaldes or Sands . . . Then you freely sail North west, without danger of the Riffe or tail sand that lieth out . . .'

This is quite strange because many of the English ships were engaged and the Spanish suffered more casualties in the engagement than in the general battle of Portland the previous day. They lost sixty killed and had seventy wounded, most of the casualties taking place aboard the *Gran Grifon*.

Two other events of this Wednesday are worth recording. In the afternoon, when the breeze fell away to nothing and the two fleets became becalmed, probably more than two hundred ships lay idly riding the waters a few miles off the Needles, barely a mile apart. Howard took the opportunity of a quiet day of enforced idleness to summon the captains for a council of war, at which he reorganized the fleet's order of battle.

The English commanders had now experienced four days of battle and skirmishing with Sidonia's seemingly impregnable formation; four days in which their constant probing had signally failed to disturb the Armada's precise formation to any extent. In a sense, the Armada, lumbering up the Channel, was winning this contest simply by preserving its fleet 'in being' while the English snapped rather ineffectually at its rearguard. Howard resolved to make efforts to disturb this apparent serenity.

He decided to divide the fleet into four divisions, and in so doing introduced the first squadronal organization into the Navy. Henceforth ships would work in relatively small groups — divisions, squadrons, call them what you will — but in manageable numbers, in a group responsible to one commander. Until now the Armada campaign had been characterized on the English side by the almost chaotic, disorganized, imprecise arrangements of the ships. The Spaniards, by comparison, had a better-integrated fleet, under squadronal commanders who could control the ships in their own squadrons far more effectively than could any of their English counterparts.

Howard decided, then, to form four squadrons of roughly 25 ships each. He would take command of one squadron himself; command of another would go to Drake, of course; John Hawkins would command a third; while Martin Frobisher, if for no other reason, had earned himself command of the fourth by his display in the *Triumph* off Portland Bill the previous day. This would make the whole fleet handier, better organized, controlled.

Although glorified by medallions, Philip II deserved censure. A fundamental strategic error of his was to direct the Armada to the English coast. It should have closely followed the French coast. 'You must keep away from the French and Flemish coasts', he had instructed Sidonia, 'because of the shoals and banks'. But he was dreadfully wrong, and hazarded the Armada even before it engaged the English ships.

The council resolved to put the new organization to the test that very night. At a given signal in the darkness each squadron was to release six armed merchantmen to assault the Spanish rearguard 'in sundry places, at one instant, in the night time, to keep the enemy waking'. It was good psychological warfare. But it came to nought: there was no wind that night, and the Armada was spared.

One other event on this day calls for comment, and it has a distinct bearing on the need to reorganize the fleet. The fighting so far — and especially on the previous day — had been expensive in terms of ammunition due to the uncoordinated attacks by ships, which fired guns at will, regardless of replenishment or of effective use of their stocks of shot. The reorganization should decrease this wastage.

*   *   *

Wednesday was a quiet day in the campaign, principally because Howard's ships had used up most of their ammunition. For this very reason it was not a quiet day along the south coast. Pinnaces, coasters, harbour craft of every description were busily engaged plying from harbour to ships, conveying not only stocks of round shot, of powder and matches, of victuals and barrels of water, but of young noblemen too, seeking glory in the battles to come at sea.

Henceforth the replenished and organized squadrons would learn how to conserve round shot and powder: ships would be better directed by squadron commanders, and would be more effectively employed; there would be less privateering and more discipline. Ships' commanders would know which vessels to follow, which to look to for orders, for support in adversity, which to keep close to for safety. The English ships in the Armada campaign were at the birth of new naval sailing tactics, better suited to the new-style naval warfare now being waged. This Wednesday may have been reasonably quiet in terms of battle, but it was in its own way a day of revolution in the Navy Royal. It was all very elementary — crude, almost — but it was a beginning.

*   *   *

The Isle of Wight hangs like a diamond pendant from the coast of England. Its southernmost point is Dunnose. To the west lies a rocky promontory, the Needles, and the western entrance to the Solent, which in the days of the Armada was not considered a safe passage. To the east the Solent opens into a broad, enticing entrance, leading through a passage navigable for even the largest vessel, up to the untold riches of Portsmouth, the safe anchorage at Spithead, and inland to Winchester, Salisbury . . . Here if anywhere were the most seductive attractions for an invader. Sidonia would not be above such enticement, surely?

Howard and Drake concentrated their minds on the attractions of an assault on the Isle of Wight: this would be the nation's greatest threat for Thursday 4 August 1588. Ships would have to be deployed for the island's defence; all would need to be concentrated on this one major danger. The pressure on the defending ships seemed to have increased following the failure to launch the twenty-four armed merchantmen at the Armada 'to keep it awake' on the previous night.

Dawn brought little improvement in the wind, which had faded to nothing at midnight, leaving both fleets becalmed.

Howard had deployed Frobisher's squadron to the landward side of the Armada — a defensive position, guarding the island, forcing the enemy to fight if he intended assaulting it. When dawn came Frobisher found his small squadron to the north and east of the Armada, ahead of its van, but with only a faint off-shore breeze, not enough to flap sails even; it was not a commanding position, neither was it dangerous.

The early-morning visibility showed two Spanish stragglers with no steerage way struggling to keep up. Hawkins in his flagship *Victory* saw them. Out went the longboats and hefty mariners began to pull the flagship to attack them. Other English ships did likewise. The enemy ships were Oquendo's hulk the *Santa Ana* and the Portuguese galleon *San Luis*. The English got close enough to fire muskets.

When the Spanish galleasses some way away awoke to what was happening they hastened to assist. This was just the venture for a galleasse; its scores of rowers would provide motive power while the enemy lay becalmed or nearly so. Three galleasses and de Leiva's *Rata Coronada* went to their colleagues' assistance. In time the *San Martin* herself reached the stragglers and joined in the action.

On the English side, the Lord High Admiral and Lord Thomas Howard in the *Golden Lion* got their longboats out and reached the scene of action, but the outcome of all this effort and activity was disappointingly inconclusive. The *Relation* records that the Spaniards were much damaged — 'one of them was fain to be carried away on the careen' — suggesting that she had been holed and was taking in water; another lost her lantern 'which came swimming by' and a third 'lost her nose'.

This sort of damage — loss of a lantern, a figurehead and a simple holing — seems small reward for some hours of close-quarter gunfire between ships, yet this is all that is recorded. The *San Martin*, incidentally, suffered some serious casualties and the loss of her mainstay but she was well supported by her rearguard and she made good her escape.

It was Frobisher who captured the headlines with almost a repeat of his Portland performance, hazarding his ship in an excess of zeal or enthusiasm. At dawn, when all this activity started, his was the landward squadron, closest inshore of all the English

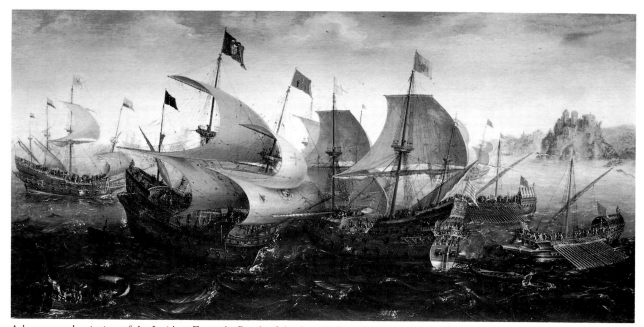

A huge panel painting of *An Incident From the Battle of the Armada* by a Dutch artist, displayed at the Rijksmuseum, Amsterdam.

and Spanish ships. The current was setting easterly at a knot — even faster the closer inshore — so, though becalmed, ships were constantly moving. When a breeze sprang up from the south-west it caught Frobisher and the leading ships of his squadron somewhere off Dunnose and to leeward of the Spanish van.

When this breeze sprang up *Triumph* and half a dozen other ships were already hotly engaged with the *San Martin*. The Spanish flagship was getting the worst of it for half an hour or so, then she was joined by a dozen or more Spanish ships now able to take advantage of the wind. The English saw the danger and turned away, most of them managing to skirt round the Spanish left wing. Frobisher's *Triumph* was in danger of being cut off so he got out the longboats, while other ships' commanders who recognized his danger hoisted out their boats too, until eleven such boats were hauling away strenuously.

In the nick of time Sheffield's *Bear* and the *Elizabeth Jonas* came round the flank to thwart the Spanish approach. The Spanish were exultant and made frantic efforts to get to the *Triumph*: they had her for sure, a huge giant of a galleon, lying to leeward of them and cut off. It was a Spanish commander's dream. Recalde's *Santa Ana* and the *San Martin* and every other Spanish ship present crowded on all sail 'certain that we would this day succeed in boarding them, wherein was the only way to victory'. But the gods smiled on Frobisher.

The wind began to get up and then to veer until it reached south-west. *Triumph* shook out every square inch of canvas, cast off her longboats and began to get under way. The wind filled her sails and she heaved herself away from danger towards the security of the rest of her squadron. The Spaniards set off in pursuit. Calderon watched the English ships in anguish and astonishment as they 'got out so swiftly that the galleon *San Juan [de Portugal]* and another quick-sailing ship — the speediest vessels in the Armada — although they gave chase seemed in comparison with her to be standing still'.

This same day's battle brought near-disaster to Sidonia, although curiously the events leading up to the climax of the battle go unrecorded in the English *Relation*. What *is* recorded needs careful scrutiny to allow a reconstruction of the events.

Drake in *Revenge* and Hawkins in *Victory* in company with the ships of their squadrons engaged the seaward wing of the Spanish formation, far from the landward wing where the main action had taken place so far. The freshening south-west wind gave Drake and Hawkins the weather gage. The 34-gun Portuguese galleon *San Mateo* bore the brunt of the initial attack, but she soon gained support from the newly built 961-ton *Florencia*, confiscated from the Duke of Tuscany for Armada service. With 52 guns she was the most heavily armed Spanish ship.

As the engagement developed, with more ships becoming involved, the set of the current and the direction of the wind combined with the pressure of the English attack in an extraordinary way to press the whole Armada in a generally northerly and easterly direction. It was forced slightly landward, gently but surely across the eastern entrance to the Solent, until, losing the wind for such a deployment, it missed the chance to enter the Solent and seize an anchorage.

Some days earlier at his war council off Cornwall Sidonia had expressed the hope of his Armada capturing the Isle of Wight and there pausing to concert plans and arrange a rendezvous with Parma. Now suddenly the chance had gone; Sidonia's long-held hopes of planning Parma's assault on Kent with Parma had evaporated, never to be

Drake's drum is 2ft in diameter and it bears his arms. It was carried into battles all over the world. Legend has it that should England ever be in danger again the drum's chilling tattoo will sound off and summon Drake to the rescue. Henry Newbolt captured this tradition in his poem:

Take my drum to England, hang et by the shore
Strike et when your powder's running low;
If the Dons sight Devon, I'll quit the port of Heaven,
An' drum them up the Channel as we drummed them long ago.

offered again. Howard, of course, was delighted. He and his commanders, unaware of the Duke's true intentions — and an assault on the Isle of Wight must have rated high — would surely have regarded this day as one of considerable victory. The Isle of Wight was the last likely landing site for the Armada.

Almost before these movements past the Solent could be observed by all the English commanders, the Armada was heading for a navigational hazard of enormous consequences. Many English commanders with a knowledge of the south coast would be aware of the impending danger of the Owers, a confusion of deadly, rocky shallows, extending miles into the Channel, to which the Armada was now being jostled by the northerly and easterly press of the battles. Was this a brilliantly executed tactical manœuvre or was it simply a case of good fortune for the English?

Some would argue that Drake and Hawkins, with their wealth of seafaring knowledge, of sailing the south coast for years, of knowing the Owers with the familiarity of their own quarterdeck, knew precisely what they were up to and came within an ace of achieving a success of incredible proportions.

It is reckoned that Sidonia avoided wrecking the fleet on the reefs by a mere 20 to 30 minutes: it was as close as that. The sight of the approaching reefs of the Owers, discernible by different coloured water and the occasional protruding rock, jolted him and his pilots into immediate action: a gun was fired to attract the fleet's attention, sails were shaken out and the *San Martin* stood out to the south-south-east. The huge formation of the Armada conformed as best it could, the distance from the Owers gradually widened as sea-room was gained and both the Isle of Wight and the English ships fell farther astern.

The battle of the Isle of Wight was over. To whom went the laurels? Certainly Sidonia must have been exasperated by the day, by the near-victory of capturing the *Triumph* (missed by the skin of its teeth) and of taking one of the enemy's senior commanders, by the failure to anchor in the Solent — if such had been his aim — and the frightening shock of near-disaster on the Owers reefs.

The records remain tantalizingly incomplete about the day's battle, with no loggings of ships damaged and casualties suffered, no explanation of Drake's and Hawkins's tactics on the southern wing of the Armada. Howard, though, was delighted. He still retained the strategic advantage in the Channel. Sidonia had been denied for several days in succession now a landing on the south coast of England: the English fleet remained totally intact, and morale was as high as a topsail. What, the English commanders reflected, would or could Sidonia do next? The climax off Calais, the battle off Gravelines, the outcome of the proposed rendezvous with Parma, the dispersal of the Armada, the flight and remorseless pursuit — all were unknown as yet, and were still to come.

14. Calais and the fireships

O N FRIDAY AND SATURDAY 5 and 6 August not a shot was fired between the two fleets. They were days of consolidation, stock-taking, munition replenishment, days of slow, methodical, disciplined progress at a speed no faster than a child's walking pace.

Howard devoted the Friday to a special congenial ceremony of celebration — a little premature, one might have thought, but it indicates his frame of mind. He summoned to the *Ark Royal* a few senior officers and, using his prerogative, bestowed the accolade of knighthood upon them. John Hawkins, architect of the Queen's ships, knelt upon the quarterdeck to receive his honour, probably long overdue; Martin Frobisher's award was in recognition of his escapades at Portland Bill and the Isle of Wight, either of which might have rewarded him with a far different fate; Lord Thomas Howard of the *Golden Lion* and Lord Edmund Sheffield of the *White Bear* received knighthoods despite their already exalted ranks. Drake was not so honoured, having been knighted by the Queen herself in 1581. Roger Townsend received his knighthood 'for special services' but these were not recorded. The most extraordinary award was that to Sir George Beeston, at eighty-nine still commanding a ship, the 400-ton *Dreadnought*.*

On this Friday and Saturday the south-coast ports and harbours were alive with activity as small vessels scurried back and forth replenishing Howard's fleet: 'the justices of the peace near the sea coast, the Earl of Sussex, Sir George Carey and the captains of the ports and castles alongst the coast sent us men, powder, shot, victuals and ships to aid and assist us.'

On these two days Howard contrived that Sidonia should sail into a trap. Sidonia was funnelling his Armada into the Dover Straits and was about to lose sea-room. If he passed the Straits he could well debouch into the North Sea and his campaign would be brought to an end. Or (and Howard conceived this to be the outcome) Sidonia would be trapped between Howard's own fleet, plucking the feathers from his rear, and the squadron now being brought round from the Downs to Dover, commanded by Lord Henry Seymour in the 500-ton *Rainbow* (54 guns), a total of fourteen Queen's ships and numerous other auxiliaries.

But Sidonia's actions were determined by one overriding consideration: the lack of communication with the Duke of Parma. On the Friday he dispatched in a pinnace yet another message, by the hand of the pilot Domingo Ochoa, in order to obtain replenishment of depleted stocks of 4, 6 and 10 lb shot.

The expenditure of shot in the Channel battles had exceeded what had been anticipated. What we know from the Spanish records is that the total round shot issued came to a grand total of 123,790 cannon balls. We know that some galleasses averaged

---

* Inexplicably, his name is not recorded in the *Relation*. He died at the age of one hundred and two.

The Ld Admirall Howard
Knighting Thomas Howard,
the Lord Sheffeild, Rog.^r Townsend,
Iohn Hawkins, and Martin
Forbisher for their good service

The twelve Spanish Shipps

Caled the 12 Apostles

The 2.^d Squadron ruled

by Sr Francis Drake

Queene Eliz: Riding in Tri=
umph through London in a
Chariot drawn by two Hor=
ses and all y.^e Companies
attending her w.th their Baners

A set of 47 Jacobean playing cards (5 are missing), all portraying incidents from the Armada campaign, have survived. They date from about 1680.

Lord Thomas Howard, kinsman of the Lord High Admiral, commanded the Queen's ship *Golden Lion* throughout the whole of the Armada campaign and was invariably in the thick of the fighting. This engraving is thought to be of his flagship.

134 shot each and we know that the urcas for example would have far fewer than the King's ships. It is generally accepted that the ships averaged about 80 shot each. While the average allocation for Howard's ships was possibly only 30 shot apiece, at least he was operating within sight of a friendly shore with replenishment stocks fairly readily available, almost like a glorified ready-use locker. Sidonia had no such logistical back-up.

Sidonia's message to Parma via Ochoa also begged for the dispatch of 40 flyboats to enable him to close with Howard's fleet, 'because our ships being very heavy in comparison with the lightness of those of the enemy it was impossible to come to hand-stroke with them'.

The message also notified Parma to be ready to come out to join the Armada the day it arrived in sight of Dunkirk. But the sands of time were now beginning to run out for Sidonia: from now on things went badly wrong for him at almost every turn and they were never to recover to his advantage, let alone his peace of mind.

His great nagging headache all along had been Parma, but he himself had never been able to understand Parma's problems — not that this excuses the soldier's lack of courteous response to his many messages of inquiry and exhortation.

Parma was perhaps the finest general in Europe, but he did not comprehend naval matters. What boats he possessed were small, barely sea-worthy, a prey to English flyboats and the Dutch Sea Beggars or the pirates of the European coastal waters. Although he occupied all the ports east of Calais, he did not possess anything like the number of small craft necessary to transport his troops, let alone to embark his army

The Lord High Admiral's tapestries

IMMEDIATELY AFTER the Armada campaign Lord Howard of Effingham set about recording his majestic victory in grand style: he had a series of ten enormous tapestries created depicting the battles and incidents in the campaign with meticulous care and accuracy while events were still fresh in his mind.

The tapestries measured between 19 and 29 feet long and 15 feet from top to bottom. The design or art-work was performed by the Dutchman Henrik Corneliszoom Vroom from Haarlem, and another Dutchman, François Spierincx from Delft, did the weaving. The resulting tapestries were works of art. Embroidered into the borders were portraits of the English commanders.

In 1616 debts forced Howard, now an octogenarian, to sell the tapestries, and the buyer was King James I, who put them on display in the House of Lords. More than a century later an engraver, John Pine, copied the entire collection at a scale of about 1 foot:1 inch, and his prints were published in 1739.

Nearly a hundred years later still, in 1834, a wrongly stoked furnace created a disastrous fire which destroyed the Palace of Westminster and all the collection of tapestries. Fortunately, their beauty and artistry was preserved in Pine's craftsmanship.

Reproduced here are three of the prints: No. 4 represents Drake's *Revenge* capturing de Valdes's *Rosario* in the foreground while the *Ark Royal*, *Mary Rose* and *White Bear* sail dangerously close to the rear of the Armada's crescent formation.

No. 7 shows the battle of the Isle of Wight with a high-castled Spanish galleon and a galleasse in the foreground while longboats try to pull English ships round.

No. 10 is one of the most dramatic, depicting Moncada's galleasse *San Lorenzo* foundering on a sandbar off Calais with English longboats pulling in for the kill.

The English commanders embroidered into the borders of Nos. 4 and 10 are the same. Reading clockwise from top left, they are:

Captain Edward Fenton *Mary Rose*
Sir Robert Southwell *Elizabeth Jonas*
Lord Sheffield *Bear*
Lord High Admiral *Ark*
Earl of Cumberland *E. Bonaventure*
Lord Thomas Howard *Lion*
Sir Francis Drake *Revenge*
Thomas Vavasour *Ark*
Sir Charles Blunt *?Ark*

Tapestry No. 4

Sir Thomas Cecill — Burghley's son (ship not listed)
Mr Knevet (?Knyvet) (ship not listed)
Sir George Beeston *Dreadnought*
Captain Christopher Baker *Foresight*
Sir John Hawkins *Victory*
Captain Benjamin Gonson (ship not listed)
Lord Henry Seymour *Rainbow*
Captain George Fenner *Galleon Leicester*
Sir Horatio Palavocini *?Ark*
Captain Robert Crosse *Hope*
Sir Edward Hoby *Ark*
Sir Martin Frobisher *Triumph*
Mr Ambrose Willoughby (ship not listed)

No. 7 portrays:

Sir Martin Frobisher *Triumph*
The Lord Admiral *Ark*
Sir John Hawkins *Victory*
Sir Thomas Garrat (?Gerard) *?Ark*
Sir Roger Townsend *E. Jonas*
Sir William Wynter *Vanguard*
Earl of Northumberland (Seymour's cousin) *?Ark*
Sir Robert Carey *E. Bonaventure*

NOTE: There is no evidence that Ambrose Willoughby and Northumberland actually served at sea during the campaign.

Tapestry No. 7

Tapestry No. 10

and keep it afloat while awaiting the arrival of Sidonia's Armada. It is apparent that Parma was totally unprepared for his part in the Enterprise of England.

On Friday evening the weather worsened, with the wind freshening from the west. The two fleets scudded before it, until Saturday morning found both of them barely a mile apart and nearing the Dover Straits. The coast of France could be seen by the lookouts, though the drizzly weather reduced visibility.

As Saturday progressed Sidonia must have viewed the lack of news from Parma with increasing gloom and foreboding. By four o'clock in the afternoon he was off Calais, indecisive, worried beyond description. Predictably, he called a council of war. The pilots as one declared that the treacherous currents farther up-Channel would at best cast the fleet upon the Flanders shoals and at worst drive it into the North Sea and away from Parma. The proper course, they advised, was to anchor now — there and then, in the broad roadstead outside Calais.

The orders went out immediately, and in a smartly executed evolution anchors crashed into the calm waters as the ships came to a standstill, bows to wind. Sidonia might conceivably have caught the English fleet unprepared by the suddenness of the Armada's anchoring: his enemy might well have stood on past the anchorage, losing the weather gage. But it would take more than this to outsmart the English mariners: it was almost as if the English also obeyed the Duke's signal. Before the Spanish cables had finished running out the English anchors were released, and Howard's fleet anchored within long culverin shot of the Armada in Whitsand Bay under the Calais Cliffs, still holding the weather gage. It was a masterly move.

If Sidonia gazed malevolently at Howard's fleet, he must have been worried too at the squadron that began to emerge from the northern haze later that evening and came to anchor with Howard's fleet. Sidonia thought it was 'Achines' (as the Spaniards called Hawkins), but unknown to the Spaniards they had had Hawkins in company all the week since they entered the Channel. It was, of course, Lord Henry Seymour, that hot-tempered son of the Duke of Somerset, Admiral of the Narrow Seas, a man probably unknown to Sidonia. Seymour was frustrated at having patrolled for days between Dover and Dunkirk, dealing with tricky Hollanders, and was anxious almost beyond endurance to get at the Armada.

One of his galleons ranged deliberately along the Armada's rear and loosed off a broadside, announcing both his arrival and his defiance in telling fashion, and then regained her station and anchored.

The combined English fleet now mustered some 140 vessels, which a Spanish captain described with a dejected honesty 'the worst, without their main-course or top sails, can beat the best sailers we have'.

*   *   *

The melancholy Sidonia had more and more bad news heaped upon him on Sunday 7 August. Soon after daybreak the first of his many messengers to Parma, Don Rodrigo Tello de Guzman, clambered aboard the *San Martin* with reports little short of catastrophic. Tello had been dispatched two weeks previously to tell Parma the Armada had reached the latitude of Ushant. Tello arrived at Dunkirk to begin his search for Parma. What he found shocked him. There was no invasion army to be seen. The expected squadron of flyboats was a pitiful handful of open canal barges secured alongside Dunkirk's quay. They had no guns, and masts were not stepped.

Worst of all, there was no Parma. He was forty miles away at his headquarters at Bruges.

When Tello met the Duke, Parma assured his visitor that some gunboats lay at Antwerp, and invasion barges were dispersed along miles of canals. There were 5,600 troops at Nieuport and 15,300 more at Dixmunde who could be embarked in about six days. From his own observations Tello reckoned a more realistic period would be fourteen days — *at least*.

Parma had not been totally honest with Tello, and the latter had not been taken in.

It is a fact that the news of the Armada's arrival caught Parma by surprise. He himself had been completely disenchanted by the invasion plans, by the whole *Empresa*, for he knew that he could not construct and equip a fleet of suitable invasion sailing craft. Those which had been built were flimsy vessels. Even Parma could see (and was impelled to warn Philip): 'Four ships of war could sink every one of my boats.' He went so far as to exhort his King to call off the Enterprise, to come to terms with Elizabeth and end the misery in the Netherlands.

Merchants of Levant, or Turkie Merchants.

Eight ships of the Levant Company of London served with Seymour's eastern squadron off 'Cape Margate' where the invasion was expected. Under a charter of 1581 the Levant Co. monopolized trade with Constantinople: the currant trade was particularly lucrative.

Parma, as we know, was no seaman, but it did not need a seaman's brain to appreciate the situation: he needed only to gaze out to sea from Dunkirk. How could he possibly transport a force of frail craft heavily laden with troops and equipment out to mid-Channel to rendezvous with the Armada before assaulting 'Cape Margate'? The prospect was absurd.

Nevertheless, Parma had persevered despite the enormous difficulties and to his credit he took action as soon as he received Tello's message. He alerted his troops, and what barges were available were mustered at Dunkirk and Nieuport. He inspected an embarkation as early as Tuesday 9 August, when he watched with mounting concern as he saw boats sink under their loads, others become uncontrollable when loaded. Meanwhile there came from seaward the unmistakable rumbling of cannon-fire as a battle raged. It is to those events that we must now turn our attention.

*   *   *

As already noted, Sidonia received the news from Tello with dismay, yet he was to continue receiving ill-tidings almost hourly for the rest of the day.

It was evident that the huge anchorage in which the Armada found itself was unsafe: advisers from ashore pointed to the natural hazards, quite apart from the presence of the English fleet. With mounting gloom, he realized that Parma and his invasion force would not make an appearance.

Unknown to Sidonia, the English were planning an attack by fireships. Such an attack had always been on the cards, and it is known that Walsingham had instructed Dover to provide some suitable vessels together with faggots and pitch in case of need. Sir Henry Palmer in the *Antelope* had been dispatched from the fleet to Dover to collect these fireships, but the English commanders meeting in council were unhappy at the delay this would cause. It would be Monday evening before an attack could be launched; they urged instead immediate preparatory action to enable an attack to be made that night, Sunday.

Drake set the scene by offering one of his 200-ton ships, while Hawkins followed with his 150-ton *Bark Bond*, as a sacrificial fireship. All told, eight were selected and prepared during the day for the midnight attack.

Feared though fireships were, even more greatly feared were vessels dubbed 'hell burners' or 'devil ships', and sometimes *maquinas de minas* — mine-machines. Just three years before, in 1585, the devil ships of Antwerp had been used by rebel Dutch forces with devastating effect. The Italian Frederigo Giambelli had devised this modern horror using ships of 70–80 tons packed with 3 tons of powder in brick-built chambers. One such floating mine had demolished a huge wooden bridge, killed 800 Spaniards and wounded countless numbers more, including the Duke of Parma himself, struck by a baulk of timber.

It was generally known that Giambelli was in England working for Queen Elizabeth, and this was interpreted to mean that he was creating new maritime mines of devilish ingenuity. Unknown to the Spaniards, he had no such assignment: he was devising a harmless boom and bridge across the Thames at Gravesend.

Medina Sidonia was, of course, prepared for a fireship attack, and when late on Sunday afternoon Seymour's ships were seen to join the English fleet, they were thought to be some new Giambelli hell burners. Sidonia nominated a number of pinnaces equipped with grapnels to grapple with fireships and tow them clear of the

A Dutch portrayal of the fireship attack off Calais entitled *The Fall of the Invincible Armada*.

fleet — out of harm's way, to the shore. The ships of the Armada, he instructed, should not move while the pinnaces were performing their duties. Should the fireships penetrate the pinnace screen, ships were to buoy and slip their cables, then stand out to sea, allowing the fireships to drift by and run ashore. Once clear, the ships would anchor again before returning at daylight to their original anchorages and recovering their buoyed anchors. It was as good a plan as could be conceived in the circumstances.

*   *   *

Monday 8 August, starting at midnight on Sunday with the attack by fireships at Calais, was a red-letter day in the annals of England's long maritime story. It was a long-drawn-out, seemingly endless day of battling, lasting from long before daybreak right through till after sunset, although at the time, in the blur of battle, sea, wind, rain, explosions and gunsmoke, it was not seen in terms of victory.

Nevertheless, it was the climactic day of the campaign, and the English were rewarded at last for their patience over the last few weeks, while the wretched Medina Sidonia finally accepted defeat, abandoned the Enterprise and fled into the North Sea on the remorseless and for many forlorn north-about voyage home.

It was at about midnight that this crucial day's events started. The Spaniards later reported: 'Two fires were seen kindled in the English fleet, which increased to eight; and suddenly eight ships with all sail set and fair wind and tide, came straight toward our *capitana* and the rest of the fleet; all burning fiercely.' The fireships had been launched.

The defensive screen of pinnaces, their crews displaying a courage probably born of desperation, grappled two of these fiery monsters and towed them ashore to burn out harmlessly. But the remaining fireships, enjoying the impetus of a spring tide, a strong wind which fanned the flames, and the set of the current, bore down on the Armada ships. The double-shotted guns began to explode, arousing new fears of hell burners, the pinnace screen faltered and the fireships broke through. Most captains viewed the scene with horror, cut their cables and with a touch of panic made for the sea as best they could. With scores of ships hastening to get to sea, it was little short of miraculous that there were so few collisions.

Sidonia's *San Martin* dropped anchor again about a mile north of her original anchorage. Four other disciplined ships — Recalde's *San Juan*, the *San Marcos*, perhaps the *San Felipe* or Oquendo's *Santa Ana* and the *San Mateo* — conformed and anchored close by.

Dawn showed a scene of dismay to the Duke. Only his five galleons in company, plus the *San Lorenzo*, the *capitana* of the galleasses, were in sight. His Armada was scattered, and its disciplined crescent formation, held as tight as a knot in the days of sailing and fighting up-Channel, had been broken at last by eight fireships during the night. For all their fearsome appearance, the fireships had not in fact set ablaze one Spanish ship: from that standpoint the attack had been a complete failure. It had, however, broken the famous formation and, secondarily — it had caused many captains to lose their primary anchors, a loss which was later to cost many of them dear in their predicaments off Ireland.

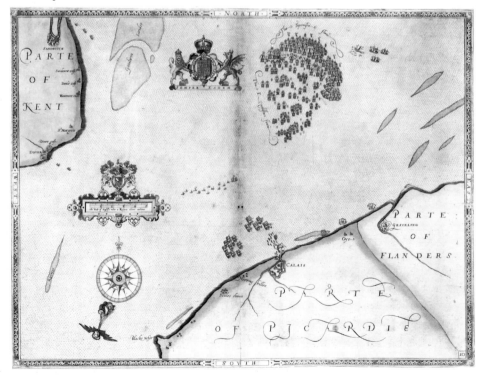

This chart is No. 10 in Robert Adams's series of eleven and shows the Armada approaching Gravelines.

Fireships of Calais

SMALL SHIPS of up to 150 tons made good fireships. Captains of such ships were willing to offer their ships for self-destruction especially if the ships were time-worn and sea-battered, because the reward for their sacrifice was probably far greater than their worth.

A fireship was filled with masses of combustible material — old spars, scrap sails, rotting cordage, used timber, pitch for caulking decks, oil for lanterns, sacking, old barrel staves. Pitch, tar and oil would be smothered overall, including the masts and yards. If the ships carried any ordnance — and they often mounted up to eight small guns — then these would be loaded for firing by the fire itself, if for no other reason than that their explosions would cause fear and spread confusion.

A fireship's role in battle, or when attacking enemy ships at anchor, was to bear down on the enemy vessels, lashing the helm to keep their ship on course. The skeleton crew would try to secure alongside with grappling irons then ignite the slow match which led via powder trains to the combustible materials, before escaping through a sally port or over the side to a boat towed astern or alongside.

Fireships were dreaded weapons in these days of sail. A ship of the wooden-wall era was a veritable fire bomb: everything about her was a fire hazard. An analogous use in modern times was the sacrifice of the old destroyer *Campbeltown* in 1942 when, crammed with explosives, she destroyed the gate of the huge dry dock at St Nazaire.

Of the eight known fireships to have been employed at Calais only six have been listed. A seventh was probably *The Angel of Hampton*, owned by Richard Goddard, ex-mayor of Southampton, and commanded by Lawrence Prowse. The town of Southampton claimed to have spent £2 17*s.* 8*d.* in equipping the ship for the campaign. The eighth has been described simply as 'Cure's ship, 150 tons.' The six listed were:

Bark Talbot, 200 tons
Thomas Drake, 200 tons, owned by Drake
Hope Hawkins of Plymouth, 180 tons, owned by William Hart
Bark Bond, 150 tons, owned by Hawkins
Bear Yonge of Lyme, 140 tons, owned by John Yonge
Elizabeth of Lowestoft, 90 tons, owned by Thomas Meldrum

The reward for the captain of a fireship successfully attacking an enemy ship of 40 guns or more was £100 (or a medal and gold chain of equivalent worth) — 'to remain as a Token of Honour to him and Posterity'. Each crew member would receive £10. If it was the enemy flagship which was destroyed the rewards were doubled.

Fireships were used fairly extensively during the seventeenth-century Anglo-Dutch wars, and for the last time by British ships against the French at anchor in the Basque Roads in 1811.

D. Valdivieso lit.ª   Lit. de J.J.Martinez. Madrid.

Hugo de Moncada, commander of the Neapolitan galleasses, who was killed aboard his flagship, the *San Lorenzo*, when she was driven ashore and plundered off Calais.

Moncada's *San Lorenzo* was in dire trouble, floundering like an injured whale. She had experienced rudder trouble earlier in the campaign, and now in the near-panic to clear the Calais anchorage during the night she collided with another ship and damaged her mainmast, while the suspect rudder fouled a cable, rendering it useless.

Moncada struggled to control her but she grounded heavily and careened over on to the shore, making her guns useless.

Sidonia saw something else, even more disquieting than Moncada's attempts to save his ship. He could see the English fleet, perhaps 140 ships strong, to the south, still in its anchorage responding to the gunshot from the *Ark* and to the braying of trumpets which could be heard across the sea. Anchors were being weighed, canvas being shaken out, flags and banners hoisted. The whole naval strength of Elizabethan England lay before Sidonia's gaze like some awesome review. England's massive naval strength was making ready for battle.

Howard's squadron held back, intent upon tackling Moncada's disabled *San Lorenzo*, while the other squadron commanders — Drake in *Revenge*, Frobisher, Hawkins, Lord Seymour and William Wynter — led their ships in pursuit of the rest of the Armada.

Howard's ships approached the *San Lorenzo* as close as they dared in the shallow waters, and began lowering boats to take the prize by boarding her. The *Ark*'s longboat, commanded by Lieutenant Amyas Preston and loaded with 60 soldiers, got away first, quickly followed by a boat from the *Margaret and John* (which itself had now grounded). When these boats reached the galleasse she towered over them and the steep sides prevented the Englishmen boarding her. Musket shots rang out, and in a half an hour's engagement the English suffered a number of casualties, including Amyas Preston.

Lieutenant Richard Tomson of the *Margaret and John*'s boat reported the odds being heavily one-sided.

Despite extra English boats arriving on the scene the sides of the *San Lorenzo* could not be scaled and the boats were preparing to retire when a musket shot hit the admiral, Hugo de Moncada, in the head and he fell dead. Resistance crumpled. Defenders jumped and scuttled ashore — 'some, and that very many, drowned' wrote Tomson. A few surrendered: 'They put up two handkerchers upon two rapiers signifying that they desired truce.'

The English managed to swarm aboard over the seaward rail and gunports. They stripped the galleasse clean of everything a man could lift and carry.

The whole engagement had been watched from ashore by many burghers of Calais and kinsmen of the Governor of the town, M. Gourdan, who called upon Tomson to take what he wished from the prize, for he had earned it. The Governor lay claim, however, by the ancient laws of war and conquest of the ship herself, her guns and rigging. He underlined his claim by pointing to the cannons of Calais Castle only a few hundred yards away. Tomson was allowed 'the spoil and pillage of the galleasse'.

The English were encouraged to depart by rounds of shot from the Castle. Howard's ships recovered their boats and loot, and stood out to sea, heading for the sound of the guns, about twelve miles to the north-east of a coastal village named Gravelines.

Margaret and John was holed twice before the flood tide floated her off the sand bar later that day. It had been a close call for the small ship and her intrepid commander.

15. Battle of Gravelines and the pursuit to Scotland

*U*NFORTUNATELY THE BATTLE of Gravelines suffers from ill-documentation by both Spanish and English sources, and the day's events are only partially recorded, leaving tantalizing gaps in the story. Here and there we get a glimpse, as if through gunsmoke, of a battle which is significant in both the story of the Armada and that of the Navy.

Monday 8 August started as we have seen with the fireship attack at midnight on the Sunday, followed by the unsavoury forenoon scramble to pillage Moncada's *San Lorenzo*. When this curious and deplorable action of Howard's was completed, he sought to recover lost time and perhaps lost chances.

All credit to the seamen squadron commanders, Drake, Frobisher and Hawkins, and indeed to the nobleman Seymour. None of them was side-tracked by the chance of acquiring a prize of the size of the *San Lorenzo*, and all four of them knew what Howard was up to; and all four left him to it while they pursued the Armada.

It seemed that Sidonia had got away well in the morning when his flagship, *San Martin*, and her four consorts cleared the straits and headed into the North Sea, running before the strong SSW wind. He tried hard to keep the squadron as far to seaward of the shoals off Dunkirk, with some success. In close pursuit of this squadron was Drake, Frobisher, Hawkins and Seymour with their squadrons.

Sidonia had several aims in mind, but first he must gain time to allow his own fleet to re-group by employing delaying tactics with the English squadrons while he headed northerly and easterly into the North Sea. Meanwhile pinnaces had been dispatched to scour the seas even as far as the shoals of Dunkirk to recover scattered ships.

Throughout the whole day's battle, from seven o'clock in the morning till about four o'clock in the afternoon, the weather remained blustery from the SSW with a lowering grey sky, giving a visibility of only a few hundred yards at times. The seas continued heavy throughout the day.

The most worrying aspect of the battle for all commanders was the desperately low levels of ammunition, especially for the Spaniards, some of whose ships were virtually out of gunshot. The English, aware of the lack of supplies, were determined to make each shot count by closing the range to ensure maximum damage to the enemy's ships.

Sidonia's efforts to gain sea-room and to protect his reassembling Armada were challenged by Drake, whose *Revenge* and the rest of his squadron gradually closed the range to almost half-musket shot (perhaps less than 100 yards), before loosing off her bow guns, then luffing up to bring her broadside to bear for a whole hail of shots, then swinging back down wind and out of range.

Ubaldini referred to this episode later; it is likely to have been this encounter that he was describing, when the *Revenge* was 'pierced through by cannon balls of all sizes above forty times'. They must have been almost the last shots in *San Martin*'s lockers.

The artist Oswald W. Brierly (1817–94) painted Drake's *Revenge* at the battle of Gravelines, capturing the intensity of the fighting during this climactic day of battle.

Ubaldini also described how Drake's 'very cabeen was twise shot thorow'. Drake related to his chronicler a tale he often told, how 'the bedde of a certain gentleman lying weary thereupon was taken quite from under him with the force of a bullet [saker ball]'. The story is probably apocryphal; it appears in many variations, all on the same theme, but it would be a pity to omit reference to it here.

The only support the *San Martin* received was from the Marquis of Peñafiel's *San Marcos de Portugal* which lay close by, taking some of the pressure off the admiral. Thomas Fenner in the *Nonpareil* followed *Revenge* in an identical manœuvre, quickly followed by nearly twenty ships of the squadron each delivering a splintering, effective broadside.

Drake's squadron headed off to the north-east and the rest of his exploits at Gravelines go unrecorded.

Frobisher witnessed Drake's squadron's in-line attack and he engaged the *San Martin* with his *Triumph*; he lay almost alongside the *San Martin*, struck his topsails and remained almost within pistol shot but not quite close enough to grapple and board. Other squadronal ships came close by and the *San Martin* received further serious damage to bows, stern and sides.

When Hawkins came up in his *Victory* way was made for him to join the fray. The damage inflicted was substantial. Altogether the *San Martin* took 200 rounds in her starboard side; her rigging and sails hung in shreds; dead and dying men littered the decks. Calderon recorded the damage in these words: 'The holes made in her hull between wind and water caused so great a leakage that two divers could hardly stop them up with hemp caulking and lead plates, working all day'.

Sir William Wynter's flagship, *Vanguard*, makes an attack at the decisive battle of Gravelines. The painting is by Oswald W. Brierly.

While the Spanish flagship was undergoing this punishment her scattered fleet began arriving at the sound of the guns to give support. Don Alonso de Leiva (*La Rata Coronada*), Recalde in his *San Juan* with his Portuguese galleons, Oquendo (*Santa Ana*), Don Diego Flores de Valdes with his Castilian galleons, the *San Juan* of Don Diego Enriquez, the *San Juan de Sicilia* of Don Diego Tellez Enriquez — all of them came, and all 'sustained the assault of the enemy as stoutly as was possible, so as all these ships were very much spoiled and almost unable to make any further resistance'.

At one stage of the battle Bertendona's great carrack *Regazona* was seen wallowing in the heavy seas, her guns silenced but musketeers still at their posts in the tops, while in the scuppers sloshing water and blood flushed overboard as she heeled in the wind and seas.

At one stage Don Francisco de Toledo in the *San Felipe* tried in vain to grapple with the English ships that 'assailed him and by shooting of ordnance brought him to great extremity'. Toledo challenged the English ships to hand-to-hand fighting but the offers were rejected and Toledo was summoned to surrender. Calderon recorded that

> one Englishman standing in the maintop with his sword and buckler called out 'Good soldiers that ye are, surrender to the fair terms we offer ye.' The only answer he got was a gunshot which brought him down in sight of everyone. And the commander then ordered the muskets and arquebusiers into action. The enemy [probably the *Rainbow*] thereupon retired, while our men shouted out that they were cowards, abusing them for want of spirit, calling them Lutheran hens, and daring them to return to the fight.

The *San Felipe* was rescued by the *San Mateo* (Don Diego Pimentel) and *San Luis*. Other Spanish ships heavily engaged in this stage of the battle were the *Valencera* (Don

This banner depicting the Crucifixion was taken from the disabled *San Mateo* before she finally foundered during the battle of Gravelines. It is now preserved in the Stedelijk Museum of Lakenhal, Leiden.

Alonso de Luzon) and *Begoña* of the Indian Guard. All were severely damaged.

A special feature of this morning's battle was the attempt made by the Spanish to recover their tight crescent formation. It was not totally successful, but it was a dramatic display of disciplined seamanship.

Justin de Nassau, the illegitimate son of William of Orange, was allied to the English during the Armada campaign. He could operate his fleet of flyboats freely among the Flemish shoals without fear of interference from the Spanish. He was a thorn in the side of the Duke of Parma.

It was in fact Wynter's *Vanguard* and Seymour's *Rainbow* which inflicted such serious damage on the *San Felipe* and the *San Mateo*. The latter became so heavily engaged that at one stage an English ship lay so close alongside that one lone Englishman boarded her in a single act of heroism, but 'our men cut him to bits instantly' the Spanish report concluded.

The *San Mateo*'s 'hull was so riddled that she was in a sinking condition, the pumps being powerless to diminish the water'. Wynter's battle report later revealed:

> Out of my ships there was shot 500 shot of demi-cannon, culverin and demi-culverin, and when I was farthest off in discharging any of the pieces, I was not out of shot of their harquebus, and most time within speech of one another. . . .

Diego Pimentel aboard the *San Mateo* begged Sidonia for one of the *San Martin*'s divers whom he could ill afford to send — but did so. However, the *San Mateo* was beyond saving, dropped astern and became beached between Ostend and Sluys. There Dutch ships attacked her. *Maestro de campo* Pimentel fought with his soldiers for two hours before surrendering. He was fortunate: his elevated rank made him ransom-worthy. There was no love lost between the Dutch and the Spanish and nearly every Spaniard other than the *maestro* 'were cast overboard . . . and slain'.

That same evening the crippled *San Felipe* was secured alongside the urca *Doncella* evacuating all her crew and soldiery when a cry went up that the urca was sinking. The *San Felipe*'s captain, Juan Poza de Santiso, and the *maestro de campo*, Francisco de Toledo, thereupon sprang back aboard their ship, Toledo declaring that if he were to be lost it would look better if he were in a galleon rather than in a hulk.

The *Doncella* did not sink, but the *San Felipe* became so heavily waterlogged that she drifted on to a beach between Nieuport and Ostend. Spanish pinnaces rushed to her rescue and the valiant *maestro* and some of the crew were rescued. Nevertheless, Dutch ships under the command of Justin of Nassau captured and refloated her. Thereupon they towed their captive towards Flushing, but she sank before reaching harbour.

One other Spanish casualty of that evening is worthy of chronicling. The *Maria Juan* was a 665-ton great ship of Recalde's squadron. She was commanded by Captain Pedro de Ugarte, who signalled to his admiral that his ship was sinking. Sidonia, hard pressed though he was even at sunset (when most of the hard fighting had finished) hurried to the rescue in worsening conditions. The *Maria Juan* was in a dreadful state and 'abandon ship' was ordered too late to save most of her crew and the soldiers aboard; she sank with the loss of perhaps 275 men, just one boatload being saved.

English ships which deserve mention for having fought valiantly during the day's battle included the *Mary Rose* (Edward Fenton), the *Hope* (Robert Crosse), *Elizabeth Bonaventure* (Earl of Cumberland and Captain George Raymond), the *Dreadnought* (commanded by the octogenarian Sir George Beeston), the *Swallow* (Richard Hawkins) and the *Elizabeth Jonas* (Sir Robert Southwell).

The fierce fighting continued throughout the afternoon until about four o'clock, and the English commanders realized that there was still time to finish off a number of damaged Spanish ships if stocks of gunshot — now heavily depleted — would last out. The Spanish, on the other hand, were in a worse plight with even less shot; their ships were in a less seaworthy condition and some means of breaking off the battle to give them an honourable escape would have been welcomed. As if in answer to their unspoken prayers, a violent rain squall brought all fighting to an end. A blackened sky

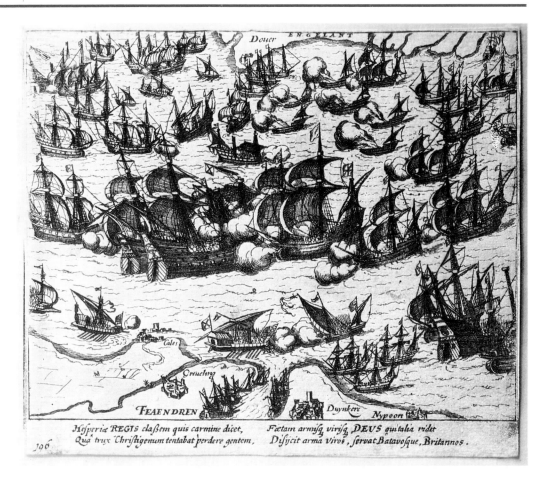

The battle of Gravelines: a Dutch portrayal.

blotted out the scene of battle. Wind lashed the rain as the front moved in, visibility dropped to nil and helmsmen struggled to keep their ships under control. It was as if a curtain had been drawn over the day's proceedings: the tragedy had been played out.

Certainly the ordeal of battle was over for Sidonia but other fierce ordeals faced him, and the onset of darkness that evening brought to him a night and following day of terror and anguish such as many mariners had never before experienced.

Recalling the dreadful day of Tuesday 9 August, Luis de Miranda, a member of Sidonia's own staff aboard the *San Martin*, painted this sombre picture of desperation aboard the flagship: 'We saw ourselves lost or taken by the enemy, or the whole Armada drowned upon the banks. It was the most fearful day in the world, for the whole company had lost all hope of success and looked only for death.'

The desperately low morale of the mariners and soldiers was worsened by a horrifying incident on the day of defeat at Gravelines. Sidonia delegated to Francisco de Bobadilla, the military officer commanding all the *tercios*, responsibility for discipline throughout the fleet following an incident earlier in the morning when more than half the Spanish vessels had apparently ignored the admiral's signal to lie to and await the English ships.

In Sidonia's name, Bobadilla issued orders that no craft was to sail ahead of the admiral's flagship, or the captain would be put to death. Either on that same evening or the following day, two ships were seen ahead of the flagship. Bobadilla sent officers to arrest the captains of the two offending ships who were brought to the flagship and summarily court-martialled. Both were sentenced to death.

Don Cristobal de Avilia, a gentleman and neighbour of Sidonia's from Sanlucar, was hanged at the yardarm of a pinnace, which sailed through the fleet with its grisly exhibit.

The other captain had friends at court. His sentence was commuted and he was dismissed his ship. He was Francisco de Cuellar, and his influential friend was none other than Martin de Aranda, Judge Advocate of the fleet, who listened to Cuellar's defence and took it upon himself to spare the captain and delivered him into his own care aboard the *La Lavia*. Cuellar's experiences and subsequent survival will be related in due course.

Pedro Calderon records that other captains and officers — some reports quote numbers as high as nineteen or twenty — were summarily court-martialled and condemned to galleys or given other harsh punishments *pour encourager les autres*.

These then were the demoralized mariners and ships of the Armada who would now be subjected to fear, not of being killed in battle but of having their ships wrecked on a hostile shore. Darkness that evening brought a continuation of the set of the current and wind which had the effect all the while of pushing the whole body of ships inexorably farther towards the Flanders sandbanks. As if to emphasize the inevitability of the impending disaster, the sea increased in its fury, the wind heightened until it blew gale force and, to compound the danger, it veered gradually from south-west to north-west. If ever the elements seemed determined to wreck a fleet, this was the time. In sailing terms, the ships — now coasting with shortened sails, as close hauled as they could — would still make dangerous leeway towards the fatal shoals away over to starboard. They could make no sea-room at all.

The *San Martin* had in company seven faithful ships: Recalde's *San Juan*, de Leiva's carrack, *La Rata Coronada*, Peñafiel's *San Marcos*, a Castilian galleon and the three galleasses. The rest of the Armada lay scattered far and wide by the storm, each ship struggling to gain sea-room as best it could, away from the breakers which could now be discerned to leeward.

The admiral's small group of ships was positioned as well as possible as a rearguard, and on its weather quarter followed the bulk of the English fleet — compact, in control of itself, standing well clear of the shoals, looking sinister to the Spaniards in its tidiness and trimmed sails.

Howard had taken time on Monday night to write to Walsingham, subscribing the letter 'From aboard her Majesty's good ship the *Ark*, the 29th July 1588 [OS], Your very loving friend. . . ' Referring to shot and powder, he wrote: 'I pray you send me with all speed as much as you can.' And in an evocative passage he continued, 'We have chased them in fight until this evening late and distressed them much; but their fleet consisteth of mighty ships and great strength . . . Their force is wonderful great and strong; and yet we pluck their feathers little and little . . .'

Drake too found time to write to Walsingham:

God hath given us so good a day in forcing the enemy so far to leeward as I hope in God the Prince of Parma and the Duke of Medina Sidonia shall not shake hands this few days; and whensoever they shall meet, I believe neither of them will greatly rejoice of this day's service.

His postscript indicated clearly an expectation of further battling: 'There must be great care taken to send us munition and victual whithersoever the enemy goeth.'

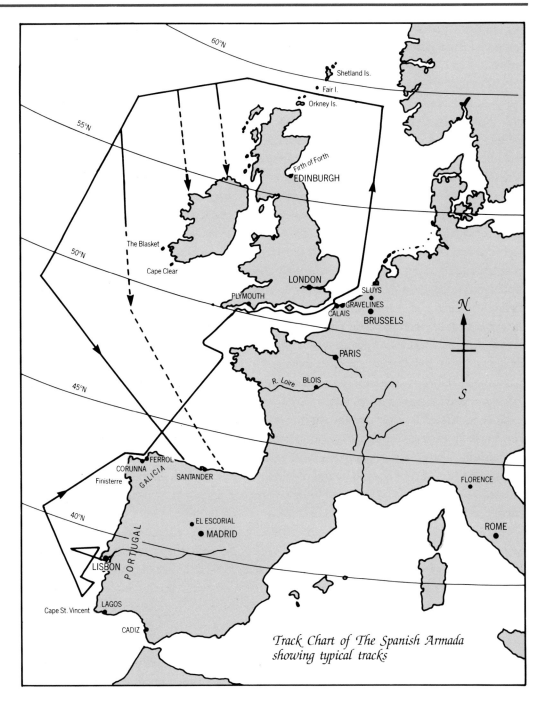

Track Chart of The Spanish Armada showing typical tracks

Howard and Drake followed Sidonia, content to keep distance of at least a culverin shot apart. After all, the elements were about to wreck the Armada, perhaps more surely than the English fleet could with their depleted stocks of shot and powder. It was apparent that under existing conditions of tide, current and wind — although it had moderated somewhat — it was only a matter of time before the ships would wreck themselves. Sidonia saw this too, and he reckoned he had about half an hour before disaster would strike.

He ordered the ships in company to lay to and prepare to battle with the English: rather a fighting death than one by shipwreck. Pinnaces were sent ahead with orders to lie to or even beat back to fight the English if they could. But although the Spaniards were lying to, the wind and current were still shunting the rearguard to leeward. Anchors lost at Calais were now being sorely missed, although in fact the loose sand lacked a firm grip for many anchors.

As the time dragged like the ships' anchors, the inevitability of wreck stared everyone in the face. The leadsmen's cries of 'Seven fathoms . . . six fathoms', when the galleons only drew five, seemed unnecessarily doom-laden. Noblemen now begged Sidonia to abandon his venture and take a pinnace ashore with his Holy Banner. Sidonia declined the offer of personal safety; rather face the heretics and die a brave death. He prepared himself for the hereafter, and was shriven by his priest. Later he recorded his thoughts at the time: 'God alone,' he wrote, 'could rescue them.'

As if in answer to his thoughts, God responded. Within minutes of a disastrous battering by the seas as his ships lay stranded, the fresh wind suddenly and incredibly backed as far as WSW. Even the leading ships in the worst condition could now stand away into deep water. Instantly all the ships came round and ran from the devilish shoals to the safety of the deep North Sea. The Duke's chaplain and Sidonia himself regarded it as an act — as a miracle — of God. Recalde thought it the bit of luck that the Armada had deserved ever since it entered the Channel.

Howard and Drake were so disappointed by the turn of events that neither of them remarked about it except casually in their reports. The English fleet had no option but to continue dogging the track of the Armada in its flight northward, like a thief in the night pursued by the constabulary.

On Thursday 11 August in the flight north both sides called for councils of war. The English one was the more congenial: victors are sweeter-tempered than the vanquished. The crisis was over, the battle done, a re-entry of the Channel was out of the question as long as the new wind blew. The council resolved to follow the Armada till it had reached the height of the Firth of Forth: they put the resolution to paper and dispatched it.

One of Howard's orders at the council provoked an angry scene. Howard instructed Seymour's squadron to return to its watch on Parma while the main fleet pursued the Armada. Seymour was furious at being deprived of possible honour in battle still to come, but of course Howard's decision to detach a squadron to watch the Thames/ Dover area was right. To have left the south-east coast of England unguarded by the navy would have been foolhardy.

The squadrons parted company between seven and eight o'clock on Wednesday evening, 10 August, when abreast of Lowestoft, Seymour's squadron then consisting of *Vanguard, Rainbow, Antelope, Bull, Tiger, Tramontana, Scout, Achates, Merlin, Sun, Cygnet, George* and Captain William Borough's galley *Bonavolia*, besides merchant ships.

When his fleet was about ninety miles off Newcastle in a position about 55°13'N Howard decided to engage in battle again on Friday 12 August. But his mind was changed, partly because it was clearly evident the battered Armada had no intention of landing its troops in Scotland — it was standing well clear of the coast to the north: partly, too, because the wind shifted to the north-west, which made it impossible for the Spanish ships to reach the Scottish coast, and partly, too, because his own ships were now desperately low in victuals and ammunition.

Howard left two pinnaces 'to dog the fleet until they should be past the isle of Scotland' and the English fleet turned about for England. Off the Norfolk coast a

Resolution at a council of war
(11 August 1588)

'WE WHOSE NAMES are hereunder written have determined and agreed in council to follow and pursue the Spanish fleet until we have cleared our own coast and brought the Frith [Firth of Forth] west of us: and then to return back again, as well to re-victual our ships, which stand in extreme scarcity, as also to guard and defend our own coast at home; with further protestation that, if our wants of victuals and munition were supplied, we would pursue them to the furthest that they durst have gone.'

The signatories of the resolution were:

C. Howard (Lord Howard of Effingham, Lord High Admiral)

T. Howard (Lord Thomas Howard aboard *Golden Lion*)

Fra. Drake (Sir Francis Drake, vice admiral, *Revenge*)

John Hawkyns (Sir John Hawkins, rear admiral, *Antelope*)

Thomas Fenner (one of three Fenners: commanding *Nonpareil*)

George Coumbreland (Earl of Cumberland: *Elizabeth Bonaventure*)

Edmund Sheffeylde (Lord Sheffield: *White Bear*)

Edw. Hoby (Sir Edward Hoby, Secretary aboard *Ark Royal*)

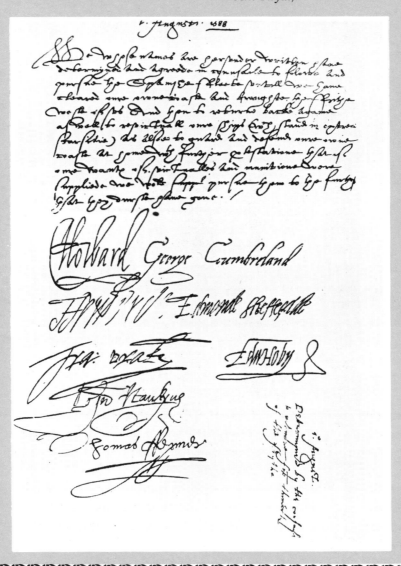

'The men sicken and die faster then ever they did'

O N 20 AUGUST 1588 when he returned to the Thames after the pursuit to the Firth of Forth, Charles Howard, Lord High Admiral wrote to Lord Burghley an alarming letter:

> Sickness and mortality begin wonderfully to grow amongst us . . . and it is a most pitiful sight to see here at Margate how the men . . . die in the streets . . . The *Elizabeth Jonas* . . . hath had a very great infection in her from the beginning, so as of the 500 men which she carried out, by the time we had been in Plymouth three weeks or a month, there were dead of them 200 or above; so as I was driven to set all the rest of her men ashore, to take out her ballast, and to make fires in her of wet broom, three or four days together; and so hoped thereby to have cleansed her of infection; and thereupon got new men, very tall and able as ever I saw and put them into her. Now the infection is broken out in greater extremity than ever it did before and the men die and sicken faster than ever they did . . .

westerly gale scattered the fleet and it ran for whatever shelter it could find: it was this gale which was responsible for the fleet arriving in piecemeal fashion in the Downs, Yarmouth, Harwich, all in battle-worn condition which gave rise to some rumours that the English fleet had lost dozens of ships and had been decisively beaten. Into Harwich on 18 August sailed the *White Bear, Victory, Nonpareil, Hope, Swiftsure, Foresight, Moon, White Lion* and *Disdain* with twenty-six ships from London.

The Spanish account of this escape into the North Sea refers to Wednesday 10 August when the Armada ran before a strong wind from the south-west, a high sea with the English fleet following. In the evening the wind fell away and the English under all sail closed the range. Sidonia, gallant to the last, struck his flagship's topsails to await his rearguard under Recalde, firing three guns to indicate that the main body of the fleet should await the rear and the flagship.

> When the enemy perceived that our flagships had brought to and that the galleasses of the rear and as many as twelve of our best ships had done likewise, their vessels also brought to and shortened sail, without firing at us. That night Juan Achines [John Hawkins] turned back with his squadron.

[It was Seymour's, of course, not Hawkins's that parted company.]

A similar manœuvre, and yet another display of bravery by the Spanish ships' commanders even when they were so evidently beaten, was made on the following day which again resulted in no exchange of fire.

The Spanish council of war held on the same day as the English council, on Thursday 11 August, differed in atmosphere from the English meeting. Tension accompanied the discussions, as one might expect from officers commanding a fleet but recently delivered from disaster by an act of God. Sidonia expressed the view that the fleet should return to the Channel to execute the original orders. History records that this was the accepted decision of the council — when circumstances permitted such a move. But one senses that no one ever had the slightest intention of turning back. It would have been suicidal, and everyone knew it. Come what may, none of them had the slightest desire or intention of facing the English fleet again. They had contested command of the Channel for days on end with their own ships in fine fettle, well armed, tactically disciplined and in an almost impregnable formation: despite these advantages they had been defeated off Gravelines. How could they possibly face the same victorious fleet now, after having suffered a brutal pounding, after being shot through time and time again, as well as depleted in victuals, ammunition and morale? It was never really a matter for honest consideration.

The Spanish account of the battles carries an apologia to account for its refusal to return to the English Channel. The wind, it claimed, continued to blow from the south-west, and so 'without having found it possible to return to the English Channel; although we desired to return until today, 10 August, when having passed the isles to the north of Scotland, we are sailing for Spain . . .'

This statement deserves a little attention. It encourages the view that the wind prevented the Armada from turning about and sailing back through the North Sea and the Channel. This is not so, and it needs refuting. On Friday 12 August, we have already seen, the English fleet gave up the northerly pursuit and headed southward, making good progress. The Spaniards could have done the same. The fact is that no one had the heart to do so, and suffer all the consequences of meeting the English fleet in battle yet again.

The Armada sailed between the Orkneys and the Shetlands, headed for the storm-bound North Atlantic and thus entered upon the final chapter of disaster, perhaps more dangerous, perplexing and climactic than the battles fought so far in their forlorn and ill-fated campaign.

Before we consider these last desperate endeavours of the Armada we need to record one or two matters if only for the sake of chronology.

16.   The Queen at Tilbury

*I*T WAS SOME months earlier — on 6 April — that Sir John Norris was appointed to supervise the land forces of the maritime counties from Dorset round to Norfolk, which was regarded as the coastline most vulnerable to seaborne attack. He established his headquarters at Weymouth. The famous system of fire beacons was inaugurated, not only as a warning to the citizens of the approach of the Spanish Armada but also as a rallying point for militiamen. Forts, trenches, gun platforms, defensive walls, barriers, all these were constructed; and plans were set afoot for cutting and flooding roads, parties of horsemen were organized — horsemen armed with petronels (heavy pistols) were organized — to drive off cattle to prevent their capture and to adopt a scorched earth policy.

Orders were issued exactly as in 1940 that persons not in actual service were to 'stay put' and not to clog roads with refugees.

Two months after Norris's appointment no less than 27,000 infantrymen, 2,000 light cavalry and 500 heavy were ready in the south to oppose a landing.

In addition three further armies had been raised: in East Anglia the Earl of Huntingdon marshalled fourteen regiments each of 2,000 men; another of 2,000 foot and 200 horse were commanded by the Queen's middle-aged Court favourite Robert Dudley, Earl of Leicester, with the intention of covering the approaches to the Thames and London. To the west of the capital Lord Hunsdon commanded an army of — on paper, at least — 34,000 men to act as a mobile striking force with three aims: firstly, to be transported immediately once the landing-site had been determined; secondly, to protect the Queen; and thirdly, to be prepared to put down any rising of Catholic support in the city.

Leicester believed that the main thrust of an invasion by Parma would be into the east of the country, and he worked slavishly to prepare his troops for the oncoming assault.

More men, some of the best trained in England, were sent to reinforce Leicester as it indeed became apparent that the biggest threat of invasion lay in his theatre. On 24 July the Queen appointed him Lieutenant-General of the Queen's Armies and Companies. She wished to appoint him Lieutenant-General of all England and Ireland in the event of anything happening to her, but she met bone when she bit upon this mouthful, entailing as it did the delicate question of succession.

There was already worry in the Council about the Queen's person: if she were taken all would be lost. Some wanted her safely hidden well inland. She was equally determined to be at the heart of things should invasion come. Leicester caught her mood and imagination in a letter dated 6 August when he suggested that she should visit her house at Havering in Essex,

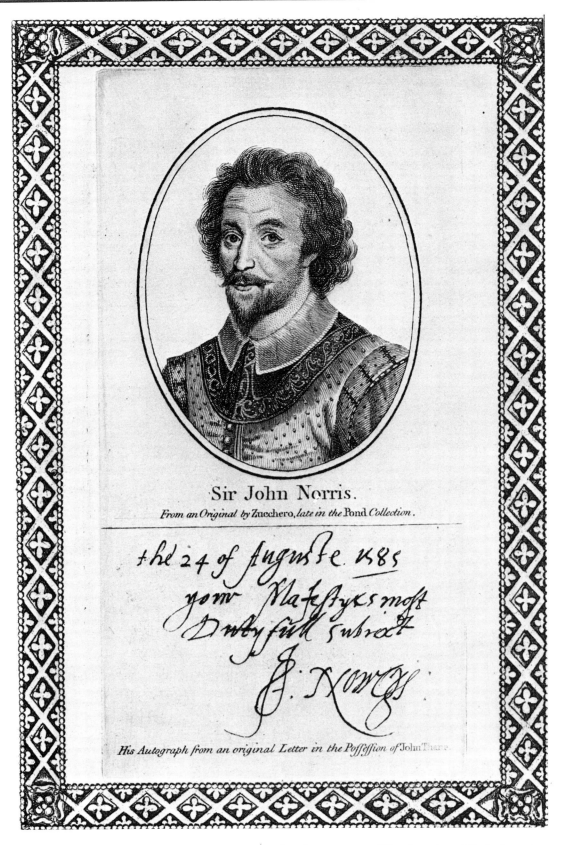

Sir John Norris.

From an Original by Zucchero, late in the Pond Collection.

His Autograph from an original Letter in the Possession of John Thane.

Sir John Norris, nicknamed 'Black Jack', was a hardened campaigner of Flanders whom Elizabeth put in command of all land troops in England. 'They all want the Spaniards to land,' he told the Queen. 'Every man is telling what feats he will do.'

and your army being about London, at Stratford, East Ham and the villages thereabout, shall be always not only a defence, but a ready supply to these counties, Essex and Kent, if need be. And in the meantime your Majesty, to comfort this army and people of these two counties, may — if it please you — spend two or three days to see both the camp and the forts. It is not fourteen miles at most from Havering and a very convenient place for your Majesty to lie by the way, and so rest you at camp. . . . You shall comfort not only these thousands, but many more that shall hear of it. And thus far and no further can I consent to venture your person. And by the Grace of God there can be no danger in this, though the enemy shall pass by your fleet. . . .

The Queen responded promptly, happy to accept the invitation, and even as she wrote the Armada lay in the Calais Roads.

Leicester worked at a feverish pace to bring some sort of order out of the chaos at Tilbury where 4,000 Essex foot soldiers were encamped with a few hundred horse and another 1,000 foot from London. It was the most advanced camp for the defence of the kingdom. The Giambelli chain barrier across the Thames had broken at the first flood tide. The barrier of boats intended for use as a carriageway for troops to cross from Tilbury Fort to Gravesend should Kent be the point of invasion (as, of course, it was intended to be) was not yet complete.

Across the Thames the Kentish camp was nothing more than a naval depot. London, with its walls, ditches and chains, was preparing with little sense of urgency for both invasion and siege.

On the morning of 18 August the Queen set out from St James's Palace for the river and there she entered the royal barge. It was a day of splendour and the river procession was a spectacle of colour and pageantry as the barge led a flotilla of small craft.

On arrival at Tilbury, Leicester received the Queen with a royal salute from the Block House, followed by the playing of fifes and drums, flags flying and the arrival of a coach 'ornamented with diamonds, emeralds and rubies in checkerwise . . .' escorted by 1,000 horse and 2,000 foot soldiers. She stayed overnight at an inn.

On the following day her inspection of the troops was a magnificent occasion. She told Leicester her pleasure was to see the troops *and to be seen*. She needed no guards, she explained, while among her own countrymen at arms.

Thus the royal party was formed: the Earl of Ormonde, carrying the Sword of State, led the procession, followed by two pages on foot dressed in white velvet, one carrying her decorated silver helmet on a cushion while the other led a horse. There followed the Queen on her docile white palfrey.

She wore white also, white velvet to make herself instantly recognizable to the troops, and a military look was given by the emblazoned and polished silver cuirass protecting her body. Her auburn wig was a-dazzle with pearls and diamonds and white feathery plumes. On her left rode her Master of Horse, Robert Devereux, Earl of Essex, a mere 21-year-old, strong, handsome, tall, the Queen's current Court favourite. He was indeed cousin of the Queen, and a Knight of the Garter.

On her other side rode Devereux's stepfather Leicester; decades earlier as Robert Dudley he had been the favourite, perhaps even the lover, of the Queen, but now he was grey-haired, bearded, tough, seasoned, still charming to and charmed by the Queen. And walking behind there came Sir John Norris.

The Queen addresses her troops at Tilbury

*I*N AUGUST Queen Elizabeth reviewed her troops at Tilbury, Essex. She rode on horseback, wearing a steel breastplate, her page bearing her helmet with white plumes. William Camden records: 'Her presence and her words fortified the courage of the captains and soldiers beyond all belief.' We now know that by this date the threat of invasion was largely past but this detracts in no way from the splendour of Elizabeth's oratory:

> My loving people, we have been persuaded by some that are careful of our safety, to take heed how we commit our self to armed multitudes, for fear of treachery; but I assure you, I do not desire to live to distrust my faithful and loving people. Let tyrants fear. I have always so behaved myself, that under God, I have placed my chieftest strength and safeguard in the loyal hearts and good will of my subjects, and therefore I am come amongst you, as you see, at this time, not for my recreation and disport, but being resolved, in the midst and heat of the battle, to live or die amongst you all; to lay down for my God, for my kingdom, and for my people, my honour and my blood, even in the dust. I know I have the body but of a weak and feeble woman, but I have the heart and stomach of a king, and of a king of England, too, and think it foul scorn that Parma or Spain or any prince of Europe should dare to invade the borders of my realm; to which, rather than any dishonour shall grow by me, I myself will take up arms, I myself will be general, Judge and rewarder of every one of your virtues in the field. I know, already for your forwardness, you have deserved rewards and crowns; and we do assure you on the word of a prince, they shall be duly paid to you. In the mean time, my Lieutenant General shall be in my stead, than whom never prince commanded more noble or worthy subject, not doubting but that by your obedience to my General, by your concord in the camp and your valour in the field, we shall shortly have a famous victory over those enemies of my God, of my kingdom, and of my people.

The picture in the possession of St Faith's Church, Gaywood, King's Lynn is painted on wood, forming part of an altar diptych. The Queen in the upper scene is thanking God for victory while the Armada is shown burning symbolically in the background below.

That was it. Four men and two boys to guard the Queen. It was audacious. It was amazing. It was adequate.

The party was received by roaring cheers that thundered around the camp as it ambled for all to see and to wonder at. This was their Queen, come among them at a time of danger — and they loved it. And they loved her. Like all great statesmen, she had a finely judged sense of showmanship about her.

She stayed overnight at a mansion four miles away and returned to the camp the following day. Again it was a day of matchless moments and unforgettable scenes and experiences. There were exercises, a review and a march past. In the multicoloured pavilion she met her army captains, who kissed her ring.

It was on this day she made her celebrated speech, as resounding as Churchill's in 1940 when daily expecting the invader. 'Let tyrants fear,' she warned, 'I have the body but of a weak and feeble woman, but I have the heart and stomach of a king — and of a king of England, too!' It was rousing, show-stopping oratory; her famous contemporary playwrights would have approved.

By Friday 19 August, when Elizabeth addressed her troops, the English ships had already secured to their moorings or anchorages in Harwich, Yarmouth and the Downs, having chased the Armada to the waters abreast of Scotland on its north-about flight. The danger was already virtually over. There still remained a slim chance that Sidonia might hazard a landing in Scotland, or perhaps Ireland, but the consensus was that the Armada would continue its flight with the intention of reaching Spanish ports.

A sad footnote to the brilliant occasion at the Tilbury camp deserves recording. Less than a month later, on 14 September, its instigator and organizer — 'your poor old servant' as he referred to himself familiarly to the Queen — died of the continual fever.

17. *Wrecks and losses*

WE LEFT THE Armada in uncomfortable straits, heading north, running before a steady NNE wind under moderate canvas and about to enter what was called the Norway Channel or Sea of Norway. Sidonia appreciated the enormity of the peril in undertaking the north-about passage, and the danger of the Armada's plight. That plight was perhaps considerably more dangerous than even Sidonia had visualized: even he could not have dreamed of the horrors yet to come.

His ships had suffered varying degrees of gunshot damage; some of the galleons, the main fighting ships, had been so heavily engaged in the battles as to be hardly seaworthy.

The gallant *San Martin* had been pierced through and through, her damage including a great 50 lb shot-hole just about the waterline. Despite the carpenter's efforts at plugging all the culverin and demi-culverin shot-holes in the flagship, she still leaked like a colander.

Recalde's *San Juan* was in a similar plight, and her mainmast was so damaged as to be unable to carry sail. Worse still, the gallant fighting admiral himself now lay in his cabin, dying slowly. Sidonia was in little better state, having been laid low by depression and by his gashed thigh, wounded in one of the battles.

This painting of the Spanish Armada off the Scottish coast depicts the situation when the Spaniards were preparing their ships for the forthcoming Atlantic experience, even to the extent of casting overboard the horses and ponies intended originally to draw the land artillery on English soil.

Sailing orders — 'For the return of the army into Spain' — given out by the Duke of Medina Sidonia to the fleet

THE COURSE that is first to be held is to the north-north-east until you be found under 61 degrees-and-a-half; and then to take great heed lest you fall upon the island of Ireland for the fear of the harm that may happen unto you on that coast. Then parting from those islands, and doubling the Cape in 60 degrees-and-a-half, you shall run west-south-west until you be found under 58 degrees, and from thence to the south-west to the height of 53 degrees; and then to the south-south-west making to the Cape Finisterre and so to procure your entrance to the Groyne (Corunna) or to Ferol or to any other port of the coast of Galicia.

This information was forwarded by Lord Deputy Fitzwilliam to Lord Burghley from Dublin Castle on 1 October 1588. The signal is said to have been recovered from one of the Spanish wrecks. It is evident that the course prescribed was not adhered to by many of the ships. Furthermore, there is a gross error of transcription in the last leg of the course. It should read SE and SSE and not SW and SSW. This may be due to the similarity of the words East and West in Spanish.

The Marquis of Peñafiel was so concerned about the state of his *San Marcos* that he had passed cables around her like binding faggots together to hold her strained timbers tight. It was clear that she would not survive the ordeal of a north-about voyage to Spain.

Two other things were casting an ominous shadow over the Armada. In addition to the worry about their structural damage, there were the ravages of sickness. Most ships were already creeping with vermin. The stench of sewage and putrescence pervaded everything: men were collapsing with disease and fever daily. When the Atlantic venture began it was estimated that there were already 3,000 men diseased with typhus, while another 1,000 lay seriously wounded from battle.

Victuals too were the other ever-constant worry. What was left that was edible became rationed. Everyone was to be treated the same, regardless of rank or status. Eight ounces of biscuit (hard tack), 1 pint of water and ½ pint of wine per man per day was the allocation. Much of the water was dank and undrinkable. Sometimes a cask would be opened to reveal a few inches of green slime: the use of green staves by the coopers had led to leakage. Drake's destruction of thousands of staves at Cadiz had its domino effect a year later off the coasts of Scotland and Ireland. In order to conserve water supplies the horses and mules aboard were sacrificed; they were jettisoned overboard like so much spoiled cargo. Why the animals were not slaughtered for fresh meat seems never to have been answered.

*   *   *

The course for Spain was determined at a war council meeting aboard the flagship. Sidonia was guided by a skilled navigator, because the instructions issued to the fleet 'For the Return of the Army Into Spain' can hardly be faulted. There had been four pilots aboard the *San Martin*, one of whom is known to have been English. Three of them died or were killed during the campaign, but the survivor's name is not known.

These Sailing Orders for the north-about route represented a distance of about 750 Spanish leagues (of 3½ nautical miles apiece) 'through stormy seas almost unknown to us', Calderon recorded.

Just how good these sailing orders were is proved by the *San Martin*'s survival. Battered though she was, and ill prepared for a voyage of such length, she escaped the worst of the storms, avoided all geographic hazards and reached Santander on 23 September. She had last sighted land in the Orkneys. Fortunate indeed were the ships which kept company with her, for they were saved.

In fact the fleet did not follow the proposed course at the outset; it took a short cut passing between the Orkneys and Fair Isle, fortunately without mishap except that the three great Levant carracks proved unable to combat the heavy seas rolling in from the Atlantic. They parted company on 14 August, heading eastward and evidently hopeful of making a landfall, but they were never heard of again. Fair Isle would in fact claim a victim — the *Gran Grifon*.

The cold, wet, misty weather and heavy sea conditions began to take an early toll. The *Gran Grifon* parted company with a number of ships of her squadron, leaving the main body of the fleet to plough westerly into heavy seas. It was beginning to look like every man for himself.

The cartographer's conception of Ireland in 1588. This map is taken from Abraham Ortelius's *Theatro de la Tierra Universal*. The Spanish captains were warned 'to take great heed lest you fall upon the island of Ireland . . .'

On Monday 25 August the bulk of the Armada was still acting more or less as an entity, progressing along the prescribed route and making two or perhaps two and a half knots. This fleet was about seventy miles north-west of Rockall when the first of a number of gales struck and scattered it. One galleon found herself as far north as latitude 63° and a great distance from the Faeroes, not so far from Iceland.

The fleet reassembled in part at least on the 27th — enough ships to justify a council of war, although who attended is not recorded. Recalde announced that Ireland offered salvation rather than damnation. His ship had suffered more than most and was in dire straits physically, but she was also lacking in victuals and water, and it was these shortages which were influencing decisions. Recalde was close to death, and this was generally known, yet still several captains rallied round him, such was his professional standing.

While Sidonia continued southward on the prescribed route Recalde altered course for north-west Ireland and collected a number of stragglers around him en route. All told he must have had upward of fifty ships now sailing in company.

Some commanders did not like what they saw of the Irish coast and managed to gain an offing and escape from the island. Others were compelled by necessity to bear down on the coastline to make a landfall. Twenty-six — or more — of these ships were to become wrecked in an episode of drama, horror, tragedy and indescribable inhumanity.

We need to turn back in time to follow the ill-fortune of some of these ships. Let it be said at the outset that the full story of what occurred in that dreadful autumn of 1588 can now never be known. Even contemporary documents cannot now help. The recurring problem of so many Spanish ships bearing the same or similar names led to errors which have never been resolved in the past, and which continue to baffle us today. Ships' names were incorrectly attributed, others were incorrectly translated, they were mistaken for similarly named vessels, wrongly identified, not identified at all . . . all these facts led to confusion and errors which have never been rectified.

At the latest count, perhaps twenty-six ships of the Armada became wrecked off the Irish coast during September and October 1588, two or three off Scotland, one off England and two off France, in addition to those that simply disappeared or foundered at sea.

Much work has been done on analysing the reasons for the great losses suffered by the Armada off the coast of Ireland, and it is possible to give some reasonable accounts of most of them. There are three fundamental reasons for this fearful disaster in Spanish naval history. Firstly, the ships were quite simply lost: goodness knows, this was easy enough, for without any means of determining longitude, and with no sighting of the sun for days and even weeks to give a latitude, positions were principally calculated by dead reckoning. The tireless Calderon in *San Salvador*, vice flagship of the urcas, has written: 'From 24 August to 4 September we sailed without knowing where we were, through constant fogs and storms.' Then quite suddenly ships came upon the coast of Ireland, the ships could not sail to windward and became embayed, totally unable to get off the coast.

Secondly, many of the severely battered ships were unseaworthy. They simply had to reach an anchorage, come what may, and the result was, more often than not, wrecking.

Thirdly, many crews were in such dire need of food and water that they anchored in bays in order to scavenge ashore, only to have their anchors drag and for the ships to

It was close to the rugged Malin Head that the *Trinidad Valencera* was wrecked, and Don Alonso de Luzon started his many adventures.

become wrecks. The loss of anchors at Calais took their toll yet again.

The earliest losses occurred in the first days of September. Some days before — about 23 August — a small group of ships fell astern of the rest of the Armada, losing touch with the main body somewhere north-west of Scotland. They were the *Gran Grifon*, *capitana* of the urcas (Don Juan Gomez de Medina), the *Castillo Negro*, the *Barca de Amburg*, and the enormous Levantine *Trinidad Valencera* of 1,100 tons with the *tercio* commander Don Alonso de Luzon aboard.

This small squadron beat against head winds which in time proved too strong for them. The *Barca de Amburg* was the first to succumb. She fired a distress shot on 1 September to announce that she was sinking. Three hundred and fifty men were rescued from her — in itself a remarkable achievement — and packed aboard the *Gran Grifon* and the *Trinidad Valencera*.

Two nights later the three remaining ships lost contact with each other, and nothing further was ever heard of the *Castillo Negro*. She foundered and was lost with all hands, presumably somewhere north of Ireland.

Twelve days later Don Alonso de Luzon sighted land and did his best to run the battered *Trinidad Valencera* ashore safely near the entrance of what turned out to be Lough Foyle in County Donegal. Most of the crew and soldiers plus a hundred survivors from the urca *Barca de Amburg* — a total of 450 men — managed to scramble ashore. That was the beginning of a story of tragedy and massacre from which no one emerged with credit save a Catholic bishop and a local clan chief.

Don Alonso de Luzon and a few others survived this fierce ordeal and lived to tell their remarkable story of endurance and survival. Don Alonso was the first to land, with five others in the only boat that remained, only to be attacked by two dozen or so 'savages' (as he called them) who robbed the Spaniards of a bag of 1,000 silver coins and a gold-embroidered cloak.

Despite this, Alonso managed to communicate with local villages, hire a boat from them and contrive to ferry off other survivors from the wreck. After two days the *Trinidad Valencera* broke up and scores of wounded and sick remaining aboard were drowned. The survivors bought ponies from the locals for slaughter, and ate them.

After some days of recuperation ashore Don Alonso assembled his men into some sort of marching order to visit a Catholic bishop named Cornelius in a castle a few miles away near Derry, but when in sight of the castle the Spaniards encountered a patrol of cavalry and infantry under the Queen's banner. It was commanded by an Irish major named Kelly and included two English captains and a number of Irish mercenaries.

The two opposing forces skirmished and parleyed for two days over a bog area. On Kelly's promises to Don Alonso for safe conduct for himself and his men to Dublin, and thence to the governor, the Spaniards surrendered. The Spanish officers and priests were then placed aside for safety by the Anglo-Irish force while they attacked the crew members with cavalry lances and arquebuses. Upward of 150 managed to escape across the bog and make their way to Bishop Cornelius's castle, where the bishop gave them refuge, and presently dispatched 100 men by boat to Scotland. The sick and wounded were tended till all were sent to a chief, Sorley Boy McDonnell of Dunluce Castle, a powerful defender of the Catholic faith who finally shipped them to Scotland.

By the time they reached Le Havre on Boxing Day the number had diminished to 32.

Meanwhile Don Alonso, the officers and priests and gentlemen, all with a potential hostage or ransom value, were force-marched to Drogheda, about a hundred miles away, where the survivors — several had died en route, including Don Alonso's brother — were interrogated by the English, and probably by the dreaded Sir William Fitzwilliam, Lord Deputy of Ireland, and Mary Stuart's former gaoler at Fotheringhay Castle.

The Don was transported under arrest to London and ransomed. He has the rare distinction of being one of only half a dozen or so Spanish officers who survived the experience of being wrecked on the coast of Ireland and making a home run to Spain.

*   *   *

The *Gran Grifon*'s perilous adventures in the saga of lost ships are the best preserved of all, having been meticulously recorded by a careful diarist.

The ship had taken a battering and had suffered seventy men killed at the hands of Drake's squadron in the battle of the Isle of Wight a month previously. Her weakened timbers were unable to withstand the Atlantic, and soon after she took aboard her share of the survivors from the *Barca de Amburg* her forward seams opened and she was only kept afloat by continual pumping and keeping wind and sea astern.

For three days she ran north-east before the wind on a course almost completely contrary to the one she wished to take. She sighted an island before the wind went round, and three days later she found herself well down the Irish coast. The weather moderated, and some of the leaks were repaired with hides and planks. But the crew became exhausted with the sheer expenditure of energy required to keep the ship afloat, and she headed back towards Scotland. On 27 September she was back in the vicinity of the Orkneys, where she had been six weeks earlier, but now both men and ship were at the end of their tether, barely able to anchor the ship in a bay where they made a landfall on the small rugged island of Fair Isle.

Tradition has it — and it is not recorded in the diary — that the *Gran Grifon* was swept by the tide against a cliff known as Stroms Hellier, lodging her main yard close to a ledge on the cliff-face. More than 300 mariners and soldiers scrambled along the yard and ledge to reach the safety of the shore.

Only a handful of families lived on the island — they were referred to as 'dirty savages' — but the two groups dwelt together harmoniously. By the time a boat arrived from the Scottish mainland to take the survivors off, they had eaten the island bare of food. Fifty of the Spaniards died there and were buried in what is known as Spanniarts Graves, while the rest reached Scotland in December. 'Thirteen score' arrived at

El Gran Grin was wrecked near here on Clare Island, County Mayo.

Anstruther, whence they were shipped to Edinburgh, where the 'young beardless men' were fêted by the Catholic community.

Edinburgh served for a time as a rallying point for survivors, and after eight months there the *Gran Grifon* refugees — now swollen to a group of about six hundred men — were transported to France en route to Spain, their year-long ordeal at an end.

*   *   *

If courage, defiance and resolution deserve reward, this — the *Girona*'s experience — must have been one of the most deserving of all.

The venture started with the great commander Don Alonso de Leiva in his ship the *Rata Coronada*. She had become detached from the main body of the fleet when off Rockall, well clear of Ireland. Sidonia had logged her departure with Recalde and fifteen other ships: 'We have counted ninety-five sail during the day . . . we are so short of provisions that if, for our sins, we are delayed, we shall all be irretrievably lost. There are now a great number of sick, and many die . . .'

Sidonia urged King Philip: 'Pray consider the distress of this Armada after such a terrible voyage . . .' But Sidonia's ill-luck dogged him even further. A few days later he recorded a severe storm — 'and we all expected to perish. I was then left with only

The *Juliana* was wrecked at Bloody Foreland in County Donegal.

eleven ships.' And at this stage even the dour, quietly courageous Duke, drained of resistance, succumbed to the fever and took to his bunk: the wonder of it is that he had resisted so long, and that he managed to survive to reach Spain.

Recalde and de Leiva sailed their ships to the Irish coast, the *Rata Coronada* making a good landfall between Achill Head and Erris Head in County Mayo. The *Rata* had in company with her the West Indiaman *Duquesa Santa Ana* which was to play an important part in the subsequent story. Both ships entered Blacksod Bay and de Leiva anchored (with his one anchor!) opposite Doona Castle, while Don Pedro Mares in the *Duquesa* also came to a single anchor in a little cove farther north in Elly Bay. It was 21 September 1588.

The *Rata* was a huge carrack, packed with people. She had 355 soldiers and 84 mariners aboard, together with 60-odd gentlemen and their servants. De Leiva, an aristocratic nobleman of courage — he had fought his ship bravely throughout the whole of the Channel pursuit — was attended by no less than thirty-six servants, while others had a dozen or more, so that in all about six hundred men were crammed into the ship.

When the *Rata* had anchored de Leiva sent fifteen of his men ashore in the only remaining boat. They were never seen again. Further trouble developed that night. Their choice of anchorage was poor. It was not protected like the *Duquesa*'s. When the

Typical of the Donegal coast. It was near here that three zabras were lost and the *Duquesa Santa Ana* was wrecked.

Sir Richard Bingham was notorious for his ruthless cruelty to Spanish prisoners in Ireland, where he ruled the western region of the island. He annihilated them by the sword, the axe and the rope — unless they were grand enough to ransom. Probably 6,000 Spaniards suffered brutal deaths in this phase of the Armada campaign.

incoming tide surged into the bay the only anchor dragged and the ship grounded hard on the shore. The ship was evacuated as quickly as possible; everyone scrambled to safety and a camp of sorts was established.

Two days later the whole company of 600 men marched round Blacksod Bay in as good order as the terrain would allow to join the *Duquesa*, whose complement had already been swollen with refugees from another sunken vessel. When they joined company de Leiva took command of the combined forces — now numbering about a thousand, a force to be reckoned with simply on weight of numbers had de Leiva wished to take on the Irish or even the English.

But it was thoughts of home that attracted the Spaniards, not an invasion. It was decided to repair the *Duquesa* as best they could then pack themselves into her. However, the repairs could only be of a temporary nature at best, and in the end it was agreed that the ship was insufficiently seaworthy to attempt the 800-mile voyage to Spain against prevailing winds. It was resolved instead to head for Scotland, only 200 miles away, with the prospect of favourable winds: furthermore, Scotland was neutral and could possibly provide means of transport to Spain.

Nearly one thousand men crammed like matches in a box into the ship. She edged cautiously out of Blacksod Bay to gain the open sea, headed northward past the string of shoals by Erris Head, across the broad sweep of Donegal Bay (which she cleared safely), and was still heading north-east when a series of westerly squalls struck her and drove her eastward towards the shore. With danger looming, she dropped an anchor, a cable parted and she was dashed on to the beach of a rocky inlet of what is now called Loughros Mor Bay.

In this incident de Leiva was injured in the leg and was unable to walk. Other casualties were suffered when the whole company — including the sick and wounded — scrambled out of the ship to the shore, bringing with them everything they could, arms, powder, shot, weapons, anything useful. The wreck was abandoned and the ship became a total wreck. Camp was established in a castle on an island in a lough.

Scouts were sent out to scavenge for food and water and they returned with news of three more ships at anchor about twenty miles south at Killybegs in Donegal Bay. In fact two of them had already been wrecked but the third, the *Girona*, rode at anchor tending her wounds and scars, cannibalizing the spares and timbers from the other two wrecks.

De Leiva marched his army of men across the rugged uplands and rough terrain to Killybegs and joined the *Girona* survivors, assuming command of a force of about 1,600 men. For three weeks they all laboured to feed themselves and repair the ship.

The galleasse *Girona* was totally incapable of accommodating so many men, so volunteers, the sick and the wounded were left ashore while 1,300 men embarked on 26 October for the attempt to reach Scotland. She weighed anchor at dawn, caught a fair south-west wind and rode steadily, despite the topweight of so many men, on an easterly course for Scotland. The following day the wind shifted north, increased in intensity and the seas rose.

The repaired rudder failed and on the afternoon of the 28th she wallowed helplessly in a stormy sea, her oars useless in such high seas. She was driven remorselessly towards the rocky northern coast of County Antrim.

Around midnight she struck the reef at the Giant's Causeway, her bottom was ripped open and she rolled over, spewing out her human cargo, and was then battered to pieces. Only nine men from the 1,300 aboard survived the ordeal. De Leiva perished.

Three hundred and eight years later the Belgian diver Robert Sténuit located the site of the wreck and recovered bronze guns, artefacts of copper, gold and silver, jewels, medallions, chains and rings. These now find a comfortable resting place in Belfast's Ulster Museum.

*   *   *

No account of the Armada's adventures in Ireland can ignore the best documented story of all. This was both written and experienced by Francisco de Cuellar, the Spanish captain sentenced by summary justice to be hanged, but spared into the custody of the Judge Advocate of the fleet, Martin de Aranda.

Cuellar's account was in the form of a letter written to a friend in 1589, and was only translated into English in late Victorian days. Its author was to prove in the days and weeks to come that he was one of life's survivors, as already proved by his reprieve from hanging at the yardarm and mere open arrest aboard the *Lavia*.

A few miles from Sligo in County Donegal there is a broad curve of fine white sandy beach with a rock at its eastern end named Carrick-na-spania (The Spaniard's Rock). It was into this bay on about 20 September 1588 that the *Lavia* sailed to seek sanctuary. She had in company two other ships, equally embattled and worn out.

All three ships anchored off the beach with its shallow, shelving shore, known as Streedagh Sound. It looked a peaceful haven, but its appearance was deceptive. Unseen by the Spaniards, Irish 'savages' lay in wait ashore. That was not all: the bay was a trap, and the chances of being able to beat out of it again were slim.

Four days after arriving a westerly gale brought huge Atlantic breakers 'running as high as Heaven' crashing into the bay, causing the anchors of the embayed ships to drag. All three grounded and were then relentlessly pounded to pieces in a matter of hours. The chance of rescue for everyone aboard was remote in the boiling surf, and it is thought that about 1,000 men died in this single incident.

A few weeks later, when Sir William Fitzwilliam rode along the strand at Streedagh, he was told that twelve or thirteen hundred bodies had been counted there.

Cuellar was on the *Lavia*'s poop deck with the Judge Advocate, and later he graphically described the scene:

> The waves and the storm were very great, and on the other hand the land and the shores were full of enemies who ran about dancing and jumping with delight at our misfortunes: and when anyone of our people reached the beach, two hundred savages and other enemies fell on him and stripped him of what he had on until he was left in his naked skin.

Cuellar watched the other two ships as they too were wrecked. There was the Levant ship *Santa Maria de Vison* of 666 tons with over 300 men aboard, commanded by Captain Juan de Bartolo, and a Castilian galleon of 530 tons, the *San Juan*, commanded by the nobleman Don Diego Enriquez, son of the Viceroy of Peru. His disappearance was described in Cuellar's account.

Enriquez, with three other grandees, got into the ship's boat, which was decked over. They went below, and were battened down. Then scores of men scrambled over the boat, seeing a chance of survival, but their press of bodies overturned it, and it floated ashore bottom up.

Cuellar himself got into the sea clutching a hatch cover, with the Judge Advocate who had filled his pockets with ducats or crown pieces. The Judge was washed off to his death. A beam of timber crushed Cuellar's legs, but somehow he managed to reach the shore and curiously he was left alone by the Irishmen. He crawled up the beach, seeing many of his countrymen 'stripped to the skin . . . shivering with the cold, which was severe. I stopped for the night in a deserted place, and lay down in great pain on some rushes.'

After surviving two other shipwrecks Don Alonso de Leiva perished with about 1,300 others when the *Girona* was wrecked at Lacada Point, County Antrim. Three hundred and eighty years later his cross of a Knight of Santiago was recovered from the sea-bed.

In the next few days Cuellar experienced an attack by an Englishman with a knife which cut a tendon in his leg, he survived stripping by the Irish, saw them robbing the rich and killing the poor, witnessed the English garrison's attack on the survivors, saw twelve Spaniards hung in the rafters of an abbey, and then, like a fairy tale, a beautiful young girl tended his wounds and fed him oatcakes and milk.

In advanced stages of collapse and surrendering to his fate he shuffled through the bogs and brambles wrapped in nothing but a rush mat and bracken. He was taken 'prisoner' by a blacksmith who put him to forced labour stoking a forge for a week before he managed to escape and befriend a priest who directed him to a castle called Rossclogher. There he sought sanctuary for three months with ten other Spanish soldiers that the Irish chief Dartry of the McClancy clan was glad to have about him in his forays against the English and other rival chiefs.

Incredibly, Cuellar and the ten soldiers in their rugged castle survived a seventeen-day siege against a great number of English soldiers under Sir William Fitzwilliam who had force-marched from Dublin to round up the hundreds of Spanish in the country. At one stage Cuellar was offered Dartry's sister in marriage as a mark of respect: the Spanish captain declined the offer.

Streedagh Strand near Donegal Bay witnessed the wrecking of three Armada vessels, all of which sank on the same day — 25 September 1588. They were the *Santa Maria de la Vison*, Don Diego de Enriquez's *San Juan* and *La Lavia*.

Cuellar escaped from Dartry's clutches and headed north with the intention of catching a boat to Scotland, an enterprise that was to last seven months while he trekked across the breadth of Ireland, begging for food and shelter as he went.

After twenty days he arrived at Sorley Boy's castle at Dunluce, but Sorley, the friend of the Spaniards, had been deposed by another chieftain by the name of O'Cahan who had joined forces with the English. At one stage Cuellar befriended the chief Brian O'Rourke, 'an important savage very friendly to the King of Spain'.

Cuellar had by now taken into his charge about seventy Armada survivors and he marched this group off to locate a Spanish ship reported to be anchored up the coast. He himself was unable to keep up with the group because of his leg injuries, and missed the ship. His good fortune held, he recorded, because it struck a reef and sank with all hands.

After a series of involvements with more beautiful peasant women, encounters with English soldiers and escapades in the mountains, he befriended a bishop friendly to the Spanish cause, who helped him escape by boat to Scotland.

Cuellar's adventures still had a long way to go. His stay in Scotland did not reach his expectations. The King of Scotland, he decided, was nothing less than a lackey of

Queen Elizabeth: 'the King of Scotland is a nobody; he does not move a step, or eat a mouthful that is not by order of the Queen of England.'

The onset of winter in 1589 brought a boat from the Duke of Parma in Flanders at the cost of five ducats a head. On approaching Dunkirk his vessel was attacked by the Dutch Sea Beggars, was grounded and became a wreck. Of the 270 Spaniards aboard only three survived, one of whom was the redoubtable Cuellar. It was almost exactly a year since his first shipwreck. He could reflect ruefully as he scrambled ashore in nothing but his shirt that it had been a year he would never forget.

Cuellar finally reached home and survived to write a narrative of his adventures.

*   *   *

It is appropriate now to relate the sad drama played out among the islands of Blasket Sound, off the Dingle peninsula in County Kerry. The principal dramatis personae were the gallant Recalde and Marcos Aramburu of the galleon *San Juan de Bautista*, vice flagship of the Castile Squadron.

Recalde deserves special mention, for he emerges from the thousands of Spaniards as the greatest hero of the Armada. He was sixty-two, a sick man, destined to die just four days after bringing his ship to the safety of Corunna. He had been in the forefront of every battle from Plymouth to Gravelines, and was a professional to his fingertips, loyal almost beyond the call of duty to the Duke, the King and his country.

Above all others he deserves an accolade for his personal conduct and his inspiration to everyone under his command. It is said that he died of shame and horror at the enormity of the defeat of the Armada. It is specially sad if this is so because no blame attaches to Recalde and the way he conducted his ship, his squadron and the fleet in his charge. He should not have lain down resigned, to die of shame, but have been honoured for acquitting himself in the best traditions of the sea, and retired to enjoy the fruits of his endeavours.

The story of the Blasket Sound incident began aboard Aramburu's *San Juan* at the end of August when in the vicinity of Rockall the ship lost touch with the main body of the Armada. Aramburu carried on struggling west and on 30 August reckoned he was in latitude 58°N and well clear of Ireland. He eased round to the south-west when the wind allowed and on 9 September managed to get a sun sight which placed the *San Juan* at 54°N, roughly on a line with Achill Head. His dead reckoning placed him about 420 miles west of the Irish coast.

The *San Juan* was in fact hundreds of miles from its dead reckoning position, just a few miles offshore; and two days later islands were sighted by lookouts. Aramburu realized the dangers, and for another two days beat out to the west to gain sea-room, but the galleon was forced to windward in the teeth of a 'most violent storm from the south' accompanied by a very wild sea and daytime darkness because of the black, lowering clouds.

On 15 September dawn brought calmer conditions, islands in sight and the mainland of Ireland to starboard. Two other ships were in sight. Aramburu recorded that they 'were beating to seaward and we recognized them now as the flagship of Juan Martinez de Recalde [the much-battered galleon *San Juan*] and a frigate. We turned towards the flagship . . . for we were totally ignorant of this coast and despaired of escaping it.'

The noble and distinguished Don Juan Martinez de Recalde.

Aramburu followed to windward of the admiral, cleared one of the islands 'and then altered course straight towards a part of the headland ahead of him . . . presuming he had some knowledge of this landfall'.

Aramburu was quite right: Recalde had in fact some knowledge of the coast. Eight years earlier he had commanded a squadron of ships which landed a force of Italian mercenaries at Smerwick less than ten miles from his present landfall. How he came to be here now has never been explained. He had last been heard of on 27 August, when he opted to head for a landfall in Ireland because of the poor state of his flagship. Sir Richard Bingham later claimed that Recalde's ship anchored in the mouth of the Shannon, but a survivor denied this and confirmed that the Blaskets was the first landfall.

Recalde rose from his bunk and saw the ships safely to an anchorage. He really did display local knowledge, for he chose the anchorage with masterly skill. Aramburu recorded that Recalde turned to what appeared to be a solid line of breakers marking a narrow channel between Great Blasket Island and the lesser islands to the north of it. The three ships entered in line ahead, through the breakers into a calm, safe anchorage off the north-eastern tip of Great Blasket Island. It is inconceivable that Recalde could have performed this manœuvre without having been there before. What was more, the anchorage gave shelter from every wind but one, the one which would enable them to clear the anchorage, gain sea-room and take them to Spain.

The ships remained at the anchorage for a week, able only to replenish water pipes from an island, for the mainland was patrolled by the English and Irish who had captured and tortured some parties sent ashore scavenging. The *San Juan* had some wine and bread aboard but 'no water but what they brought out of Spain, which stinketh marvellously, and the meat they cannot eat [it was so salty], the drought is so great'.

There was worse to come. On 21 September a severe westerly gale stormed in and the ships' anchors began to drag in the poor holding ground. The flagship was the first to suffer; she drifted down on to Aramburu's *San Juan* and smashed her stern lantern and mizzen riggings.

In the middle of all this storm and travail an extraordinarily eerie incident occurred. The *Santa Maria de la Rosa* (also known as the *Nuestra Señora de la Rosa*) entered the anchorage and fired a gun as if to draw attention to herself and her plight. She looked in a terrible state; her sails tattered and rent, with only the foresail in use. She fired another shot and came to a single anchor.

As soon as the tide turned the wind and tide combined and the *Santa Maria* dragged her anchor, struck a rock and began to sink. 'In an instant,' Aramburu records, 'we could see she was going down, trying to hoist her foresail. Then she sank, with all on board, not a man being saved . . .' Within two hours of making her appearance she was gone: and apart from the two gunshots it had all happened in unnatural and almost sepulchral silence.

In point of fact, one young man was saved, while hundreds of others perished. He was a lad named Giovanni. He reached shore safely, was captured by the Irish, was interrogated brutally, fabricated some stories of grandees aboard, and then suffered hanging like the rest of the captured refugees.

Later that same day two more ships of the Armada entered the anchorage. The first was a pinnace — not named — and the second was yet another *San Juan* — the

Scene of the wrecking of the *Nuestra Señora de la Rosa* and the 650-ton Castilian *San Juan Bautista*. Several other Spanish ships, including Recalde's, anchored here briefly in Blasket Sound before the last leg of their voyage to Spain.

Bautista of the Indian Guard, nominally a stout ship but now minus her mainmast and with her hull battered beyond all bounds of safety. Her captain realized she had no chance of reaching Spain and told Recalde so. The admiral agreed to transfer all personnel from the *Bautista* — the mariners to the flagship and the soldiers to the other ships. When this was done the *Bautista* was probably burnt and allowed to sink.

Aramburu's ship, now loaded with another hundred or so men, made an attempt to quit the anchorage, cutting her fouled anchor, then experiencing a nightmare of a voyage to clear the islands. By the following day she was clear and got away, clear away and back to Spain. Aramburu survived the experience and went on to enjoy a distinguished naval career.

Recalde's flagship escaped the Blaskets and also made good her flight to Spain. Recalde was languishing again in his bunk. He saw his beloved Spain again when the *San Juan* anchored at Corunna, but a few days later he died.

*   *   *

The Shannon estuary was kinder to the Armada than many other sites. Four large Spanish ships and three pinnaces entered its sheltered waters and anchored in Scattery Road. They all seemed to be in reasonably seaworthy condition except the galleon *San Marcos*, a valiant participant in most of the Armada battles. She was so heavily damaged that she was almost settling. Indeed, she was soon abandoned and set ablaze and allowed to sink. The rest of the ships sailed out on a north-easter on 11 September and there is every reason to believe they reached Spain.

A few miles away to the north two other ships met their doom. One was the *San Esteban* of Oquendo's squadron. She was wrecked off Doonbeg, many of her crew and

Armada treasures

THERE WERE NO 'treasure ships' in the Armada in the sense that there were no ships laden with chests of treasure such as jewellery, coins, gems, gold and silver. Treasure of a sort existed in terms of personal jewellery, gold chains, rings, ship's gold plate and ornaments, silver candlesticks and artefacts, but all this was rather inconsequential.

After all, why should there have been hoards of treasure? The Armada was a battle fleet intent on invasion, plunder and the spoils of war: there was no reason to saddle the fleet with chests of treasure except for the thousands of ducats necessary to pay the soldiery and mariners in the fleet. This was thought to have amounted to about 600,000 ducats — about £150,000 — a vast sum, it is true, but it was distributed throughout most of the flagships of the Armada, perhaps ten ships or more.

There were no doubt other treasures of a sort for use as bribes for James VI and for influential English Catholics and Quislings as an inducement to co-operation, but nothing of the scale you would expect to find aboard a true treasure ship, let alone the reported '30,000,000 of money' allegedly stowed away aboard the 'Tobermory treasure ship'.

There was no figure given for the consignment of coinage in this alleged 30,000,000 of money, which is typical of the stories surrounding this most legendary, most mysterious, most written about and debated of all the Armada wrecks.

One of the first references appeared in 1641, just fifty-three years after the event; by 1677 it was accorded this 30,000,000 figure, plus other elaborate detail. The 'treasure ship' was named as the *Florida*, the *almirante* or vice-flagship of the fleet. Neither of these 'facts' were correct. The *almirante* was Recalde's royal Portuguese galleon *San Juan*, whose progress home we have already followed, while the *Flordia* was not a name on the Armada list at all. *Florentia* existed, and soon this name became adopted for the story — which is also curious, because she can be shown to have arrived back in Spain safely.

In point of fact the Tobermory wreck was the *San Juan de Sicilia*, a ship of the Levantine squadron from Ragusa (present-day Dubrovnik), commanded by Don Diego Tellez Henriquez. She was not a flagship, and therefore was unlikely to have carried even a share of the ducats for wages.

Indeed, the artefacts she has disgorged — anchors, guns, plates and ornaments — have lacked the value and sparkle of precious metal treasure trove.

Other wrecks have been located and 'worked' with more rewarding success. The Belgian diver Robert Sténuit discovered the wreck of the *Girona* in 1967 and recovered a beautiful collection of hundreds of items, including Renaissance jewellery plus more than a thousand gold and silver coins. One poignant item was a gold ring decorated with a hand holding a heart and inscribed '*No tengo mas que dar te*' — 'I have nothing more to give thee'. Another gold ring inscribed 'Madame de Champagney 1524' was proof that the wreck was the *Girona*: the ring belonged to the grandson Don Tomas Perrenoto known to have perished in the ship.

Other wrecks which have been discovered are the *Santa Maria de la Rosa*, lost in Blasket Sound with only one survivor; the *Gran Grifon*, wrecked on Fair Isle; and *La Trinidad Valencera*, driven ashore on a reef near Lough Foyle: all have given up a host of interesting guns and artefacts, and a wealth of knowledge — treasure of a kind — but not one of them by any stretch of the imagination can be described as a treasure ship.

Philip II is readily recognized on this gold coin recovered from the *Girona*, together with lengths of gold chain and the gold salamander pendant encrusted with rubies.

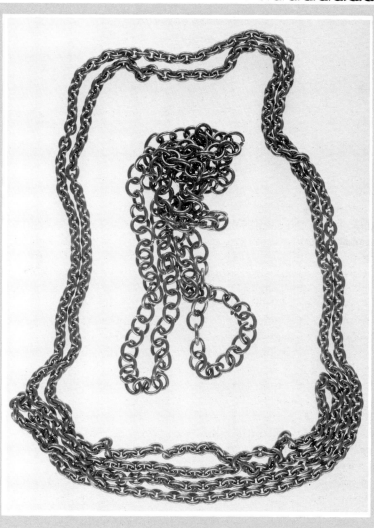

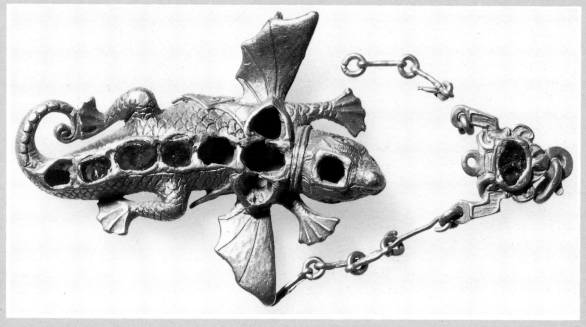

soldiers were drowned and those who managed to scramble ashore were rounded up and summarily executed by the Sheriff of Clare.

A similar fate was meted out to those who survived the wrecking nearby under Tromra Castle at Milltown — it might have been the *Anunciada* — and their bones, like those of their compatriots from the *San Esteban*, were buried at Spanish Point near Milltown Malbay.

It was from this hostile coast that the *Zuñiga* managed to set out on a voyage as remarkable as any to be found in Victorian books of boys' yarns.

The galleasse *Zuñiga* has no tonnage recorded for her, and her captain is not identified. That is a pity because he was a most resourceful officer who showed great steadfastness in his ordeals.

The *Zuñiga* had serious rudder trouble and was only saved from almost certain shipwreck by the use of her oars to find safe anchorage off Liscanor Castle. During the north-easter of 11 September she managed to clear the land and steered for Spain. When she entered the mouth of the Channel she resigned herself to her fate during the westerly which blew up — she was, after all attempts at repair, rudderless and virtually without victuals. She arrived at Le Havre in a sinking condition to join the *Santa Ana*, which had been there now for several weeks.

Stores and spares from Moncada's galleasse *San Lorenzo*, beached after the Calais fireship attack, were scrounged to help repair her. Fifty-six men were also brought from Calais to the *Zuñiga*, together with another twenty refugees from Ireland, described as 'naked'.

It was mid-April 1589 before she was seaworthy and cleared Le Havre, only to run into a storm which almost battered her back to the condition in which she had arrived months before. No sooner had she clawed her way back to port than the dispirited crew mutinied, and refused to take her out again. So immobile did she become that by mid-July she had become silted up at her moorings. Interest in her seems to have flagged at this point, for nothing more is heard of her, no record has survived as to her fate. It is thought likely that she finally made a home port, so determined was her captain.

*   *   *

Another Armada loss deserves passing mention. The 581-ton urca *San Pedro Mayor*, serving as a hospital ship ('there was put into her as much drugs and pothecary stuff as came to 6,000 ducats'), had lived through the horrors of the Atlantic storms, had even made a landfall in Dingle Bay when Recalde's *San Juan* was there, and — like the admiral — had managed to beat out to sea again. She seemed to give up when on the threshold of safety. Despairing of ever seeing Spain again, and with his ship packed with dead and dying men, short of food and water, the captain decided to head into the Channel and seek a French port.

The gods were not smiling on the *San Pedro Mayor*: soon after entering the Channel she wrecked herself on the Bolt Tail by Bigbury Bay in Devon. She was 'spoiled' — pillaged — by the locals, and the Spaniards were taken prisoner.

Perhaps it was fitting that it was a Devon harbour which received the first Spanish ships to be lost to the Armada in the Channel — the splendid *Rosario* in far-off July and symbolically still, this the last one, the bedraggled urca *San Pedro Mayor*, lying wrecked and pillaged on the Bolt Tail.

18. Postscript

WHEN MEDINA SIDONIA'S flagship sighted Spain on 21 September the Duke's pilot thought it was Corunna but in fact he was a couple of hundred miles out, an understandable error after a voyage of the dimensions experienced by the Armada. It was Santander that everyone was gazing at. Since the wind had dropped away and the *San Martin* was in danger of drifting ashore, a gun was fired to summon boats to her assistance to tow her into harbour.

The ailing Duke, broken in body and spirit, was ferried ashore in a boat, leaving Diego Flores to bring the once splendid flagship into harbour. Sidonia was a very sick man, having suffered fever and other illnesses for more than three weeks.

On 23 September he wrote a long letter to the King explaining his incapacities and inabilities to face the accumulation of problems.

The troubles and miseries we have suffered cannot be described to your Majesty. They have been worse than have ever been seen in any voyage before. On board some of the ships that are in [about 20 had made port or were lying off shore at this date] there has not been a drop of water to drink for a fortnight. On my own ship 180 men have died of sickness . . . and all the rest of the people on board are ill, many of typhus and other infectious diseases . . . Great as the miseries have been, we are worse off than before for . . . the little biscuit and wine we have left will be finished in a week. We are therefore in a wretched state and I implore your Majesty to send some money quickly to buy necessities . . . Everything is in disorder . . . I am in no condition to attend to business.

Sidonia sent Bobadilla with this letter and another one to the King in the Escorial to give an eye-witness account of the campaign. Sidonia begged to be relieved of his command and the King treated the good Duke compassionately — as well he might, for Sidonia had performed his duties with devout faith in his God, with deep loyalty to his King and country, bravely and courageously. He was a man to be treated with compassion and kindness, and the King to his credit did just that. Sidonia was released. He left Santander on 10 October to travel the gruelling whole length of the country to his home at Sanlucar near Cadiz in a curtained horse litter.

His journey home across Castile, one authority reports, was 'a procession of ignominy'. The street boys in Salamanca and Medina del Campo pelted him with stones. The litter avoided noblemen's homes, most of which would be in mourning for the loss of a son or husband — he would not be welcome there. Once home at Sanlucar he recovered his bodily health and was soon riding through the orange groves in the warm spring, though he remained scarred in spirit for the rest of his life, some thirty years.

The country sought a scapegoat, and logically Sidonia was the choice. The army, the senior service at the time, as represented by Bobadilla, blamed the navy for its inability to beat the Queen's Navy Royal, and this stigma lasted for a long time. Those in the Armada knew better where to lay the blame.

The Duke of Parma had let down Sidonia left, right and centre. His failure to communicate with him in the days after the departure from Corunna right up to his appearance in the Calais anchorage was shameful, and must have kept the admiral in an agonized frame of mind for weeks on end. His failure to have ready a flotilla of small boats was a disgrace.

Even when the truth began to dawn, and realization came of Parma's failure in the crucial phase of the Armada's Channel venture, the latter resorted to lies to cover his shortcomings.

In truth the greatest blame lay not with Sidonia or Parma, with God, the elements, the English ships and commanders who inflicted the defeat of the Spanish Armada, but on the man besotted with the need to bring the heretical English and their Queen back into the great Catholic fold, King Philip II himself.

Even Philip entertained some doubts as the horrific losses of the north-about route mounted day after day, as reports from his ambassador-spy Mendoza in Paris corrected his earlier optimistic reports of euphoric victory to reports excusing the losses. Philip had never been greatly impressed by Mendoza's reports, and he saw through a good many of them, annotating them caustically in the margin.

The King's reaction was calm and dispassionate to the reports as they accumulated, telling a story of mounting disaster as the ragged remnants of his once proud Armada limped into harbour.

Hakluyt later wrote with a degree of artistic licence: 'The magnificent, huge and mighty fleet of the Spaniards vanished into smoake: to the great confusion and discouragement of the authors thereof.'

Another quotation, unmatched for its callous insensitivity, came from the King himself: 'I give thanks to God by whose hand I have been so endowed that I can put to sea another fleet as great as this we have lost whenever I choose. It does not matter if a stream is sometimes choked, as long as the source flows freely.'

*   *   *

In England realization that the landings in Ireland were not a concerted invasion attempt dawned slowly over a period of some weeks, as did the knowledge that a great and glorious victory had been gained. Spontaneous celebrations spread over the land, and balladeers had a field day. Silver coins were struck depicting the Queen's head, with a Latin phrase referring to the storms and winds: *Flavit deus et dissipati sunt* (God blew and they were scattered.)

Queen Elizabeth used the same sort of allusion in a Song of Thanksgiving which she wrote and which was set to music specially composed for the occasion: it was sung at a service at St Paul's Cathedral* in December. The service served a dual purpose: a lavish thanksgiving for the victory over the Armada and a celebration of the thirtieth anniversary of Elizabeth's coronation.

Elizabeth, with more than a touch of showmanship, moved through London in a canopied chariot drawn by white-caparisoned horses and escorted on either side by mounted attendants, noblemen, courtiers, gentlemen. The citizens of London loved it all; their drab lives were brightened and enlivened by their Queen who brought a touch

* Some say at Temple Bar in Fleet Street.

This medallion was struck to commemorate the defeat of the Spanish Armada. It is 51mm in diameter. It bears the Latin legend: 'God blew and they were scattered.'

of magic into their existence. The streets were en fête, with colourful banners, flags and bunting giving a warm holiday atmosphere despite the cold weather.

Look and bow down thine ear, oh Lord,
From thy bright sphere behold and see
Thy handmaid and thy handiwork
Among my priests offering to thee
Zeal for thy incense reaching to the skies
My self and sceptre sacrifice

My soul ascended to holy place.
Ascribe him strength and sing Him praise,
For He refraineth Princes' spirits
And hath done wonders in my days.
He made the winds and waters rise
To scatter all mine enemies.

This Joseph's lord and Israel's god,
The fiery pillar and day's cloud,
That saved his saints from wicked men
And drenched the honour of the proud,
And hath preserved in tender love
The spirit of his Turtle dove.

It is unfortunate that the Latin tag on the coin and Elizabeth's own verses perpetuate the belief that God and the winds had more to do with the defeat of the Armada than did the skill of England's seamen, their ships and guns.

It was to take years, even a generation or more, to appreciate the real magnitude of the English victory. It was a watershed in the story of England, the birth of a new patriotism, and the beginning of a new belief in the Navy, a belief that was to grow in intensity in future centuries. Although tested time and time again in the furnace of battle, that Navy was never to be found wanting. Three and a half centuries after the Armada Admiral Sir Andrew B. Cunningham was considering whether to send in the Navy against fearful air attacks for another day's rescue operation of troops from the embattled island of Crete: 'It takes three years to build a destroyer and three hundred to build a reputation. We cannot let the Army down. Send in the Navy!' After the defeat of the Armada the destiny of England rested confidently with the sea and the Navy.

Supplement 1
The opposing fleets

These lists and figures are based upon Professor Sir John Laughton's, W. Laird Clowes's and Fernandez Duro's works listed in Supplement 4. They have been up-dated and an attempt has been made to rectify some of their more blatant discrepancies: Laughton confesses they are 'in a hopeless muddle'. Many other arithmetical errors still exist and probably now cannot be reconciled. Few sources agree in many details but none disputes the magnitude of the enterprise which the figures, even with their relatively minor errors, present.

In the case of the Spanish ships it was thought inappropriate in this volume to give all the Spanish officers' names: they can be referred to in Duro's study of the campaign; but some officers' names are given where there is some relevance to the text.

Summaries of the two fleets

ENGLISH

Divisions	Ships	Tonnage	Total Men
Her Majesty's Ships	34	12,320	6,269
Merchant ships under Sir Francis Drake	34	5,170	2,394
Ships paid by the City of London	30	4,530	2,180
Merchant ships under the Lord High Admiral:			
For about 8 weeks	8	1,390	540
For the whole campaign	10	756	221
Victuallers	15		810
Coasters under the Lord High Admiral	20	1,931	993
Coasters under Lord Henry Seymour	23	2,243	1,090
Voluntary ships	23	1,806	1,044
TOTALS	197	30,146	15,541

SPANISH

Divisions	Ships	Tonnage	Total Men
Portuguese Squadron	12	7,737	4,623
Biscayan Squadron	14	6,543	2,692
Castilian Galleons	16	8,714	4,147
Andalusian Squadron	11	8,292	3,105
Guipuzcoan Squadron	12	6,691	2,600
	(2)	unknown	unknown
Levantine Squadron	10	8,754	3,637
Hulks or Urcas	23	10,251	3,729
Pataches & Zabras (Pinnaces)	22	1,426	1,168
Galleasses of Naples (incl. 1,200 rowers)	4		2,541
Galleys of Portugal (incl. 880 rowers)	4		1,250
TOTALS	128 (130)	58,408	29,492

In the list of English ships, the ° denotes the date of modernization of the ship.

Other explanations are:

** = *Capitana general* = C-in-C's flagship
* = *Capitana* = admiral's flagship
\+ = *Almirante* = vice admiral or second in command
N.S. = *Nuestra Señora*
S.M. = *Santa Maria*
Tercio = A brigade of about 3,000 men
Maestro de campo = MC = Officer commanding a *tercio*

THE ENGLISH FLEET: Commander-in-Chief Charles, Lord Howard of Effingham, Lord High Admiral.

Queen's Ships	Built or or Modern-ized	Tons	Men				Guns
			Mariners	Gunners	Soldiers	Total	Guns
1 *Ark Royal*	1587	800	270	34	126	430	55
2 *Elizabeth Bonaventure*	1581°	600	150	24	76	250	47
3 *Rainbow*	1586	500	150	24	76	250	54
4 *Golden Lion*	1582°	500	150	24	76	250	38
5 *White Bear*	1563	1,000	300	40	150	490	40
6 *Vanguard*	1586	500	150	24	76	250	54
7 *Revenge*	1577	500	150	24	76	250	43
8 *Elizabeth Jonas*	1559	900	300	40	150	490	56
9 *Victory*	1586°	800	270	34	126	430	42
10 *Antelope*	1581°	400	120	20	30	170	30
11 *Triumph*	1561	1,100	300	40	160	500	42
12 *Dreadnought*	1573	400	130	20	40	190	32
13 *Mary Rose*	1556	600	150	24	76	250	36
14 *Nonpareil*	1584°	500	150	24	76	250	38
15 *Hope*	1584°	600	160	25	85	270	48
16 *Bonavolia*, galley	1584					250	
17 *Swiftsure*	1573	400	120	20	40	180	42
18 *Swallow*	1573°	360	110	20	20	150	8
19 *Foresight*	1570	300	110	20	20	150	37
20 *Aid*	1562	250	90	16	14	120	18
21 *Bull*	1570°	200	80	12	8	100	
22 *Tiger*	1570°	200	80	12	8	100	30
23 *Tramontana*	1586	150	55	8	7	70	21
24 *Scout*	1577	120	55	8	7	70	10
25 *Achates*	1573	100	45	8	7	60	13
26 *Charles*	1586	70	32	6	7	45	16
27 *Moon*	1586	60	30	5	5	40	9
28 *Advice*	1586	50	30	5	5	40	9
29 *Merlin*	1579	50	26	5	4	35	7
30 *Spy*	1586	50	30	5	5	40	9
31 *Sun*	1586	40	24	4	2	30	5
32 *Cygnet*	1585	30				20	3
33 *Brigandine*	1583	90				35	
34 *George*, hoy		100				24	
34 ships		12,320	3,817	539	1,558	6,269	894

Officers, Noblemen, Volunteers and others aboard the Queen's Ships

1 Lord Howard of Effingham,
Lord High Admiral.
Sir Edward Hoby, Secretary
Thomas Gray, Master
Amyas Preston, Lieutenant
Morgan, Captain of soldiers
Samuel Clerke, Master gunner
John Wright, Boatswain
Richard Leveson, Volunteer
Thomas Gerard, Volunteer
William Harvey, Volunteer
John Chidley, Volunteer
Thomas Vavasour, Volunteer
Francis Burnell, Admiral's man
Newton, Admiral's man
2 Earl of Cumberland
George Raymond, Captain
James Sewell, Master
Tristram Searche, Boatswain
Robert Carey, Volunteer
3 Lord Henry Seymour
Richard Laine, Boatswain
Sir Charles Blunt, Volunteer
Francis Carey, Volunteer
Brute Brown, Volunteer
4 Lord Thomas Howard
5 Lord Sheffield
H. Sheffield, Lieutenant
? Richard Poulter, Master
Robert Baxter, Boatswain
6 Sir William Wynter
John Wynter, Lieutenant

7 Sir Francis Drake, Vice Admiral
John Gray, Master
Jonas Bodenham, Lieutenant
? Martin Jeffrey, Purser
Richard Derrick, Boatswain
Nicholas Oseley, Volunteer
8 Sir Robert Southwell
? John Austyne, Master
John Woodroffe, Boatswain
9 Sir John Hawkins, Rear Admiral
? Barker, Master
John Edmonds, Boatswain
10 Sir Henry Palmer
11 Sir Martin Frobisher
? Eliot, Lieutenant
Simon Fernandez, Boatswain
12 Sir George Beeston
? Harvey, Boatswain
13 Edward Fenton
Lawrence Cleer, Boatswain
Henry Whyte, Volunteer
14 Thomas Fenner
L___ C____, Boatswain
15 Robert Crosse
? John Sampson, Master
John Vayle, Boatswain
16 William Borough
17 Edward Fenner
William Mychell, Boatswain
18 Richard Hawkins
John Borman, Boatswain
19 Christopher Baker
James Andrews, Boatswain

20 William Fenner
? Richard Blucke, Purser
John Russell, Boatswain
21 Jeremy Turner
Myhyll Pyrkyne, Boatswain
22 John Bostocke
23 Luke Ward
John Pratte, Boatswain
24 Henry Ashley
25 Gregory Riggs
26 John Roberts
William Monson, Volunteer
27 Alexander Clifford
28 John Harris
Tristram George, Boatswain
28 Walter Gower
30 Ambrose Ward
31 Richard Buckley, Master
32 John Sheriff, Master
George Wilkynson, Boatswain
33 Thomas Scott
34 Richard Hodges, Master

Merchant ships appointed to serve westward under Sir Francis Drake

Ship	Tons	Men	Captain, Officer & Remarks
35 *Galleon Leicester*	400	160	George Fenner
36 *Merchant Royal*	400	160	Robert Flicke. Levant Company ship
37 *Edward Bonaventure*	300	120	James Lancaster. Levant Company ship: first to sail to India and back 1591–3
38 *Roebuck*	300	120	Jacob Whiddon. Raleigh's ship.
39 *Golden Noble*	250	110	Adam Seager
40 *Griffin*	200	100	William Hawkins: Samuel Norfolk, Master

Ship	Tons	Men	Captain, Officer & Remarks
41 *Minion*	200	80	William Wynter: Nicholas Maunder, Master
42 *Bark Talbot*	200	90	Henry Whyte: John Hampton, Master. Calais fireship.
43 *Thomas Drake*	200	80	Henry Spindelow: John Tranton, Master. Drake's ship and Calais fireship.
44 *Spark*	200	90	William Spark: Richard Loarie, Master
45 *Hopewell*	200	100	John Marchant
46 *Galleon Dudley*	250	96	James Erisey. Of Barnstaple.
47 *Virgin God Save Her*	200	70	John Grenville. Sir Richard Grenville's ship.
48 *Hope Hawkins*	200	80	John Rivers: Roger Haley, Master. Owned by William Hart. Calais fireship. A Plymouth ship.
49 *Bark Bond*	150	70	William Poole: John Rock, Master. Owned by Sir John Hawkins. Calais fireship
50 *Bark Bonner*	150	70	Charles Caesar: William Loggin, Master
51 *Bark Hawkins*	150	70	—— Prideaux: William Snell, Master
52 *Unity*	80	40	Humphrey Sydenham: William Cornish, Master.
53 *Elizabeth Drake*	60	30	Thomas Cely: Thomas Clerke, Master. Of Lyme.
54 *Bark Buggins*	80	50	John Langford
55 *Elizabeth Founes*	80	50	Roger Grant
56 *Bark St Leger*	160	80	John St Leger
57 *Bark Manington*	160	80	Ambrose Manington
58 *Heartsease*		24	Hannibal Sharpham
59 *Golden Hind*	50	30	Thomas Fleming. Not Drake's ship. First to sight the Armada.
60 *Makeshift*	60	40	Piers Lemon
61 *Diamond*	60	40	Robert Holland. Of Dartmouth
62 *Speedwell*	60	14	Hugh Hardinge, Master
63 *Bear Yonge*	140	70	John Yonge. Of Lyme. Calais fireship.
64 *Chance*	60	40	James Founes: Hugh Cornish, Master
65 *Delight*	50	40	William Coxe. Sir William Wynter's ship
66 *Nightingale*	40	30	John Grisling: Habbakuk Percy, Master
67 Small Caravel	30	20	
68 *Yonge,* flyboat	50	50	Nicholas Webb
34 ships	5,170	2,394	

Ships fitted out and paid for by the City of London

Ship		Tons	Men	Captain, Officer & Remarks
69	Hercules	300	120	George Barne
70	Toby	250	100	Robert Barrett
71	Mayflower	200	90	Edward Bancks
72	Minion	200	90	John Dale
73	Royal Defence	160	80	John Chester
74	Ascension	200	100	John Bacon
75	Gift of God	180	80	Thomas Luntlowe
76	Primrose	200	90	Robert Bringborne
77	Margaret and John	200	90	John Fisher: John Nash, Master: Richard Tomson, Lieutenant: John Watts, Volunteer, who owned her. He was knighted 1603 and became Lord Mayor of London in 1606.
78	Golden Lion	140	70	Robert Wilcox
79	Diana	80	40	Edward Cock
80	Bark Burr	160	70	John Serocold
81	Tiger	200	90	William Caesar
82	Brave	160	70	William Furthow
83	Red Lion	200	90	Jervis Wilde
84	Centurion	250	100	Samuel Foxcraft
85	Passport	80	40	Christopher Colthurst
86	Moonshine	60	30	John Brough
87	Thomas Bonaventure	140	70	William Aldridge. Levant Company ship
88	Release	60	30	John King
89	George Noble	120	80	Henry Bellingham: Richard Harper, Master
90	Anthony	100	60	George Harper: Richard Dove, Master
91	Toby	120	70	Christopher Pigot: Robert Cuttle, Master
92	Salamander	110	60	——Damford: William Goodlad, Master. Of Leigh.
93	Rose Lion	100	50	Bartholomew Acton: Robert Duke, Master. Of Leigh.
94	Antelope	120	60	——Denison: Abraham Bonner, Master.
95	Jewel	110	60	——Rowell: Henry Rawlyn, Master. Of Leigh.
96	Pansy	100	70	William Butler, Master
97	Prudence	120	60	Richard Chester, Master. Of Leigh.
98	Dolphin	110	70	William Hare, Master. Of Leigh.
30 ships		4,530	2,180	

These London ships were armed with sakers, minions, falcons and fowlers, while Nos. 89–98 carried a variety of calivers and muskets, too.

Merchant Ships which served under the Lord High Admiral, paid for by the Queen

Ship		Tons	Men	Captain, Officer & Remarks
99	*Susan Parnell*	220	80	Nicholas Gorges. Levant Company ship
100	*Violet*	220	60	Martin Hawkes
101	*Solomon*	170	80	Edmund Musgrave
102	*Anne Frances*	180	70	Charles Lister
103	*George Bonaventure*	200	90	Eleazer Hickman. Levant Company ship
104	*Jane Bonaventure*	100	50	Thomas Hallwood
105	*Vineyard*	160	60	Benjamin Cooke
106	*Samuel*	140	50	John Vassall
8 ships		1,390	540	

The above served for about 8 weeks; the following served the whole time:

		Tons	Men	Captain, Officer & Remarks
107	*White Lion*	140	50	Charles Howard
108	*Disdain*	80	45	Jonas Bradbury
109	*Lark*	50	20	Thomas Chichester
110	*Edward*	186	30	William Pierce. Owned by Edward Peek. Of Maldon.
111	*Marigold*	30	12	William Newton, Master
112	*Black Dog*	20	10	John Davis, Master
113	*Katharine*	20	10	
114	*Fancy*	50	20	John Paul, Master
115	*Pippin*	20	8	
116	*Nightingale*	160	16	John Doate, Master
10 ships		756	221	

Ships which transported victuals westward

		Tonnages not known	Men	Captain, Officer & Remarks
117	*Mary Rose*		70	Francis Burnell: William Parker, Master
118	*Elizabeth Bonaventure*		60	Richard Start
119	*Pelican*		50	John Clarke
120	*Hope*		40	John Skinner
121	*Unity*		40	John Moore
122	*Pearl*		50	Lawrence Moore
123	*Elizabeth*		60	William Bower. Of Leigh
124	*John*		70	Richard Rose. Of London
125	*? Bearsabe*		60	Edward Bryan
126	*Marigold*		50	Robert Bowers
127	*White Hind*		40	Richard Browne
128	*Gift of God*		40	Robert Harrison
129	*Jonas*		50	Edward Bell
130	*Solomon*		60	George Street. Of Aldborough
131	*Richard Duffield*		70	William Adams
15 ships			810	

Coasters serving the Lord High Admiral and paid for by the Queen

Ship		Tons	Men	Captain, Officer & Remarks
132	Bark Webb	80	50	
133	John Trelawney	150	30	Thomas Meek
134	Hart	60	70	James Houghton or Houston: Thomas Anthony, Master. Of Dartmouth.
135	Bark Potts	180	80	Anthony Potts
136	Little John	40	20	Laurence Clayton
137	Bartholomew	130	70	Nicholas Wright. Of Topsham.
138	Rose	110	50	Thomas Sandye. Of Topsham
139	Gift	25	20	Of Topsham.
140	Jacob	90	50	Of Lyme
141	Revenge	60	30	Richard Bedford. Of Lyme
142	Bark of Bridgwater	70	30	John Smyth
143	Crescent	140	75	John Wilson: Christopher Weymouth, Master
144	Galleon of Weymouth	100	50	Richard Miller
145	John	70	50	John Young. Of Chichester
146	Katharine	66	30	Of Weymouth
147	Hearty Anne	60	30	John Wynnall
148	Minion	230	110	John Sachfield. He owned Nos. 148-151. Sometimes spelt Sackvile. All of Bristol
149	Unicorn	130	66	James Langton
150	Handmaid	80	56	Christopher Pitt
151	Aid	60	26	William Megar
20 ships		1,931	993	

Coasters under Lord Henry Seymour, some paid for by the Queen but most by the ports

152	Daniel	160	70	Robert Johnson
153	Galleon Hutchins	150	60	Thomas Tucker
154	Bark Lamb	150	60	Leonard Harbell
155	Fancy	60	30	Richard Fearne
156	Griffin	70	35	John Dobson
157	Little Hare	50	25	Matthew Railstone
158	Handmaid	75	35	John Gattenbury
159	Marigold	150	70	Francis Johnson. Of Hull
160	Matthew	35	16	Richard Mitchell
161	Susan	40	20	John Musgrave
162	William	140	50	Barnaby Lowe. Of Ipswich
163	Katharine	125	50	Thomas Grymble. Of Ipswich.
164	Primrose	120	40	John Cardinal
165	Anne Bonaventure	60	50	John Conny
166	William	80	60	William Coxon. Of Rye

Ship		Tons	Men	Captain, Officer & Remarks
167	Grace of God	50	30	William Fordred. Of Dover
168	Elizabeth	120	70	John Lidgen. Of Dover
169	Robin	110	65	William Cripps. Of Sandwich
170	Hazard	38	34	Nicholas Turner. Of Feversham
171	Grace	150	70	William Musgrave. Of Yarmouth
172	Mayflower	150	70	Alexander Musgrave. Of King's Lynn
173	William	100	50	Thomas Lambert. Of Colchester
174	John Young	60	30	Reynold Vesey
23 ships		2,243	1,090	

Voluntary Ships paid for by the Queen

175	Sampson	300	108	John Wingfield. Owned by the Earl of Cumberland
176	Frances	140	60	John Rashley, who owned her. Of Fowey
177	Heathen	60	30	Of Weymouth
178	Golden Rial (or Ryall)	120	50	Owned by Thomas Middleton. Of Weymouth
179	Bark Sutton	70	40	Hugh Pearson. Of Weymouth
180	Carouse	50	25	
181	Samaritan	250	100	Of Dartmouth
182	William	120	60	Of Plymouth
183	Gallego	30	20	Of Plymouth
184	Bark Halse	60	40	Grenfield Halse
185	Unicorn	76	30	Ralph Hawes. Of Dartmouth
186	Grace	100	50	Walter Edney. Of Topsham
187	Thomas Bonaventure	60	30	John Pentire. Of Lyme
188	Rat	80	60	Gilbert Lee. Of Wight
189	Margaret	60	46	William Hubbard
190	Elizabeth	40	30	
191	Raphael	40	40	
192	Flyboat	60	40	
193	John	–	65	Owned by Sir Richard Grenville. Of Barnstaple
194	Greyhound		40	Michael Pullison. Of Aldborough
195	Elizabeth	90	30	Of Lowestoft. Owned by Thomas Meldrum. Calais fireship
196	Jonas		25	Of Aldborough
197	Fortune		25	Of Aldborough
23 ships		1,806	1,044	

THE SPANISH ARMADA: *Commander-in-Chief the Duke of Medina Sidona*

Portuguese Squadron	Tons	Guns	Men			Officers, Fate and Remarks
			Soldiers	Mariners	Total	
1 San Martin **	1,000	48	300	177	477	Duke of Medina Sidonia, Prince Ascoli, Francisco de Bobadilla (MC General), Captain Marolin de Juan. Arrived Santander. 180 dead.
2 San Juan + [de Portugal]	1,050	50	321	179	500	Recalde's flagship after 24 July. Arrived Galicia. Captured in Drake's raid April 1589.
3 San Marcos	790	33	292	117	409	Marquis de Peñafiel. Lost off Ireland.
4 San Felipe	800	40	415	117	532	Juan Poza de Santiso, Don Francisco de Toledo (MC). Captured by the Dutch then sank.
5 San Luis	830	38	376	116	492	Don Agustin Mexia (MC). Arrived Santander.
6 San Mateo	750	34	277	120	397	Don Diego Pimentel (MC), Don Rodrigo de Vivero, Don Luis Vanegas. Captured by the Dutch and sunk.
7 Santiago	520	24	300	93	393	Arrived Santander.
8 Florencia	961	52	400	86	486	Confiscated from Grand Duke of Tuscany. Gaspar de Sosa (MC). Constructive total loss.
9 San Cristobal	352	20	300	78	378	Arrived Santander.
10 San Bernardo	352	21	250	81	331	Arrived Galicia.
11 Augusta (zabra)	166	13	55	57	112	Arrived Santander.
12 Julia (zabra)	166	14	44	72	116	Arrived Santander.
12 ships	7,737	387	3,330	1,293	4,623	

Castilian Squadron   Don Diego Flores de Valdes

		Tons	Guns	Men			Officers, Fate and Remarks
				Soldiers	Mariners	Total	
13	San Cristobal *	700	36	205	120	325	Flagship of Diego Flores, though as chief of staff to the C-in-C he spent entire campaign aboard *San Martin*. Arrived Santander.
14	San Juan Bautista +	750	24	207	136	343	Marcos Aramburu. Arrived Santander.
15	San Pedro	530	24	141	131	272	Probable command of Francisco de Cuellar.
16	San Juan	530	24	163	113	276	Don Diego Enriquez, son of Vicery of Peru. Wrecked at Streedagh Sound.
17	Santiago el Mayor	530	24	210	132	342	Arrived Santander.
18	San Felipe y Santiago	530	24	151	116	267	Arrived Santander.
19	La Asuncion	530	24	199	114	313	Arrived Santander.
20	N.S. del Barrio	530	24	155	108	263	Arrived Santander.
21	San Medel y Celedon	530	24	160	101	261	Arrived Santander.
22	Santa Ana	250	24	91	80	171	Arrived Santander.
23	N.S. de Begoña	750	24	174	123	297	Indian Guard merchantman. Arrived Galicia.
24	La Trinidad	872	24	180	122	302	Last seen 15 September. Probably wrecked Tralee.
25	La Santa Catalina	882	24	190	159	349	Arrived Santander.
26	San Juan Bautista	650	24	192	93	285	Gregoria Melandez, Diego de Bazan, Don Juan Maldonado, Don Luis de Maeda, Captain F. Horra. Scuttled off Ireland.
27	N.S. del Socorro (patache)	75	24	20	25	45	Lost.
28	Antonio de Padua (patache)	75	12	20	46	66	Lost.
16 ships		8,714	384	2,458	1,719	4,147	

Biscayan Squadron   Don Juan Martinez de Recalde

		Tons	Guns	Men			Officers, Fate and Remarks
				Soldiers	Mariners	Total	
29	Santa Ana *	768	30	256	73	329	Nicolas de Isla (MC). Recalde's flagship till 21 July. Sheltered in La Hogue Bay. Became total loss.
30	El Gran Grin +	1,160	28	256	73	329	Don Pedro de Mendoza. Captain A. Felipe. Wrecked off Clare Island. Survivors executed.
31	Santiago	666	25	214	102	316	Arrived Guipuzcoa.
32	La Concepcion de Zubelzu	486	16	90	70	160	Reported missing but arrived Guipuzcoa.
33	La Concepcion de Juanes del Cano	418	18	164	61	225	Reported missing; also as having arrived Guipuzcoa. Captain Juan del Cano. Now, believed wrecked Co Galway.
34	La Magdalena	530	18	193	67	260	Arrived Guipuzcoa.
35	San Juan	350	21	114	80	194	Arrived Santander.
36	La Maria Juan	665	24	172	100	272	Captain Pedro de Ugarte. Sunk off Gravelines.
37	La Manuela	520	12	125	54	179	Arrived Santander.
38	S.M. de Monte-Mayor	707	18	206	45	251	Arrived Santander.
39	La Maria de Aguirre (patache)	70	6	20	23	43	Missing.
40	La Isabela (patache)	71	10	20	22	42	Safe.
41	Patache de Miguel Suso	36	6	20	26	46	Missing.
42	San Esteban (patache)	96	6	20	26	46	Safe.
14 ships		6,543	238	1,870	822	2,692	

Andalusian Squadron   Don Pedro de Valdes

| | | Tons | Guns | Men | | | Officers, Fate and Remarks |
				Soldiers	Mariners	Total	
43	N.S. del Rosario *	1,150	46	304	118	422	Don Pedro de Valdes. Surrendered in the Channel to Drake's *Revenge*.
44	San Francisco +	915	21	222	56	278	Arrived Santander.
45	San Juan	810	31	245	89	334	Arrived Santander.
46	San Juan de Gargarin	569	16	165	56	221	Arrived Santander.
47	La Concepcion	862	20	185	71	256	Arrived Santander.
48	Duquesa Santa Ana	900	23	280	77	357	Don Pedro Mares, Don Alonso de Leiva. Wrecked Loughros Mor Bay, Co Donegal.
49	Santa Catalina	730	23	231	77	308	Arrived Santander.
50	La Trinidad	650	13	192	74	266	Arrived Santander.
51	S.M. del Juncal	730	20	228	80	308	Arrived Santander.
52	San Bartolomé	976	27	240	72	312	Arrived Galicia.
53	El Espiritu Santo (patache)			33	10	43	Lost.
11 ships		8,292	240	2,325	780	3,105	

Guipuzcoan Squadron   Don Miguel de Oquendo

	Tons	Guns	Men			Officers, Fate and Remarks
			Soldiers	Mariners	Total	
54 Santa Ana *	1,200	47	303	82	385	Miguel de Oquendo died of wounds on arrival San Sebastian. After anchoring the ship blew up, killing 100.
55 N.S. de la Rosa +	945	26	233	64	297	Martin de Villafrance. Wrecked Blasket Sound. Wreck located July 1968.
56 San Salvador	958	25	321	75	396	Magazine exploded killing 200. Hulk captured by English and towed to Weymouth.
57 San Esteban	736	26	196	68	264	Wrecked off Ireland. Survivors executed.
58 Santa Marta	548	20	173	63	236	Arrived Guipuzcoa.
59 Santa Barbara	525	12	154	45	199	Arrived Guipuzcoa.
60 San Buenaventura	379	21	168	53	221	Arrived Guipuzcoa.
61 La Maria San Juan	291	12	110	30	140	Arrived Lisbon.
62 Santa Cruz	680	16	156	32	188	Arrived Santander.
63 Doncella (urca)	500	16	156	32	188	Sank at Santander.
64 La Asuncion (patache)	60	9	20	23	43	Lost.
65 San Bernabe (patache)	69	9	20	23	43	Safe.
66 N.S. de Guadalupe		1		15		Lost.
67 Magdalena		1		14		Lost.
14 ships	6,691	241	2,010	619	2,600	

Levantine Squadron   Don Martin de Bertendona

		Tons	Guns	Men			Officers, Fate and Remarks
				Soldiers	Mariners	Total	
68	La Regazona *	1249	30	344	80	424	Don Martin de Bertendona. Ship arrived Spain.
69	La Lavia +	728	25	203	71	274	Judge Advocate General Martin de Aranda, Francisco de Cuellar. Wrecked Streedagh Sound, Co. Sligo.
70	La Rata (En)coronada	820	35	335	84	419	Don Alonso de Leiva. Wrecked Blacksod Bay.
71	San Juan de Sicilia	800	26	279	63	342	Don Diego Tellez Enriquez. The ship wrecked in Tobermory Bay
72	La Trinidad Valencera	1100	42	281	79	360	Don Alonso de Luzon. Wrecked in Glenagivney Bay. Wreck located February 1971.
73	La Anunciada	703	24	196	79	275	Captain O. Iveglia. Scuttled in Shannon estuary.
74	San Nicolas Prodaneli	834	26	374	8	455	Captain Maria Prodaneli. Wrecked Co. Kerry.
75	La Juliana	860	32	325	70	395	Don F. de Aranada. Wrecked off Donegal.
76	Santa Maria de Vison	666	18	236	71	307	Captain J. de Bartolo. Wrecked off Co Sligo.
77	La Trinidad de Scala	900	22	307	79	386	Arrived Santander.
	10 ships	8,754	280	2,880	757	3,637	

Squadron of Hulks or Urcas   Don Juan Gomez de Medina

| | | Tons | Guns | Men | | | Officers, Fate and Remarks |
				Soldiers	Mariners	Total	
78	El Gran Grifon *	650	38	243	43	286	Gomez de Medina's flagship. Wrecked on Fair Isle. Wreck located June 1970.
79	San Salvador +	650	24	218	43	261	Pedro Coco Calderon. Arrived Santander.
80	Perro Marina	200	7	70	24	94	Believed wrecked but evidently arrived Santander.
81	Falcon Blanco Mayor	500	16	161	36	197	Listed missing, but captured by English in January 1589.
82	Castillo Negro	750	27	239	34	273	Captain Pedro Ferrat. Foundered north of Ireland.
83	Barca de Amburg	600	23	239	25	264	Captain Juan de San Martin. Foundered north of Ireland. Most of crew rescued by the Valencera and El Gran Grifon.
84	Casa de Paz Grande	650	26	198	27	225	Sailed from Lisbon but not at Corunna muster. Unlikely she took part in the campaign.
85	San Pedro Mayor	581	29	213	28	241	Hospital ship. Wrecked Bigbury Bay after completing north-about voyage to the Channel.
86	El Sanson	500	18	200	31	231	Arrived Galicia.
87	San Pedro Menor	500	18	157	23	180	Missing.
88	Barca de Anzique	450	26	200	25	225	Captain Pedro de Arechaga.
89	Falcon Blanco Mediano	300	16	76	27	103	Don Luis de Cordoba. Wrecked off Ireland.
90	Santo Andres	400	14	150	28	178	Arrived Santander.
91	Casa de Paz Chica	350	15	162	24	186	Arrived Santander.

		Tons	Guns	Men			Officers, Fate and Remarks
				Soldiers	Mariners	Total	
92	Ciervo Volante	400	18	200	22	222	Captain Juan de Permato. Wrecked off Ireland.
93	Paloma Blanca	250	12	56	20	76	Arrived Galicia.
94	La Ventura	160	4	58	14	72	Evidently arrived Santander.
95	Santa Barbara	370	10	70	22	92	Missing.
96	Santiago	600	19	56	30	86	Captain J.H. de Luna. Wrecked off Ireland.
97	David (Chico)	450	7	50	24	74	Listed missing but not at Corunna muster and did not serve in the campaign.
98	El Gato	400	9	40	22	62	Arrived Santander.
99	Esayas	260	4	30	16	46	Arrived Santander.
100	San Gabriel	280	4	35	20	55	—
	23 ships	10,251	384	3,121	608	3,729	

Pataches and Zabras   Don Antonio Hurtado de Mendoza

		Tons	Guns	Men			Officers, Fate and Remarks
				Soldiers	**Mariners**	**Total**	
101	*N.S. del Pilar de Zaragoza* *	300	11	109	51	160	Lost
102	*La Caridad*	180	12	70	36	106	Lost
103	*San Andres*	150	12	40	29	69	
104	*El Crucifijo*	150	8	40	29	69	Lost
105	*N.S. del Puerto*	55	8	30	33	63	
106	*La Concepcion de Carasa*	70	5	30	42	72	Lost
107	*N.S. de Regoña*	64		20	26	46	Lost
108	*La Concepcion de Capetillo*	60	10	20	26	46	
109	*San Jeronimo*	50	4	20	37	57	Lost
110	*N.S. de Gracia*	57	5	20	34	54	Arrived Santander.
111	*La Concepcion de Francisco de Latero*	75	6	20	29	49	Lost
112	*N.S. de Guadalupe*	70		20	42	62	Arrived Santander.
113	*San Francisco*	70		20	37	57	Lost
114	*Esperitu Santo*	75		20	47	67	Arrived Santander.
115	*Trinidad*, zabra		2		23	23	Lost off Ireland
116	*N.S. de Castro*		2		26	26	Lost
117	*Santo Andres*		2		15	15	
118	*La Concepcion de Valmaseda*		2		27	27	Lost
119	*La Concepcion de Somanila*				31	31	Lost
120	*Santa Catalina*				23	23	Lost
121	*San Juan de Carasa*				23	23	Lost
122	*Asuncion*				23	23	Lost
	22 ships	1,426				1,168	

Galleasses of Naples   Don Hugo de Moncada

| | | Tons | Guns | Men | | | Officers, Fate and Remarks |
				Soldiers	Mariners	Total	
123	*San Lorenzo* *	—	50	262	124	386	Foundered at Calais. Ship taken by the French. Moncada killed.
124	*Patrona Zuñiga*	—	50	178	112	290	Arrived Le Havre in distress after north-about voyage. Out of commission for at least a year.
125	*Girona*	—	50	169	120	289	Captain Fabricio Spinola. Wrecked west of Giant's Causeway. Wreck located June 1967.
126	*Napolitana*	—	50	264	112	376	Arrived Santander.
	4 ships					1,341	

Portuguese Galleys   Don Diego Medrano

| | | Tons | Guns | Men | | | Officers, Fate and Remarks |
				Soldiers	Mariners	Total	
127	*Capitana* *	—	5	—	106	106	Withdrew from the campaign before reaching England.
128	*Princesa*	—	5	—	90	90	Withdrew from the campaign before reaching England.
129	*Diana*	—	5	—	94	94	Wrecked at Bayonne Bay.
130	*Bazana*	—	5	—	72	72	Withdrew from the campaign before reaching England.
	4 ships					362	

Supplement 2
The Armada guns

Let it be said at the outset that the whole subject of Armada gunnery and guns is beset with anomalies and inaccuracies and that there is no means of resolving the many discrepancies which abound.* Consider some of the problems: firstly, calibres are nominal. All dimensions, in fact, are open to question. In the sixteenth century there were no accurate standards as regards calibre, weight of shot, diameter of bore, length of cannon, range of shot — all were approximate and largely empirical.

Consider, for example, the inside diameter (calibre) of a gun and the diameter of a shot. The difference could measure as much as half an inch, and this gap was called 'windage'. The size of gap could have a bearing on the range of shot. Furthermore, the quality of powder could also help determine the range. Thus every shot from every gun had a character of its own which made engagements fought at long range a matter of luck rather more than a matter of efficiency.

The table overleaf clearly shows that the English fleet preferred the long-range culverin and demi-culverin to the heavier and comparatively unwieldy cannon class of weapon favoured by the Spanish ships. There was thus an English preponderance in the demi-culverin, saker and minion classes: these were all with medium to long range capability, weak in weight of shot but quite strong on range. A potential disadvantage, of course, was that these guns were essentially man-killers, and in the ship-smasher category the Spaniards dominated. In the top three categories of guns — cannon, demi-cannon and cannon-perier — the total number of guns the Spaniards carried approached 500, against less than 100 English guns of the same categories. Even in the culverin class of 17 lb weight of shot, the English could barely reach parity. The English advantage becomes dominant in the demi-culverin class, but with a modest weight of only 9 lb of shot.

These observations lead to the comment that if the encounters between the two fleets were to be at long range, then ship losses would be minimal. The English had the range to inflict death and injury to personnel with minimal damage to the actual ship, while the Spanish had the capability of inflicting considerable damage to ship structures, yet their lack of range would restrict damage to English ships to a bare minimum. Close encounters, in fact, would favour the ship-smashing Spanish guns while at the same time give the massive advantage in men-killers to the English.

If calibres and shot diameters gave rise to discrepancies, the question of ranges too was hedged about with imponderables and inconsistencies. Reports of actions were

*The best source on the subject is Professor Michael Lewis's *Armada Guns*, 1961, originally published in eight parts in *The Mariner's Mirror*, the quarterly journal of the Society for Nautical Research. See vols XXVIII and XXIX, 1942–3.

Gun	Calibre (inches)	Weight of shot (lb)	Range: Point-blank and Random (paces)	No. of guns	
				Spanish Fleet	English Fleet
CANNON DEMI-CANNON	$7\frac{1}{4}$ $6\frac{1}{4}$	50 32	340/2,000 340/1,700	163	55
CANNON-PERIER	8	24	320/1,600	326	43
CULVERIN	$5\frac{1}{4}$	17	400/2,400	165	153
DEMI-CULVERIN	$4\frac{1}{2}$	9	400/2,500	137	344
SAKER	$3\frac{1}{2}$	5	340/1,700	144	662
MINION	$3\frac{1}{2}$	4	320/1,600	189	715

	Spanish	English
Total guns over 4 lb	1,124	1,972
Number of gun-carrying ships	124	172
Average weight of shot per ship	156lb	85 lb
Total weight of shot thrown	19,369 lb	14,677 lb

described as between two ships 'a long-culverin shot away'. Reference to the accompanying table will show that a culverin could fire a 17 lb shot at point-blank distance of about 400 paces (say 330 yards) and at random 2,400 paces (say about 1 mile). Thus, a long-culverin shot would translate to about one mile. But note the reference to paces instead of yards. Historians and compilers regularly used the phrase to describe demi-culverin shots of 9 lb being thrown 2,500 paces without having the least idea exactly what a pace was or what precisely was meant by a pound — or whether they were using the same values as the source from which they were copying. One Elizabethan source quotes a gunner's pace as an absurdly long 5ft, which would give a culverin random shot the equally absurd range of over 2 miles. Another source defined it more properly as $2\frac{1}{2}$ ft, giving a more acceptable random range of a little over 1 mile.

Within all these limitations and constraints, we can simplify the presentation of naval guns of the period by dividing the two main types of guns, the heavy, muzzle-loading ship-smashers of the main batteries and the small breech-loading man-killers (the smeriglio or robinet firing a shot of between 8 oz and 1 lb), into just seven specific guns in most common use.

It is worth noting, incidentally, that it was the Armada campaign which proved to be a testing ground for decades of new shipbuilding and gunnery techniques not significantly demonstrated previously under war conditions. When the English and Dutch galleons made their appearance in the early sixteenth century their sides were pierced with gunports. It is said that Henry VIII himself suggested the idea of mounting cannons on the lower decks, reducing centres of gravity, firing through ports which could be securely fastened against the sea when not in use for gunnery. This was not new to shipbuilding, but it was innovative to England and north-western Europe. Also, as time went on the Tudor period saw an improvement in the quality and power of gunpowder, allowing quicker combustion and smaller charges. This enabled the length of culverins to be reduced.

Philip II's coat of arms enrich this bronze 50 lb siege gun recovered from the wreck of Don Alonso de Luzon's 1,100-ton *La Trinidad Valencera*, located in 1971 in Glenagivney Bay, County Donegal.

At this time too guns began to be mounted on to small wooden carriages or trucks, running on solid wooden wheels. Naval warfare was beginning to move into a new era. The centuries-old practice was to employ soldiers and army officers to fight with muskets, long-bows, pikes and other hand weapons, in close fighting against the enemy, because boarding the enemy ship was fundamental to the engagement. This practice was beginning to change for good, since broadsides fired from a relatively long range so severely damaged an enemy ship that the necessity for boarding was obviated or at least reduced. The effectiveness of this emerging mode of naval warfare was first demonstrated in the Armada campaign.

Let us now cast a glance over these new naval weapons that were to change the whole character of war at sea.

Cannon: As can be seen from the composite table, these were heavy-shotted guns of large calibre, medium length and medium-to-long range of shot. These guns were originally land pieces used almost exclusively for battering — i.e. demolishing walls. When taken to sea they were intended to smash ships. Their heavy projectiles of about 50 lb were capable of rendering enormous damage to ships at short-to-medium range, but their accuracy was to some extent reliant on luck. The lengths of the guns were about 18–24 times the calibre, giving an average of about 11 feet. Although there were many varieties of this group we need only consider two:
(a) Cannon: about 7"–7½" calibre, 11ft long and firing a 50 lb iron shot, muzzle-loaded. Smooth bore. Strengthened with circular bands sweated on to the barrels. Favoured by the Spanish.
(b) Demi-Cannon: about 6"–6½" calibre with a length about 20–22 calibres. Muzzle-loading round shot of about 32–33 lb. Also favoured by the Spanish.

Perier or cannon-perier: A short-barrelled gun of about eight calibres in length; medium-shotted, short-range and of fairly light construction, throwing a relatively heavy shot. A typical perier would be 8" calibre, about 5ft long, firing a stone ball weighing about 24 lb to a distance of between 200 and 1,250 yards.

Culverins: These guns were long in proportion to their calibres, and consequently had the advantage of a greater range: in general the greater the length of the barrel, the greater the range and the more accurate the shot. This class of weapon can be conveniently subdivided into five categories:
(a) Culverin: a typical example is a 5"–5¼" calibre, firing a 17–18 lb shot, with a length varying from only 8 or 9ft for a broadside gun and 13ft for a bow chaser. Favoured equally by the Spanish and English ships.
(b) Demi-Culverin: a 4½" calibre gun firing a 9 lb shot with a gun length of about 11ft. Much favoured by the English, who possessed a preponderance of this weapon in the campaign.
(c) Saker: a 3½" calibre gun firing a 5 lb shot with a barrel length of about 9ft. The English had a dramatic superiority in numbers of sakers aboard their ships.
(d) Minion: a gun very similar to the saker but firing a slightly lighter weight of shot, about 4 lb. The English ships were armed with great numbers of these light weapons, which were effective anti-personnel guns.
(e) Falcon: these guns fired a shot of only 2–3 lb, while the smaller cousin, the falconet, was even lighter, with a shot weighing between 1 and 2 lb.

Supplement 3
The Armada losses

Four hundred years after the battle, scholars cannot agree on the exact losses suffered by the Spanish — not in ships and certainly not in personnel. The basis on which all losses and survivals are compiled are two documents lodged in the Simancas Archives in Spain (on which Captain Fernandez Duro based his subsequent work *La Armada Invencible*, 2 vols., Madrid, 1885) which were evidently compiled in October 1588 while some of the exhausted ships were still floundering home. The lists are numbered 180 — those ships which returned safely to Spanish ports — and 181 — those ships presumed to have been lost.

One would think, therefore, armed with these two documents it would be easy enough to reconcile both lists and figures. Not a bit of it. Firstly, the lists are not reliable. Some ships appear on one list as having returned safely, and on the other lists as being lost. Other ships appear on either list. It will be appreciated, too, the 'Missing' in October 1588 does not necessarily mean that a ship was lost. A few still had to reach safety — and subsequently did so later that month. Others — the *Girona* for example — were still fighting for their lives later in October: *Girona* was wrecked off Ireland on 26 October. And the *Zuñiga*, as we have seen, lingered for a whole year, neither totally lost nor returned to safety in the Baie de la Seine. Some ships, notably the urcas, may have made good their escape to Baltic ports quite unknown to the Spanish authorities, while quite a number of pataches and zabras may have sought shelter in friendly ports along the Channel and survived the campaign.

The compilation of these lists was beset with errors and confusion arising from the duplication of names of ships in the Armada. For example, a swift glance through the list of Spanish ships will soon reveal that there are six *San Juans*; there were two *San Juan Bautistas* (John the Baptist) and no less than eight *Concepcions*, some of them known by one name and sometimes by another. In Recalde's squadron there were two great ships, both *Concepcions*, one sometimes known as *Concepcion Mayor* and at other times as *Concepcion Zubelzu*: the other, known as *Concepcion Menor*, was also known as *Concepcion de Juanes del Cano*. List No. 180 clearly shows *Mayor* and *Menor* home safely. However, List No. 181 records also both *Concepcions* of *Zubelzu* and *Juanes del Cano* as lost.

Thus there are still some question marks that can now never be resolved. Most authorities agree a figure of between about 60 and 65 ships of the Armada as having been lost through a variety of causes. Professor Mattingley argued cogently for a lesser figure, but Professor Laughton, also an impressive authority, regards Duro's statement of 65 ships lost, of which about 35 are marked 'fate unknown', 'probably as fair an approximation as can be arrived at'. Professor Lewis, whose authority is dominant, summarizes the Spanish losses as follows:

Galleons	4
Flagships of auxiliary warships	8
Other auxiliary warships	10
Hulks	11
Small craft	15
Galleasses	2
Galley	1
Total	51

Much of the original work on the losses off Ireland was done by William Spotswood Green, a chief inspector of Irish fisheries, whose work was published in learned journals around the turn of the century. More recently the losses have been analysed by Niall Fallon, who considers that the total losses on the Irish coasts number 26. All Armada squadrons lost at least one ship there, except the galleys, which did not reach Ireland.

Levant 7	Zabras 4	Andalusia 1
Hulks 5	Guipuzcoa 2	Naples 1
Castile 3	Portugal 1	Biscay 2

These figures include two ships sometimes excluded from other lists: the hulk *Doncella* was wrecked at Santander immediately on arrival, and the Guipuzcoan flagship of that volatile Admiral Oquendo — another *Santa Ana* — blew up in the little bay of San Sebastian. Miguel de Oquendo, like his ship, had survived countless dangers but was lost due to an accidental explosion.

It is worth noting the heavy losses of the Levantine squadron. The only two ships of this squadron to reach Spain were the flagship *La Regazona* and the *Trinidad de Scala*. These ships were of lighter construction than the galleons, perfectly good enough for the Mediterranean conditions for which they were built, but manifestly unsuited to the heavier sea and weather conditions of the North Atlantic in autumn. Nor were the hulks or urcas weatherly enough for these conditions. It is significant that the magnificent Portuguese galleons suffered only one loss, and that was due to burning in the river Shannon rather than at the hands of the elements.

Of the twenty-six wrecks off Ireland only three have been officially worked by research and recovery teams: the *Girona*, which was found on the coast of Antrim in 1967; the *Santa Maria de la Rosa* which was located in the following year near the Blaskets, Co Kerry, while the third was the *Trinidad Valencera*, located in Donegal Bay in 1971.

Unofficially several more have been found and worked: the *Juliana* off Bloody Foreland, the *Duquesa Santa Ana* off Donegal, the *Concepcion del Cano* in Galway Bay and, nearby, an unknown small vessel in the Rosses.

*   *   *

The English losses in ships, in severe contrast, amounted to none. A contemporary report sometimes attributed to Drake summed it up: 'They [the Spaniards] did not in all their sailing round about England, so much as sink or take one ship, bark, pinnace or cock-boat of ours, or even burn so much as one sheepcote in this land.'

As regards losses in personnel, all figures are conjectural. Of the nearly 30,000 men who set out from Lisbon on this venture, only one in three ever returned to Spain:

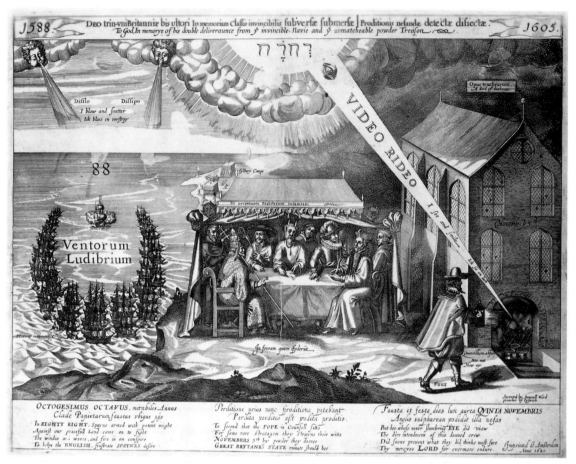

Allegorical reference to both the Armada campaign and to the Gunpowder Plot in a Dutch publication of 1621. The Latin phrases mean 'sport of the winds' and 'I see and smile'.

20,000 men died. More than half perished through sickness, starvation, disease: probably 6,000 died in shipwrecks, 1,000 by murder and probably 1,500 in battle. How many more died even once they had made their landfall in Spain is anyone's guess, but the lingering nature of many of the diseases and the low state of health of everyone suggests that perhaps thousands more succumbed.

The English battle losses in personnel were minuscule by comparison. No official figures were issued, but it was generally believed that the number killed probably only reached 68, possibly reached three figures, but certainly not more.

Deaths from sickness outnumbered these by hundreds. Professor Lewis has calculated (from what are admittedly sparse figures) that the likely losses in the English ships from disease, starvation, the putrescent food and the filthy living conditions imply deaths at the hands of the enemy should be multiplied a hundred times to arrive at a true figure of the English casualties: he is suggesting then a figure of about 6,800 at its lowest. If true, it is a horrifying indictment of the living conditions to which the English mariners were subjected, and of the authorities which allowed them.

Armada wrecks on the coast of Ireland

Ship		Tonnage	Site	Date
83	Barca de Amburg	600	At sea N of Malin Head, Donegal	1 Sept
82	Castillo Negro	750	Foundered at sea NW of Donegal	?4 Sept
115	Trinidad, zabra		Valentia Is, Co Kerry	15 Sept
74	San Nicolas Prodaneli	834	Toorglass, Curraun Peninsula, Co Mayo	16 Sept
72	La Trinidad Valencera	1,100	Glenagivnev Bav. Innishowen Peninsula, Co Donegal	16 Sept
24	La Trinidad	872	Tralee, Co Kerry	?18 Sept
73	La Anunciada	703	Scattery Roads, River Shannon	20 Sept
57	San Esteban	736	Doonbeg, Co Clare	20 Sept
3	San Marcos	790	Reef between Mutton Is and Lurga Point, Spanish Point, Co Clare	20 Sept
55	N. S. de la Rosa	945	Stromboli Reef, Blasket Sound, Co Kerry	21 Sept
70	La Rata Encoronada	820	Fahy Strand, Ballycroy, Blacksod Bay, Co Mayo	21 Sept
96	Santiago	600	Inver, Broadhaven Bay, Erris, Co Mayo	?21 Sept
30	El Gran Grin	1,160	Clare Is, Clew Bay, Co Mayo	22 Sept
92	Ciervo Volante	400	Tirawley, North Mayo	?22 Sept
26	San Juan Bautista	650	SW of Blasket Islands, at sea	?24 Sept
69	La Lavia	728	Streedagh Sound, near Grange, Co Sligo	25 Sept
16	San Juan	530	Streedagh Sound, near Grange, Co Sligo	25 Sept
89	Falcon Blanco Mediano	300	Freaghillaun South Is. Ballynakill, Co Galway	?25 Sept
76	Santa Maria de Vison	666	Streedagh Sound, near Grange, Co Sligo	25 Sept
33	La Concepcion del Cane	418	Duirling Na Spainneach, Ards, near Carna, Co Galway	?25 Sept
48	Duquesa Santa Ana	900	Rosbeg, Loughros Mor Bav. Co Donegal	26 Sept
75	La Juliana	860	Mullaghderg, Arranmore, Co Donegal	? Sept
125	Girona	700	Lacada Point, Port na Spaniagh, Co Antrim	28 Oct
	Unknown Zabra	?	Cloughglass, Arranmore, Co Donegal	?
	Unknown Zabra	?	Outside Killybegs Harbour, Co Donegal	?
	Unknown Zabra	?	Outside Killybegs Harbour, Co Donegal	?
	Unknown Ship	?	Near Gola Island, Co Donegal	?
	Unknown Ship	?	Near Brandon Point, Dingle Peninsula Co Kerry	?
	Unknown Ship	?	North Sound, Galway Bay – possibly No, 33	?

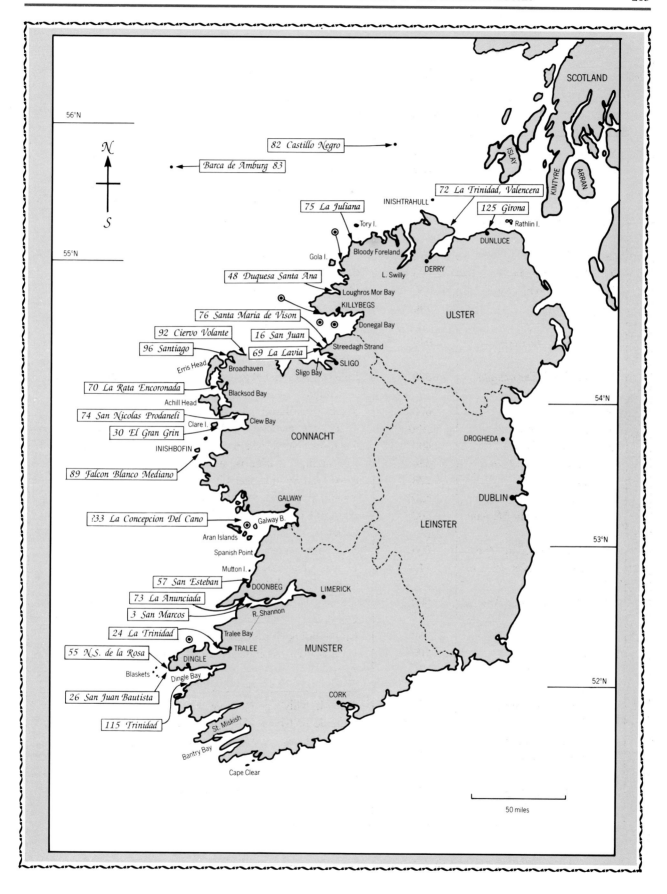

82 Castillo Negro

Barca de Amburg 83

SCOTLAND

ISLAY

KINTYRE

ARRAN

72 La Trinidad, Valencera

125 Girona

INISHTRAHULL

Rathlin I.

75 La Juliana

Tory I.

DUNLUCE

Gola I.

Bloody Foreland

DERRY

L. Swilly

48 Duquesa Santa Ana

Loughros Mor Bay

KILLYBEGS

ULSTER

76 Santa Maria de Vison

Donegal Bay

92 Ciervo Volante

96 Santiago

16 San Juan

69 La Lavia

Streedagh Strand

SLIGO

Erris Head

Broadhaven

Sligo Bay

70 La Rata Encoronada

Blacksod Bay

Achill Head

74 San Nicolas Prodaneli

Clare I.

Clew Bay

30 El Gran Grin

CONNACHT

DROGHEDA

INISHBOFIN

89 Falcon Blanco Mediano

GALWAY

DUBLIN

?33 La Concepcion Del Cano

Galway B.

Aran Islands

LEINSTER

Spanish Point

Mutton I.

57 San Esteban

DOONBEG

LIMERICK

73 La Anunciada

3 San Marcos

R. Shannon

24 La Trinidad

Tralee Bay

55 N.S. de la Rosa

TRALEE

MUNSTER

DINGLE

Blaskets

Dingle Bay

26 San Juan Bautista

CORK

115 Trinidad

St. Miskish

Bantry Bay

Cape Clear

56°N

55°N

54°N

53°N

52°N

N

S

50 miles

Supplement 4
Further reading: one hundred books on the Armada

The literature on the Armada is extensive, and runs to many hundreds of books alone — quite apart from the thousands of references in magazines, periodicals, journals and other publications of a minor nature. The following list provides a selection of important, interesting and absorbing books which will give the reader a first-class view of the campaign; predominantly from the British point of view, of course. More serious students who wish to research in greater depth should consult the *Bibliography of British History: Tudor Period 1485–1603*, compiled by Conyers Read; the second edition published at Oxford in 1959 classifies about 4,000 books and periodical articles on the period of Queen Elizabeth I's reign, 1558–1603.

ALLINGHAM, Hugh *Captain Cuellar's Adventures in Connaught and Ulster 1588*. This picture of the times, drawn from contemporary sources, carries an introduction and translation of Captain Cuellar's narrative of the Spanish Armada and his adventures in Ireland. Published 1897. The translation by Robert Crawford is from the Spanish text of Captain Fernandez Duro. See Cuellar and Duro.

ANDREWS, K.R. *Drake's Voyages*, 1967. *Elizabethan Privateering*, 1964

BARROW, John *Memoirs of the Naval Worthies of Queen Elizabeth's Reign*, 1845

BESANT, Sir Walter *London in the Time of the Tudors*, 1904

BIRCH, Thomas *Memoirs of the Reign of Elizabeth*, 2 vols., 1751

BLACK, J.B. *The Reign of Elizabeth, 1558–1603* (Oxford History of England) 2nd revised edition, 1959

BOURNE, H.R. Fox *Sir Philip Sydney*, 1891

BRIDGE, Sir Cyprian *Sea Power And Other Studies*, 1910

BRUCE, J. *Naval Equipments*, 1798

BURGHLEY, Lord *The Spanish Invasion, 1588*

CHEYNEY, E.P. *A History of England From the Defeat of the Armada to the Death of Elizabeth*, 2 vols., 1914, 1918

CLOWES, Sir William Laird *The Armada. The Elizabethan Navy. The Royal Navy*, 7 vols., 1897–1903: see Vol.1, chapter on the Armada, pp 539–604: a masterly condensation.

CORBETT, Sir Julian Stafford *Authorities for The Armada Campaign*, 1898. *Drake And The Tudor Navy*, 2 vols., 1898

CUELLAR, Captain Francisco *Narrative of the Armada*, 1897 see Hugh ALLINGHAM

CUSTANCE, Sir R. *Invasion Overseas*, 1905

DURO, Captain Cesareo Fernandez *La Armada Invencible*, Madrid, 2 vols., 1884–5 The standard Spanish history. Never fully translated, but a selection of the documents appears in Hume's *Calendar of State Papers* (q.v.)

DYER, F.E. *The Elizabethan Sailorman*, 1924

EWALD, A.C. *The Invincible Armada*, 1882

FALLON, Niall *The Armada in Ireland*, 1978

FISKE, J. *The Elizabethan Sea Kings*, 1895

FROBISHER, Sir Martin *Letters to Lord Burghley*, 1592

FROUDE, J.A. *History of England From the Fall of Wolsey to The Defeat of the Spanish Armada*, 1856–70, Vols vii–xii. Also published in Everyman's Library. *The Spanish Story of the Armada*, 1882 and subsequent editions. Based on Duro

GOLDINGHAM C.S. *The Personnel of the Tudor Navy and The Internal Economy of Ships*, 1918

GRAHAM, Winston *The Spanish Armadas*, 1972

GREVILLE, Sir Fulke *The Life of the Renowned Sir Philip Sidney*, 1907

GUZMAN, Alonso Perez de, 7th Duke of Medina Sidonia *Orders Set Downe by the Duke of Medina, Lord general of the King's Fleet*, 1588

HADFIELD, A.M. *Time To Finish The Game*, 1964

HAKLUYT, Richard *Principal Navigations*, 12 vols. 1903–05 edited W. Raleigh. Also available in Everyman's Library

HALE, J.R. *The Great Armada*, 1913

HAMILTON, H.C. (Ed) *Calendar of State Papers Relating to Ireland*, Vol IV, 1885

HANNAY, David *Short History of the British Navy*, 2 vols., 1898, 1908

HARDIE, R.P. *The Tobermory Argosy*, 1912

HARDY, Evelyn *Survivors of the Armada*, 1966

HARING, C.M. *The Spanish Empire*, 1914

HARRISON, C.B. *The Life and Death of Robert Devereaux, Earl of Essex*, 1937

HART, Roger *Battle of the Spanish Armada*, 1973

HAWKINS, M.W.S. *The Armada*, 1888 (With reproductions of Pine's engravings)

HOFFMAN, Ann *Lives of the Tudor Age 1485–1603*, 1977

HOWARTH, David *The Voyage of the Armada: The Spanish Story*, 1981

HUME, Major Martin A.S. (Editor), *Calendar of State Papers Relating to English Affairs*, Vol. IV, 1899 Contains the bulk of the Spanish documents in English translation. *The Defeat of the Armada*, 1896. *Evolution of the Armada*, 1896

JERDAN, W. *Documents Relating to the Spanish Armada and the Defences of the Thames and Medway*, 1854 First appeared in *British Arch. Assoc.*, ix, 1853, pp. 330–6

KEMPE, A.J. *Particulars of the Armada and Preparations Against the Invasion*, 1835. Contemporary documents

KESTEVEN, G.R. *The Armada*, 1965

LAUGHTON, Sir John K. *The Elizabethan Naval War with Spain* (to 1598), 1904. *State Papers Relating to the Defeat of the Spanish Armada*, 2 vols, 1894, reprinted 1981. The bulk of the English documents have been presented and edited in a masterly fashion by Professor Laughton. *The Invincible Armada: A Tercentenary Retrospect*, 1888

LAUGHTON, L.G.C. *The Navy: Ships and Sailors* (Elizabethan), 1916

LEWIS, Michael *Armada Guns*, 1961. See also *The Mariner's Mirror. The Hawkins Dynasty*, 1969. *The Spanish Armada*, 1960

LLOYD, Christopher *The British Seaman*, 1969

McFEE, William *Sir Martin Frobisher*, 1928

McKEE, Alexander *From Merciless Invaders*, 1963; revised 1987

McLEAN, Alison *The Tobermory Treasure*, 1986

MARTIN, Colin *Full Fathom Five*, 1975. Carries an appendix on guns and shot by Sidney Wignall

MARTIN, Colin and PARKER, Geoffrey, *The Spanish Armada* 1988

MATTINGLEY, Garrett *The Defeat of the Spanish Armada*, 1959

MONSON, Sir William *Account of the Navy 1585–1641*. Yearly account of the English and Spanish fleets, 1585–1602

MOTLEY, J.L. *History of the Netherlands*, 1860. Correspondence of Philip II and Parma

NAISH, George P.B. *The Spanish Armada* Contains a translation of Ubaldini's *Commentary* published in 1589

NEALE, Sir John E. *Queen Elizabeth*, 1934

NOBLE, T.C. *The Names of those Persons who Subscribed toward the Defence of this country at the time of the Spanish Armada, 1588, and the Amounts they contributed*, 1886

OMAN, Sir Charles *A History of the Art of War in the Sixteenth Century*, 1937

OPPENHEIM, Michael *History of the Administration of the Navy*, 1896

PIERSON, Piers *Philip II of Spain*, 1975

PINE, John *The Tapestry Hangings in the House of Lords: representing the several engagements between the English and Spanish fleets in the ever memorable year MDLXXXVIII*, 1739. This 24 page booklet contains 16 double-page engravings

READ, Conyers *Lord Burghley and Queen Elizabeth*, 1960. *Mr Secretary Cecil and Queen Elizabeth*, 1960. *Mr Secretary Walsingham and the Policy of Queen Elizabeth*, 3 vols., 1925

RICHMOND, Herbert *The Navy as an Instrument of Policy 1558–1727*, 1953

ROBINSON, Gregory *The Elizabethan Ship*, 1956

ROUND, J.H. and OPPENHEIM, M. *Royal Navy Under Elizabeth*, 1955

ROWSE, A.L. *The Expansion of Elizabethan England*, 1955. *Sir Richard Grenville of the 'Revenge'*, 1937

SOUTHEY, Robert *Lives of the British Admirals*, 5 vols., 1833–40

SPOTSWOOD GREEN, W. See Green, W. Spotswood

STÉNUIT, Robert *Treasures of the Armada*, 1972

THOMSON, George Malcolm *Sir Francis Drake*, 1972

THURSFIELD, J.R. *The Spanish Armada*, 1895

UBALDINI, Petruccio *A discourse Concerning the Spanish Fleet Invading England*, trans. Robert Adams, 1590

UDEN, Grant *Drake at Cadiz*, 1969

UNWIN, Rayner *The Defeat of Sir John Hawkins*, 1960

WALKER, W.H.K. *The Seafarers: The Armada*, Time-Life Books, 1982

WALLACE, Willard M. *Sir Walter Raleigh*, 1959

WATERS, David *The Art of Navigation in England in Elizabethan and Early Stuart Times*, 1958

WERNHAM, R.B. *Before the Armada: The Growth of English Foreign Policy 1485–1588*, 1966

WILLIAMS, Neville *Elizabeth I, Queen of England*, 1967. *Francis Drake*, 1973

WILLIAMSON, G.C. *George 3rd Earl of Cumberland, 1558-1605*, 1920

WILLIAMSON, J.A. *Sir John Hawkins*, 1927, revised 1949. *The Age of Drake*, 1970

WOODROOFE, Thomas *The Enterprise of England*, 1958

WRIGHT, W.H.K. *The Spanish Armada*, 1887. It carries reproductions of Pine's tapestries

Index

The names of ships and men appearing in SUPPLEMENTS 1 and 4 are not included in the Index unless they have already featured in the main body of the text.